Emily Brontë: *Wuthering Heights*

ANALYSING TEXTS

General Editor: Nicholas Marsh

Further titles are in preparation

Emily Brontë:
Wuthering Heights

NICHOLAS MARSH

St. Martin's Press
New York

EMILY BRONTË

St. Martin's Press, Scholarly and Reference Division, 175 Fifth Avenue, New York, N.Y. 10010

First published in the United States of America in 1999

This book is printed on paper suitable for recycling and made from fully managed and sustained forest sources.

Printed in Hong Kong

ISBN 0–312–22376–5 clothbound
ISBN 0–312–22377–3 paperback

Library of Congress Cataloging-in-Publication Data
Marsh, Nicholas.
Emily Brontë—Wuthering Heights / Nicholas Marsh.
p.   cm. — (Analysing texts)
Includes bibliographical references and index.
ISBN 0–312–22376–5 (cloth). — ISBN 0–312–22377–3 (pbk.)
1. Brontë, Emily, 1818–1848. Wuthering Heights—Examinations–
–Study guides.   I. Title.   II. Title: Emily Brontë.   III. Series.
PR4172.W73M36   1999
823'.8—dc21   99–18935
                                                              CIP

For Bertie

Contents

PART 2: THE CONTEXT AND THE CRITICS

General Editor's Preface

This series is dedicated to one clear belief: that we can all enjoy, understand and analyse literature for ourselves, provided we know how to do it. How can we build on close understanding of a short passage, and develop our insight into the whole work? What features do we expect to find in a text? Why do we study style in so much detail? In demystifying the study of literature, these are only some of the questions the *Analysing Texts* series addresses and answers.

The books in this series will not do all the work for you, but will provide you with the tools, and show you how to use them. Here, you will find samples of close, detailed analysis, with an explanation of the analytical techniques utilised. At the end of each chapter there are useful suggestions for further work you can do to practise, develop and hone the skills demonstrated and build confidence in your own analytical ability.

An author's individuality shows in the way they write: every work they produce bears the hallmark of that writer's personal 'style'. In the main part of each book we concentrate therefore on analysing the particular flavour and concerns of one author's work, and explain the features of their writing in connection with major themes. In Part 2 there are chapters about the author's life and work, assessing their contribution to developments in literature; and a sample of critics' views are summarised and discussed in comparison with each other. Some suggestions for further reading provide a bridge towards further critical research.

Analysing Texts is designed to stimulate and encourage your critical and analytic faculty, to develop your personal insight into the author's work and individual style, and to provide you with the skills and techniques to enjoy at first hand the excitement of discovering the richness of the text.

NICHOLAS MARSH

A Note on Editions

References to *Wuthering Heights* give the page number from the Penguin Classics edition of 1995, edited with an Introduction and Notes by Pauline Nestor. This edition keeps the original numbering of chapters, beginning at a 'Chapter 1' for each of the three volumes that were originally published. Where there might be any confusion as to which chapter is referred to, I have specified thus: 'Volume 2, Chapter 3'.

PART 1

ANALYSING *WUTHERING HEIGHTS*

1
The Narrative Frame

The story of *Wuthering Heights* centres on a group of characters – Catherine and Hindley Earnshaw, Heathcliff, Edgar and Isabella Linton, and their three children. We can say that this 'story' begins when Heathcliff is brought into the Earnshaw family, when Catherine and Hindley are children; and ends with the marriage of Hareton Earnshaw and Catherine Linton/Heathcliff, and the death of Heathcliff himself. It is an exciting story, full of passions, marriages, births and deaths. However, it is important to remember that the author does not tell us this story: *Wuthering Heights* has a **narrative frame**. Another character, Nelly Dean, tells the story to Mr Lockwood, and he tells it to us. The first-person narrator of *Wuthering Heights*, then, is a long way removed from the actual experiences of the story. He only meets three of the main characters (Hareton and young Cathy, the two survivors of the younger generation; and Heathcliff), and he meets them as an unperceptive stranger, preoccupied by his own affairs, in the final year of their forty-year story.

Emily Brontë has devised an elaborate 'frame' for her story, then. In *Wuthering Heights*, the normal act of reading a fable related by an author is trebled: we read a fable narrated by a man who was told the story by a woman who was peripherally involved. This form places an insistent focus on the act of storytelling, and raises numerous questions: What is a 'story'? What kind of an activity is 'storytelling'? How should we navigate the complex relationship between any narrative account, and the thing – life – itself. An equally heavy emphasis is placed on the act of reading or 'hearing' the story, so we are provoked to question our own activity when we are engaged in reading the novel. How do we hear the things that are related to us? Do we accept a truth that has been filtered through the prejudices, and is imprisoned in the language, of successive narrators? Or do we believe we can reconstruct the original event, compensating for the different viewpoints that have coloured it? Is it reasonable to attempt such a reconstruction? Can a story exist independent of the language that tells it?

These questions go to the heart of how literature is written and read. Many modern critics are particularly interested in analysing the actions of language, in order to throw light onto literary activity itself. Some concentrate on words as the constituent elements of language, treating them as 'signs' which refer to a reality we can never reach because it can never be fully represented to us. Others see language and the act of storytelling as a 'code', which readers are eager to break in order to reach through to the reality behind it. In this view, writers 'encode' a story which we attempt to 'decode'. Yet other critics focus on the act of reading, as a hopeless search for 'mastery' of the text: hopeless because the authority of the story is constantly undermined by the act of narration, so that meaning retreats from us.

It is not our purpose to indulge in modern critical controversies in our first chapter. But we do begin with the recognition that *Wuthering Heights* tells its story in a particularly elaborate and questionable way, within a double frame. In this chapter we look at extracts which highlight the influence of the different narrators. From analysing specific passages, we hope to understand more about how and why Emily Brontë introduces such complex relationships between the original story and the reader, and how she plays the narrators off against each other.

Narrators

[a] Lockwood

We start with the first-person narrator, Mr Lockwood. He arrives in the story almost by chance, as a gentleman who has casually rented Thrushcross Grange, but who might have 'fixed on' a completely different part of 'all England'. He has never been to that part of the country before, and immediately identifies himself as a newcomer by exclaiming 'This is certainly a beautiful country!'; while the aura of diary or travelogue is enhanced by the bald statement of the date '1801' followed by a dash, which is the first mark of the novel.

He writes because he has just visited Heathcliff at Wuthering Heights, and wishes to record his impressions. We will look at his description of the house, which is given on pages 4–6:

> 'Joseph, take Mr Lockwood's horse; and bring up some wine.'
> 'Here we have the whole establishment of domestics, I suppose,' was the reflection, suggested by this compound order. 'No wonder the grass grows up between the flags, and cattle are the only hedge-cutters.'
> Joseph was an elderly, nay, an old man, very old, perhaps, though hale and sinewy.
> 'The Lord help us!' he soliloquised in an undertone of peevish displeasure, while relieving me of my horse: looking, meantime, in my face so sourly that I charitably conjectured he must have need of divine aid to digest his dinner, and his pious ejaculation had no reference to my unexpected advent.
> Wuthering Heights is the name of Mr Heathcliff's dwelling, 'Wuthering' being a significant provincial adjective, descriptive of the atmospheric tumult to which its station is exposed in stormy weather. Pure, bracing ventilation they must have up there, at all times, indeed: one may guess the power of the north wind, blowing over the edge, by the excessive slant of a few, stunted firs at the end of the house; and by a range of gaunt thorns all stretching their limbs one way, as if craving alms of the sun. Happily, the architect had foresight to build it strong: the narrow windows are deeply set in the wall, and the corners defended with large jutting stones.
> Before passing the threshold, I paused to admire a quantity of

grotesque carving lavished over the front, and especially about the principal door, above which, among a wilderness of crumbling griffins, and shameless little boys, I detected the date '1500,' and the name 'Hareton Earnshaw.' I would have made a few comments, and requested a short history of the place from the surly owner, but his attitude at the door appeared to demand my speedy entrance, or complete departure, and I had no desire to aggravate his impatience, previous to inspecting the penetralium.

One step brought us into the family sitting-room, without any introductory lobby, or passage: they call it here 'the house' pre-eminently. It includes the kitchen and parlor, generally, but I believe at Wuthering Heights the kitchen is forced to retreat altogether into another quarter, at least I distinguished a chatter of tongues, and a clatter of culinary utensils, deep within; and I observed no signs of roasting, boiling, or baking, about the huge fire-place; nor any glitter of copper saucepans and tin cullenders on the walls. One end, indeed, reflected spendidly both light and heat from ranks of immense pewter dishes, interspersed with silver jugs and tankards, towering row after row, in a vast oak dresser, to the very roof. The latter had never been underdrawn: its entire anatomy lay bare to an inquiring eye, except where a frame of wood laden with oatcakes, and clusters of legs of beef, mutton and ham, concealed it. Above the chimney were sundry villainous old guns, and a couple of horse-pistols, and, by way of ornament, three gaudily painted canisters disposed along its ledge. The floor was of smooth, white stone: the chairs, high-backed, primitive structures, painted green: one or two heavy black ones lurking in the shade. In an arch, under the dresser, reposed a huge, liver-coloured bitch pointer surrounded by a swarm of squealing puppies, and other dogs haunted other recesses.

The apartment and furniture would have been nothing extraordinary as belonging to a homely, northern farmer with a stubborn countenance, and stalwart limbs set out to advantage in knee-breeches and gaiters. Such an individual, seated in his armchair, his mug of ale frothing on the round table before him, is to be seen in any circuit of five or six miles among these hills, if you go at the right time, after dinner. But, Mr Heathcliff forms a singular contrast to his abode and style of living. He is a dark-skinned gypsy in aspect, in dress and manners a gentleman – that is, as much a gentleman as many a country squire: rather slovenly, perhaps, yet not looking amiss, with his negligence, because he has an erect and handsome figure – and rather morose – possibly some people might suspect him of a degree of under-bred pride – I have a sympathetic chord within that tells me it is nothing of the sort; I know, by instinct, his reserve springs from an aversion to showy displays of feeling – to manifestations of mutual kindliness. He'll love and hate, equally under cover, and esteem it a species of impertinence to be loved or hated again – No, I'm running on too fast – I bestow my own attributes over-liberally on him. Mr Heathcliff may have entirely dissimilar reasons for keeping his hand out of the way, when he meets a would-be acquaintance, to those which actuate me. Let me hope my constitution is almost peculiar: my dear mother used to say I should never have a comfortable home, and only last summer, I proved myself perfectly unworthy of one.

(Wuthering Heights, pp. 4–6)[1]

We are interested in the way Mr Lockwood expresses himself, first of all, as the story of *Wuthering Heights* comes to us through the filter of his language. What are the noticeable features of his language in this extract, and what conclusions about him can we draw based on these?

One insistent feature in this passage is Lockwood's speculations. The language is filled with guesswork: 'I suppose', 'perhaps' and 'I conjectured' govern the three main statements about Joseph (that he is the only servant; his age; and that he repeatedly calls on God) when Lockwood meets him. When the narrative turns to describe the exterior of the house, Lockwood assumes the wild weather they 'must have', and uses the slanting vegetation to 'guess' the power of the wind. Amusingly, he attributes the same speculative approach to the housebuilder three-hundred years before, who 'happily' (meaning *luckily*) built the house strongly and with small windows. When Lockwood sees the date '1500', he is curious and 'would have . . . requested a short history of the place'; but the pattern of the extract, where Lockwood speculates but has no definite information, is maintained. Heathcliff looks morose, so Lockwood is deterred from asking his question.

---

[1] Page-references to *Wuthering Heights* are to the Penguin Classics edition, edited by Pauline Nestor (London, 1995). Page references to this text will appear alone, in brackets.

The next paragraph, describing the interior of the house, further develops the sense that we observe phenomena and guess their explanation. Here, Lockwood 'believes' that the kitchen is a separate room. He can 'distinguish' kitchen noises but 'observed no signs' of cooking in the main room. Towards the end of this paragraph, vague and unexplainable distances again appear in the narrative: chairs and dogs are described, but more chairs are 'lurking in the shade'; and 'other dogs haunted other recesses'.

Finally we arrive at the description of Heathcliff, in the last paragraph of our extract. Notice that the first 73 words are devoted to describing an imagined farmer who is *not* like Heathcliff. Then comes the statement that he contrasts with his surroundings, and a much shorter description (47 words) of Heathcliff. The whole of the last half of the paragraph (144 words) is then given over to speculation about Heathcliff's character, and revelation of Lockwood's. Meanwhile, the motif of hesitant, uncertain language is continued in 'perhaps', 'possibly', 'suspect' and 'may have'. In this paragraph, then, the narrator attempts to describe Heathcliff, but fails.

The effect of this style is to focus our attention on the act of narration itself. Lockwood is an observer who takes in sense-impressions and thinks about them, as does any person travelling through life; and he struggles to translate these impressions into words for us. Brontë's repeated use of the language of guesswork and hesitant deduction never allows us to forget that the thing itself – Heathcliff and his house – is only relayed to us by means of a clumsy, struggling observer.

So far, then, we have found a consistent seam in Lockwood's language which emphasises the act of narration, reminding us that the story comes to us via a narrative frame. We have also noticed that the Lockwood 'filter' only allows a small amount of solid material to reach us. So, for example, we saw that the paragraph about Heathcliff was 278 words long, but only 47 of these words conveyed reliable information. So, the frame restricts our information. The next question is: does it also change, distort or suppress information?

Two features of the extract suggest answers to these questions. First, Brontë begins to establish a contrast between the diction of the story itself, and the more elaborate language of the narrator; and secondly, the speculation about Heathcliff's character which ends the extract also analyses the relationship between narrator and character, and contains a warning about judgements of character in general. The 'diction of the story itself' is found in the characters' direct speech, and in two words which Lockwood puts in quotation marks. This language comes to us direct from the story without interference, and is markedly plain. Heathcliff and Joseph both speak in monosyllables apart from the two names 'Joseph' and 'Lockwood'. Heathcliff includes two imperatives, 'take' and 'bring'. Their short, plain words are in sharp contrast to Lockwood's narrative. Immediately after Heathcliff speaks, Lockwood uses 'establishment' and 'domestics'; and following Joseph's speech he uses 'soliloquised', 'undertone' and 'displeasure'.

The two words in quotation marks are 'wuthering', the local term for wild stormy weather; and 'house'. The first of these is a most suggestive word which provokes us to think of 'weathering' and 'withering', and has an indefinably onomatopoeic effect, the first syllable being reminiscent of a gust of wind. Lockwood's commentary is typically elaborate, in contrast: it is 'a significant provincial adjective, descriptive of the atmospheric tumult' and so on. 'House', the local word for the main room in a farmhouse, is directly contrasted to the most pompous, precious term in this part of Lockwood's narrative. He calls the interior the 'penetralium'.

In the final paragraph Lockwood becomes uncharacteristically sure of himself. Faced with Heathcliff's 'morose' expression, he claims to understand the other man: 'I know, by instinct', he says, and then gives an analysis of Heathcliff's character: 'He'll love and hate, equally under cover, and esteem it a species of impertinence to be loved or hated again.' When we have finished reading the novel, we are struck by the simultaneous perception and blindness of Lockwood's instinct. However, Lockwood stops himself and returns to the guesswork that is typical of his narrative: 'I bestow my own attributes over-liberally on him', he says, and acknowledges that Heathcliff may have motives he (Lockwood) has never imagined.

This is a fascinating passage, raising as it does the relationship between the storyteller and the character – whether they are real or imagined people. Brontë has established that the narrator cannot be neutral, that authors express their own characters in the stories and people they create. At the same time, the unknowable mystery of other people is affirmed. Heathcliff, like any character, has separate, free existence and infinite potential: he 'may have entirely dissimilar reasons' for appearing the way he does – reasons his author cannot imagine. The passage is particularly important as it arrives so close to the beginning of the novel, and marks Brontë's concern with the question of narrative. It is like a declaration of her intention, to exploit the doubled narrative framework to the full.

We could notice further features of Lockwood's style in this extract. Examining his sentences, for example, would show that he uses elaborate and educated constructions, and that he uses circumlocution and writes euphemistically (notice, for example, that 'atmospheric tumult' stands for 'storm'). However, we have already discovered a great deal about Brontë's use of the narrator's voice and character, and it is time to summarise what we have found.

The narrator is openly uncertain, and only a small amount of reliable material filters through him from the story to us. We are constantly reminded of how little we know, and how speculative all our interpretations must be. So, it seems at first that Brontë has created a very thin and rarefied story, and we might expect the effect of this narrative to be reductive or economical. This is not the effect, however. The explicit, insistent lack of thorough information in the story paradoxically creates the opposite effect. As we are reminded how thin our information is, we are at the same time reminded, continually, of the fullness of vague distances which contain more but unknown information. Heathcliff's 'entirely dissimilar' motives, the unknowable infinite mystery of another individual, are like the 'other dogs' which 'haunted other recesses': they are things we are vaguely aware of which create an unlimited but obscured environment around the story itself.

At the same time, Brontë has carefully allowed some scraps of material to pass through unchanged by the narrator. In this extract, there were two very short speeches and two local words. Later in the novel, we will find the characters' voices speaking to us directly through the narrative frames. In this extract, a contrast between real speech and Lockwood's elaborately precious style enhances the directness, the realism, of these scraps, so that they stand out powerfully.

[b] Nelly Dean

Nelly Dean was a girl-servant at Wuthering Heights when Mr Earnshaw returned from a visit to Liverpool with the orphan child, Heathcliff. When Lockwood records the story, she is the middle-aged housekeeper at Thrushcross Grange. Most of the novel is narrated to Lockwood by her. Our next extract is from Mrs Dean's narrative, and comes just after the death of Catherine:

. . . My mind was never in a holier frame, than while I gazed on that untroubled image of Divine rest. I instinctively echoed the words she had uttered, a few hours before, 'Incomparably beyond, and above us all! Whether still on earth or now in heaven, her spirit is at home with God!'

I don't know if it be a peculiarity in me, but I am seldom otherwise than happy while watching in the chamber of death, should no frenzied or despairing mourner share the duty with me. I see a repose that neither earth nor hell can break; and I feel an assurance of the endless and shadowless hereafter – the eternity they have entered – where life is boundless in its duration, and love in its sympathy, and joy in its fulness. I noticed on that occasion how much selfishness there is even in a love like Mr Linton's, when he so regretted Catherine's blessed release!

To be sure one might have doubted, after the wayward and impatient existence she had led, whether she merited a haven of peace at last. One might doubt in seasons of cold reflection, but not then, in the presence of her corpse. It asserted its own tranquillity, which seemed a pledge of equal quiet to its former inhabitants.

'Do you believe such people *are* happy in the other world, sir? I'd give a great deal to know.'

I declined answering Mrs Dean's question, which struck me as something heterodox. She proceeded:

'Retracing the course of Catherine Linton, I fear we have no right to think she is: but we'll leave her with her Maker.'

The master looked asleep, and I ventured soon after sunrise to quit the room and steal out to the pure, refreshing air. The servants thought me gone to shake off the drowsiness of my protracted watch; in reality my chief motive was seeing Mr Heathcliff. If he had remained among the larches all night he would have heard nothing of the stir at the Grange, unless, perhaps, he might catch the gallop of the messenger going to Gimmerton. If he had come nearer he would probably be aware, from the lights flitting to and fro, and the opening and shutting of the outer doors, that all was not right within.

I wished yet feared to find him. I felt the terrible news must be told, and I longed to get it over, but *how* to do it I did not know.

He was there – at least a few yards further in the park; leant against an old ash tree, his hat off, and his hair soaked with the dew that had gathered on the budded branches, and fell pattering round him. He had been standing a long time in that position, for I saw a pair of ousels passing and repassing, scarcely three feet from him, busy in building their nest, and regarding his proximity no more than that of a piece of timber. They flew off at my approach, and he raised his eyes and spoke:

'She's dead!' he said; 'I've not waited for you to learn that. Put your handkerchief away – don't snivel before me. Damn you all! She wants none of *your* tears!'

I was weeping as much for him as her: we do sometimes pity creatures that have none of the feeling either for themselves or others; and when I first looked into his face I perceived that he had got intelligence of the catastrophe; and a foolish notion struck me that his heart was quelled, and he prayed, because his lips moved, and his gaze was bent on the ground.

'Yes, she's dead!' I answered, checking my sobs, and drying my cheeks. 'Gone to heaven, I hope, where we may, everyone, join her, if we take due warning, and leave our evil ways to follow good!'

'Did *she* take due warning, then?' asked Heathcliff, attempting a sneer. 'Did she die like a saint? Come, give me a true history of the event. How did –'

He endeavoured to pronounce the name, but could not manage it; and compressing his mouth, he held a silent combat with his inward agony, defying, meanwhile, my sympathy with an unflinching, ferocious stare.

'How did she die?' he resumed, at last – fain, notwithstanding his hardihood, to have a support behind him, for, after the struggle, he trembled, in spite of himself, to his very finger-ends.

'Poor wretch!' I thought; 'you have a heart and nerves the same as your brother men! Why should you be so anxious to conceal them? Your pride cannot blind God! You tempt him to wring them, till he forces a cry of humiliation!' 'Quietly as a lamb!' I answered, aloud. 'She drew a sigh, and stretched herself, like a child reviving, and sinking again to sleep; and five minutes after I felt one little pulse at her heart, and nothing more!'

'And – and did she ever mention me?' he asked, hesitating, as if he dreaded the answer to his question would introduce details that he could not bear to hear.

'Her senses never returned – she recognised nobody from the time you left her,' I said. 'She lies with a sweet smile on her face; and her latest ideas wandered back to pleasant early days. Her life closed in a gentle dream – may she wake as kindly in the other world!'

'May she wake in torment!' he cried, with frightful vehemence, stamping his foot, and groaning in a sudden paroxysm of ungovernable passion. 'Why, she's a liar to the end! Where is she? Not *there* – not in heaven – not perished – where? Oh! you said you cared nothing for my sufferings! And I pray one prayer – I repeat it till my tongue stiffens – Catherine Earnshaw, may you not rest, as long as I am living! You said I killed you – haunt me, then! The murdered *do* haunt their murderers. I believe – I know that ghosts *have* wandered on earth. Be with me always – take any form – drive me mad! only *do* not leave me in this abyss, where I cannot find you! Oh, God! it is unutterable! I *cannot* live without my life! I *cannot* live without my soul!'

He dashed his head against the knotted trunk; and, lifting up his eyes, howled, not like a man, but like a savage beast getting goaded to death with knives and spears.

I observed several splashes of blood about the bark of the tree, and his hand and forehead were both stained; probably the scene I witnessed was a repetition of others acted during the night. It hardly moved my compassion – it appalled me; still I felt reluctant to quit him so. But the moment he recollected himself enough to notice me watching, he thundered a command for me to go, and I obeyed. He was beyond my skill to quiet or console!

(*Wuthering Heights*, pp. 164–7)

Our first extract introduced us to Emily Brontë's concern with the narrative frame. In particular, we noticed three features. First, the narrator's guesses and interpretations of the story are repeatedly emphasised; secondly, the narrator's character interferes with the story (Lockwood projects his own character onto Heathcliff); finally, Brontë establishes a contrast between the narrator's language and the language of the story, which sets off the direct strength of the story itself.

The present extract shows a more complicated situation. Brontë's manipulation of the narrative frame has developed, and this extract is narrated through the two 'filters' of Mrs Dean and Lockwood. We can begin by asking: are the three features we noticed in the previous extract, present here as well?

Mrs Dean does use guesswork, and interprets on the basis of what she observes. When she approaches Heathcliff and announces Cathy's death, for example, she tells us that 'a foolish notion struck me that his heart was quelled, and he prayed' because Heathcliff's mouth is moving. This is a straightforward example of the narrator guessing about the character's state of mind, and by calling her guess a 'foolish notion', Mrs Dean reminds us that we cannot rely on her. A more complex situation surrounds her picture of the dead Cathy as 'that untroubled image of Divine rest'. This is a conventional view of the dead, yet in the context of *Wuthering Heights*, Mrs Dean's description raises unanswerable questions. We will discuss these later in our analysis. For now, we simply notice that she does guess about the characters, and that she repeatedly reminds us not to rely on her guesses. In this case, she goes so far as to ask Lockwood whether Cathy is in heaven ('Divine rest') or not.

Does the narrator's character interfere with the story? Yes, again. Mrs Dean is an active participant in this part of the story, and she acts on the basis of what she believes, introducing her concepts of good, evil, and Heathcliff's character, into her words. She admonishes him pompously ('if we . . . leave our evil ways'), and rubs salt into his wounds by saying that Cathy died 'Quietly as a lamb' and without mentioning his name. These are hostile actions. As with her guesswork, Mrs Dean's interference will provoke further discussion below.

It is more difficult to identify a contrast between the narrator's language and that of the story, in this extract, because Mrs Dean's language spreads into the dialogue in which she takes part. However, two features stand out. First, there is a marked contrast between her language and Heathcliff's. Their disagreement over Cathy comes through in the contrast between Mrs Dean's 'sweet smile' and 'kindly', and Heathcliff's peremptory 'May she wake in torment!' They even insult each other in contrasting diction: Mrs Dean is pompously self-righteous ('if we take due warning . . . etc.'), Heathcliff biting and hostile: 'Don't snivel before me. Damn you all!' Secondly, Brontë includes a pure Lockwood-ism, similar to the precious 'penetralium' we picked out from the earlier extract. Here, Lockwood thinks the housekeeper's speculations about salvation are 'something *heterodox*' (my italics). This classically-derived, academic word introduces to the passage the full linguistic distance the story travels before reaching the reader. It begins in the direct emotion of Heathcliff's words, then passes through Mrs Dean's bland pomposities and Lockwood's prissy academia, before reaching us. We can suggest that this linguistic journey is reflected in a parallel journey of experience and attitudes, from the story to us.

We have established, then, that the three features we noticed from the first extract are all present again here. However, the situation between narrators and story seems to be much more complicated in this extract; and we have set aside two questions for further discussion, the first of which concerns Mrs Dean's guessing.

The narrative frame in *Wuthering Heights* throws up complicated and ambiguous ironies. This is only a short extract, but we have deferred full discussion because there are so many implications that it is difficult to hold them all in our heads at the same time. In these circumstances it is helpful to summarise exactly what happens in relation to the narrative. Here is an attempt to reduce the implications of Mrs Dean's guesswork to manageable proportions, by summarising.

Mrs Dean guesses about the internal states and opinions of three characters: she guesses about Heathcliff, Cathy, and God. We will begin with the most straightforward of these.

Guesses about Heathcliff. Mrs Dean has a consistent opinion of Heathcliff, that he is a bad man who feels no pity and commits evil actions. So, she calls her notion that he prays 'foolish', refers to his 'evil ways', and opines that he was one of those who had 'none of the feeling [pity] either for themselves or others'. She explains his hardheartedness as originating in his pride, and declares 'Your pride cannot blind God!' She compares him to 'a savage beast', and his grief 'appalled' her rather than inspiring pity. On the other hand, she has an involuntary 'foolish notion' that his heart was 'quelled', admits that she was 'weeping as much for him as her', and pities him ('Poor wretch!') because he is human as she is: 'you have a heart and nerves the same as your brother men!' Even when his savage words and behaviour have appalled her, towards the end of the extract, Mrs Dean feels 'reluctant to quit him so', as if she is responsible for him in some way. In short, Mrs Dean is affected by Heathcliff's grief, and feels an involuntary sympathy towards him, despite her opinion that he is evil and savage.

Why, then, does she treat him so badly, rubbing salt in his wounds? It is reasonable to suggest that she defends herself against the appeal of his emotion, and bolsters her bad opinion of him, by pitting her moral platitudes against his angry grief. Here, then, we have a narrator who is at war within herself. Her psychological needs drive her behaviour, and distort her narrative.

Guesses about Cathy. Mrs Dean wonders where Cathy is, but concludes that she is at peace: 'her spirit is at home with God!' she says, and imagines a place where 'life is boundless . . . , and love in its sympathy, and joy in its fulness'. Having speculated about Cathy's restless character when she was alive, our narrator still thinks that the body 'asserted its own tranquillity'. Brontë highlights how doubtful these visions of paradise are, when Mrs Dean quotes Cathy herself. She remembers Cathy's words 'incomparably beyond, and above us all', and these lead her to the conclusion that her 'spirit is at home with God'. However, we remember that Cathy's vision of the afterlife was ambiguous. She desired 'escape into that glorious world', but claimed that she would 'not be at peace' until Heathcliff joined her in death (pp. 159–60). Earlier, she had said 'they may bury me twelve feet deep, and throw the church down over me; but

I won't rest till you are with me . . . I never will!' (p. 125). Cathy's afterlife, then, means continued existence leading to final union with Heathcliff, and no rest until that union occurs. This is consistent with the dream she told to Mrs Dean, in which angels threw her out of heaven for weeping, and she awoke on the heath above Wuthering Heights, 'sobbing for joy' (see p. 80). So, Mrs Dean's emphasis on peace and reconciliation, full of love's 'sympathy', is not like Cathy's own belief. The narrator's belief supplants the character's.

Guesses about God. The questions Mrs Dean raises about God are really an expansion of her thoughts on Cathy's death. She asks Mr Lockwood whether 'wayward and impatient' people are happy in heaven. This is, indeed, a 'heterodox' question, and belongs with major themes in the novel: the contrast between Joseph's and Edgar's versions of Christianity, and the lovers' ambiguous beliefs. We must read Mrs Dean's question carefully because it is, in fact, two different questions. First, Mrs Dean is asking about the extent of God's mercy: is God merciful enough to allow a wayward girl like Cathy into heaven? This is the question that Lockwood finds 'heterodox'. We may also quail at an attempt to define the limits of God's mercy! Secondly, Mrs Dean seems to ask whether Cathy would be happy in heaven. This is an entirely different question, and harks back to Cathy's own feelings: her dream of misery among the angels, and her supreme goal of union with Heathcliff. In effect, Cathy's emotional connection to Wuthering Heights and Heathcliff is so basic to her nature, that Mrs Dean finds it hard to imagine her happy away from these physical presences – even in heaven.

We have summarised Mrs Dean's speculations, then. If we now think of them as a whole, we may be struck by the way they circle and elaborate central themes of the novel. Heathcliff's character is an enigma. Is he human, or a creature of savage, elemental passion? Is he evil, or does his violence derive from agony and early abuse? These questions provoke a bitter conflict within Mrs Dean, and they also trouble the reader. Cathy's vision of life after death is equally contentious. At issue is the fundamental bond between her, Heathcliff, and Wuthering Heights, that is such a powerful element in the novel as a whole. Is their union pagan or romantic, a delusion or a wonder transcending life and breaking through the gates of the grave? Readers and critics have argued these questions hotly ever since *Wuthering Heights* first appeared. Again, then, our questions echo Mrs Dean's. Finally, how infinite is God's love? One of the major questions of the novel concerns the infinity or limitation of love, and love's unlimited demands. The importance of this theme will be enlarged on in Chapter 5, where we discuss the significance of Lockwood's dreams and the sin called the 'first of the seventy-first'.

Features of the narrative frame we noticed in our first extract appear here in a much more complicated form, then. They have the effect of exploring and elaborating central themes of the novel, but there is one consistent element: however much the narrator guesses, interferes, or imposes a different language on events, Brontë never allows the narrative to solve the fundamental problems of the book. The narrative framework simply passes its questions up the line to us, and leaves the reader in a state of uneasy doubt about the nature of reality. The two narrators we have analysed are typically unable to control the story they tell: it unsettles and overwhelms them, and they pass on to the reader their disturbed inability to master it. If we can express the effect of this in a simile, it is as if the story is a flood, and the narrator a hose, attempting to contain the flood and channel it through its meagre pipe to us.

Two further features of this passage are worthy of remark before we pass on. First, some parts of 'the thing itself' – the story and the main characters' experiences – are directly and powerfully conveyed. This happens in Heathcliff's speech, and we have already noted that his diction is contrastingly more vigorous than Mrs Dean's. It also happens through the use of imagery, and in the power of descriptions. In this extract, the detail of the ousels, which build their nest oblivious of Heathcliff's presence, is an extraordinary evocation of his long stillness; and the image of him as 'a savage beast getting goaded to death with knives and spears' is both vivid, and arguably a figure which expresses the course of Heathcliff's whole life. Mrs Dean's images often have this quality: their effect spreads outward, expressing something of much wider significance than the moment they purport to describe.

Secondly, the subject of storytelling, and the distortion that any narrative imposes on life itself, is brought up between the characters. Here, Heathcliff objects to the moralistic slant Mrs Dean adds to her account of Cathy's death. He asks for 'a true history of the event'. Such a narrative may not be possible, and it is certainly beyond Mrs Dean's powers, so Heathcliff never hears a 'true history'. Instead, she continues to goad him with pictures of peace and mildness until he can bear it no more and bursts out, dismissing narrator and story at once: 'Why, she's a liar to the end!'

Describing the effect of Lockwood and Mrs Dean, we likened the story to a flood trying to get through a hosepipe. Here again, Brontë presents the violent conflict between life and true experience, on the one hand, and narrative on the other. These two elements of the text seem to rub against each other in potentially explosive conflict, throughout the novel. In this extract, sparks fly because Heathcliff refuses to allow truth to be distorted and diluted in its telling.

So far, we have taken samples of the two narrators who constitute the main 'frame' of the novel – the storytellers who enable the story to reach us. Another servant, Zillah, whose relation to the events is similar to that of Mrs Dean, narrates a part of the story also; but in the next section we want to focus on those times when the main characters take over the narrative and tell their own experience. We already noted that some dialogue contrasts with Lockwood's and Mrs Dean's language, establishing direct contact between the reader and characters. This effect occurs on a larger scale when the characters' voices are used in extended monologues.

[c] Other narrators

There are a number of narratives spoken by the participating characters in *Wuthering Heights*. We will look at two of them. We begin with Heathcliff's account of his marriage and life with Isabella. Afterwards, we will examine an extract from Isabella's account of the same period. Here is what Heathcliff says:

> 'She abandoned them [the . . . comforts, and friends of her former home] under a delusion,' he answered, 'picturing in me a hero of

romance, and expecting unlimited indulgences from my chivalrous devotion. I can hardly regard her in the light of a rational creature, so obstinately has she persisted in forming a fabulous notion of my character, and acting on the false impressions she cherished. But, at last, I think she begins to know me – I don't perceive the silly smiles and grimaces that provoked me at first; and the senseless incapability of discerning that I was in earnest when I gave her my opinion of her infatuation, and herself – It was a marvellous effort of perspicacity to discover that I did not love her. I believed, at one time, no lessons could teach her that! and yet it is poorly learnt; for this morning she announced, as a piece of appalling intelligence, that I had actually succeeded in making her hate me! A positive labour of Hercules, I assure you! If it be achieved I have cause to return thanks – Can I trust your assertion, Isabella, are you sure you hate me? If I let you alone for half-a-day, won't you come sighing and wheedling to me again? I dare say she would rather I had seemed all tenderness before you; it wounds her vanity to have the truth exposed. But, I don't care who knows that the passion was wholly on one side, and I never told her a lie about it. She cannot accuse me of showing a bit of deceitful softness. The first thing she saw me do, on coming out of the Grange, was to hang up her little dog, and when she pleaded for it, the first words I uttered were a wish that I had the hanging of every being belonging to her, except one: possibly, she took that exception for herself – But no brutality disgusted her – I suppose she has an innate admiration of it, if only her precious person were secure from injury! Now, was it not the depth of absurdity – of genuine idiocy, for that pitiful, slavish, mean-minded brach to dream that I could love her? Tell your master, Nelly, that I never, in all my life, met with such an abject thing as she is – She even disgraces the name of Linton; and I've sometimes relented, from pure lack of invention, in my experiments on what she could endure, and still creep shamefully cringing back! But tell him, also, to set his fraternal and magisterial heart at ease, that I keep strictly within the limits of the law – I have avoided, up to this period, giving her the slightest right to claim a separation; and what's more, she'd thank nobody for dividing us – if she desired to go she might – the nuisance of her presence outweighs the gratification to be derived from tormenting her.'

(pp. 148–9)

Let us look at the language Heathcliff uses. When we begin to assess his style, we may be surprised at the breadth and complexity of his vocabulary, since our first observation of his speech commented on short words and simple physical verbs. This speech seems much more elaborate. Close analysis soon shows us that the plain language is still there, but is one of two distinct styles in Heathcliff's speech.

We know from previous extracts that Heathcliff commands a rough, violent diction that contrasts with Nelly's and Lockwood's. For example, we heard him say 'don't snivel' to Nelly, and 'May she wake in torment!' of Cathy. The present passage includes some choice insults aimed at Isabella. She is a 'mean-minded brach' and an 'abject thing' who showed 'silly smiles and grimaces', for example; and Heathcliff's concise colloquial energy is apparent in forceful phrases such as 'she'd thank nobody for dividing us' and 'I never told her a lie about it.' These expressions could not possibly come from either Lockwood or Nelly – they are purely Heathcliff's rough, energetic style.

We have also heard Heathcliff's sarcasm before. He asked Nelly 'Did *she* take due warning, then?', angrily deflating her pompous moralising over Cathy's death. In the present passage, Heathcliff uses sarcasm intensively. Perhaps the strongest impression we form of his language, is his trick of hijacking the vocabulary of others and using it sneeringly against them. So, Isabella expected 'unlimited indulgences' from his 'chivalrous devotion'. He tried hard to show her his hatred, but it was 'a marvellous effort of perspicacity' for her to discover this truth. She reveals her hatred of him as if it is an 'appalling intelligence', and Heathcliff satirically comments on the 'positive labour of Hercules' it has been to open her eyes. He treats Edgar Linton with equal sarcasm, talking of his 'fraternal and magisterial heart'. These phrases have in common that they employ an elaborate, literary vocabulary and tend to be hyperbolic.

Where does this elaborate style of speech come from? Heathcliff's intention is clearly to parody others — but he does not meet Lockwood for another nineteen years. Who else speaks formally and stiffly? Here is a speech of Edgar's:

'I have been so far forbearing with you, sir . . . not that I was ignorant of your miserable, degraded character, but, I felt you were only partly responsible for that; and Catherine, wishing to keep up your acquaintance, I acquiesced – foolishly'

(p. 113)

The phrases of the magistrate 'I have been so far forbearing' and 'wishing to keep up your acquaintance' lead to the precise literary word: 'acquiesced'. Edgar speaks well, but he often uses a formal diction that reveals his class. This is the language Heathcliff satirises, and he does so with a weight of contemptuous irony (think of Edgar's 'fraternal and magisterial heart') that is devastating.

We have described two distinct styles in Heathcliff's speech, then: sarcastic pomposity and plain roughness. How do they work together? Heathcliff uses them to contrast with each other, and this heightens the satirical effect. For example, there is strong linguistic bathos between Isabella's 'marvellous effort of perspicacity' and the obvious monosyllables of her discovery 'that I did not love her'. The speech constantly plays upon this contrast, so the reader seems to be carried up to a false height, sneeringly intoned, then dropped harshly down to the real ground of rough truth. The overall effect, then, is energetic and violent: the reader is repeatedly thrown back down to reality from a pretentious linguistic height.

Clearly, Emily Brontë has created a distinct dramatic 'voice' for Heathcliff. Analysis has shown us more than this, however. His voice is surprisingly wide-ranging. It takes and uses the narrators' diction, exposes its hollowness and throws it away with contempt; and in contrast, Heathcliff speaks through the narrative frame in his own forceful, plain style. So, not only does he make direct contact with us, like a dramatic character speaking straight to the audience; he also shreds the linguistic pretensions of the narrators, at the same time. The effect is peculiarly powerful, and suggests the idea that the story of *Wuthering Heights* is too strong, too powerfully alive, to be contained within the storytellers' frame. It – the story itself – actively breaks the frame through which we read it.

Here is Isabella's description of a scene during her life at Wuthering Heights. She feels 'a certain sense of superiority and satisfaction' when she finds Heathcliff and Hindley grief-stricken and sick respectively. She attributes her pleasure to 'the comfort of a quiet conscience within me', then describes Heathcliff:

'Heathcliff did not glance my way, and I gazed up, and contemplated his features, almost as confidently as if they had been turned to stone. His forehead, that I once thought so manly, and that I now think so diabolical, was shaded with a heavy cloud; his basilisk eyes were nearly quenched by sleeplessness – and weeping, perhaps, for the lashes were wet then: his lips devoid of their ferocious sneer, and sealed in an expression of unspeakable sadness. Had it been another, I would have covered my face, in the presence of such grief. In *his* case, I was gratified: and ignoble as it seems to insult a fallen enemy, I couldn't miss this chance of sticking in a dart; his weakness was the only time when I could taste the delight of paying wrong for wrong.'

'Fie, fie, Miss!' I interrupted. 'One might suppose you had never opened a Bible in your life. If God afflict your enemies, surely that ought to suffice you. It is both mean and presumptuous to add your torture to his!'

'In general, I'll allow that it would be, Ellen,' she continued. 'But what misery laid on Heathcliff could content me, unless I have a hand in it? I'd rather he suffered *less*, if I might cause his sufferings, and he might *know* that I was the cause. Oh, I owe him so much. On only one condition can I hope to forgive him. It is, if I may take an eye for an eye, a tooth for a tooth, for every wrench of agony, return a wrench, reduce him to my level. As he was the first to injure, make him the first to implore pardon; and then – why then, Ellen, I might show you some generosity. But it is utterly impossible I can ever be revenged, and therefore I cannot forgive him.'

(pp. 178–9)

First, does Isabella have a distinctive style of speaking? If we look at her vocabulary in this extract, there seems to be no characteristic style: she uses a wide range of words, including both the physical 'wrench' of agony and more literary words such as 'ignoble', 'gratified' and 'implore'. However, there is no sense of a gap between the truth and her diction – she is neither pompous nor sarcastic, and seems to speak with power and feeling. In this extract we also find Isabella using words metaphorically, with a vivid descriptive effect. The picture of Heathcliff's forehead 'shaded with a heavy cloud' and the idea of his eyes 'quenched' are examples of this.

There is, however, a difference between her speech and Heathcliff's. Look back to Heathcliff's sentence beginning 'Tell your master, Nelly, that I never, in all my life, met with such an abject thing . . .'. Heathcliff's sentence is loosely constructed, and contains a second description ('she even disgraces the name of Linton') as well as his further thought that he ran out of ideas for torturing her. Heathcliff begins his next sentence as if he has rambled, and adds a further sarcastic message for Linton, saying 'But tell him, also . . .'. In Heathcliff's speech, then, the sentences are loose and often change direction as new ways of expressing his feelings and new thoughts occur to him. Isabella's sentences are more structured, and each sentence follows the previous one in a logical way, as if she is explaining herself, or arguing her case. So, for example, she begins a sentence 'Had it been another', and the next sentence completes her deliberate contrast: 'In *his* case'. Isabella's style is so analytical that her conclusion follows from the attitudes she has expressed, logically connected by the conjunction 'therefore': 'it is utterly impossible I can ever be revenged, and therefore I cannot forgive him'.

Brontë has distinguished the speech of these two characters effectively, then. We can describe Isabella's speech as more 'rationalised' than Heathcliff's. He speaks at the moment of feeling and thinking; whereas Isabella speaks in analytical, structured sentences, explaining and justifying herself.

In comparing these two extracts, we should now consider the content of each. They are both accounts of the same events, and Brontë has given us two versions, from two characters' points of view. The obvious question for us to ask is: why has the author provided us with two narratives? We may find answers to this question by comparing the different statements the two characters make. What do they both say about their relationship?

Heathcliff emphasises that Isabella persisted in loving him, despite his obvious indifference. His sarcasm is brought into play to portray her irrational crush on him. Heathcliff correctly perceives her simple romantic notions. When he satirises her as 'picturing in me a hero of romance, and expecting unlimited indulgences from my chivalrous devotion', this picture of Isabella's idealistic love is not simpler than her own statement: 'I love him more than ever you loved Edgar; and he might love me if you would let him' (p. 101). Isabella rises vividly out of Heathcliff's account, with her 'silly smiles and grimaces', and her propensity to 'come sighing and wheedling to me again'. He even understands Isabella's mind and its self-deceptions, that she 'took that exception for herself' when he said he wanted to hang her entire family excepting one; and that 'it wounds her vanity to have the truth exposed'. Further, Heathcliff guesses at darker impulses in Isabella, saying 'no brutality disgusted her – I suppose she has an innate admiration of it'. This is a particularly perceptive thrust: we reconsider pages 176–8, when Isabella watches Heathcliff beat and kick Hindley near to death, then wakes with 'the comfort of a quiet conscience'; and pages 180–1, when she goads Heathcliff to such fury that he throws a knife at her. So, Heathcliff's account gives a vivid description of Isabella, and a perceptive analysis of even hidden elements of her character.

Heathcliff makes two statements about himself, both of which raise questions. First, it has been a 'labour of Hercules' to make her hate him, he says, implying that he has worked hard to cause her pain. This impression is enlarged upon when he claims to have run out of ideas for torturing her ('I've sometimes relented, from pure lack of invention'), and refers to 'tormenting her', at the end of his speech. He presents himself as a man devoting time and concentration to torturing Isabella; but this impression is suspect. After the fight with Hindley, for example, he only notices her when she laughs: he exclaims 'Oh, I forgot you', and only then does he remember to treat her roughly. His own account suggests the same picture, since the 'gratification' from torturing her is not strong enough to outweigh the annoyance she causes – he would rather ignore her altogether. Secondly, Heathcliff claims to have been honest to her: 'I never told her a lie', he says, and he refers to when he 'gave her my opinion of her infatuation, and herself'. On the other hand we remember Ellen and Cathy watching him embrace Isabella in the garden of Thrushcross Grange, so his behaviour has not been as unwaveringly honest as he suggests. Heathcliff, then, makes two doubtful statements about himself – and he says nothing about Cathy's death and his grief, which took place at this time.

What does Isabella say? First, she gives us a moving and thoroughly believable account of Heathcliff. We have remarked on how effectively she describes his eyes 'nearly quenched by sleeplessness', and the detail of his wet lashes. Isabella is clearly sensitive to the depth of Heathcliff's agony: 'I would have covered my face, in the presence of such grief.' Comparing this picture with Heathcliff's own, we notice that he leans silently against the chimney, looking 'gaunt and ghastly,' and ignores Isabella when she draws near to the fire, which she calls an 'unusual liberty'. This is not a torturing tyrant, but a forgetful man engrossed in his grief.

Secondly, Isabella is as suspect about her own character as Heathcliff is about his. She talks astonishingly of her 'quiet conscience', and in the same speech declares the 'delight of paying wrong for wrong'. The moral discussion goes into more detail in the final paragraph, when Isabella makes herself an exception to the Christian rule against vengeance; yet, at the same time, she seems to be aware that she cannot hurt Heathcliff deeply ('it is utterly impossible I can ever be revenged').

We can draw the conclusion, then, that the two accounts present two opposed points of view. Each of them is perceptive about the other but opaque about themselves. The effect of this is to highlight the self-deceptions of both characters, by comparison of the two accounts; and to increase the dramatic qualities of the novel, creating that three-dimensional play between points of view that exists on stage, and is commonly called 'dramatic irony'.

The observations we have made about the narrators of the 'framework' and the other narrators are tending in one direction: we find ourselves increasingly looking at *Wuthering Heights* in terms of its 'dramatic' qualities. A brief discussion of some other dramatic features will develop this line of thought.

A 'Dramatic' Work

We have thought of the reader being spoken to 'directly' by the characters, as if they speak 'through' the framework of Ellen Dean and Lockwood, the supposed narrators. We can take the analogy between *Wuthering Heights* and a play further, as there are several features of the way Brontë constructed her novel, reminiscent of techniques used by dramatists. In the present chapter, we will merely list and describe some of these, which are worth following up when studying the novel.

[a] **Set scenes.** The story of *Wuthering Heights* seems to revolve around a series of scenes which take place in static settings. We should notice that some scenes are viewed in the way an audience might 'view' a play (for example, Heathcliff and Cathy 'view' the quarrel about a dog, between the Linton children, through the lighted window of Thrushcross Grange; and Ellen and Cathy 'view' Heathcliff embracing Isabella through another window). More important, there are several crucial scenes which take place within a single setting, to which characters enter and from which they leave, while the narrative – like the audience's attention at a play – remains continuously in the same place. One example of this effect is the scene in Cathy's bedchamber, when Ellen enters and finds her delirious. This lasts between pages 119 and 125, and the last part of the scene follows Edgar's entry.

[b] **Self-revealing speeches.** These are a frequent device, similar to monologues or soliloquies on stage. For example, Cathy gives a deeply personal account of her delirious dreams on pages 123 and 124, beginning 'Well, it seems a weary number of hours'. She is speaking to Ellen, but clearly the feelings she communicates are beyond Mrs Dean's understanding. This is emphasised by Cathy towards the end of the speech, when she says: 'Shake your head, as you will, Nelly', knowing that her listener cannot 'fancy a glimpse of the abyss where [she] grovelled' (p. 124). The effect of this speech, then, is like that of a soliloquy on stage – it is as if Cathy is speaking her innermost feelings aloud.

There are several other examples of the same effect, including Heathcliff's description of his state of mind that begins on p. 319. Here, the effect of soliloquy is even more openly defined. In the middle of his speech, Heathcliff observes:

'But you'll not talk of what I tell you, and my mind is so eternally secluded in itself, it is tempting, at last, to turn it out to another.'

(p. 320)

Heathcliff has no purpose in talking of these things to Mrs Dean, then, except to relieve his own feelings. Again, we feel that the character is simply relieving his innermost feelings for his own purposes, as if talking to himself, and the supposed 'audience' (Mrs Dean) is irrelevant. We, the readers, share the soliloquy with the character.

[c] **Direct speech narrative of 'offstage' events.** We have already observed that many of the scenes described in *Wuthering Heights* are static, interior settings which are like the constant location of a scene in a play. Brontë also limits the amount her narrative point of view moves around, by bringing narrators into the set location to narrate events which have happened elsewhere. A moment's thought will provide you with many examples of this technique. Notable among them are Heathcliff's narrative of his and Cathy's foray to Thrushcross Grange (pp. 47–51), and the younger Cathy's narrative of her visits to Wuthering Heights (pp. 244–51).

The way in which narrators are regularly 'brought in' to the set scene, in order to narrate events that have taken place elsewhere, enhances the effect of a theatrical drama. Plays often suggest that the limited 'stage' is only a visible focus for events which extend through an apparent wider world, around and outside that limited 'stage'.

[d] **Unity of place.** This phrase comes from neo-classical theories about tragic plays. Interpreting the idea strictly, neo-classicists of the seventeenth and eighteenth centuries believed that the best tragedy had a single dramatic setting: the scene should not change at all throughout the play. The original idea derives from Aristotle's *Poetics*, where he proposes the idea of 'unity', saying that the 'action' of a tragedy is best when it is 'a complete unit, and the events of which it is made up must be so plotted that if any of these elements is moved or removed the whole is altered and upset'.[2] It is this, more

---

[2] Aristotle, *On the Art of Fiction: An English Translation of 'The Poetics'*, trans. and ed. L. J. Potts (Cambridge, 1962), p. 28.

sophisticated concept of 'unity' that I believe Brontë was seeking in the way she arranged the setting for *Wuthering Heights*.

Emily Brontë was clearly anxious to prevent her narrative point of view from being too mobile. She judged that the intensity of the story might dissipate and be lost, if she introduced too many locations and changes of scene. This would explain the liberal use she makes of narratives from 'offstage', mentioned in [c] above. The same point is underscored by the way she handles journeys outside the localities of Wuthering Heights and Thrushcross Grange. Old Mr Earnshaw, Hindley, Heathcliff, Isabella, and Edgar Linton, all go away at one point or another in the story. Old Mr Earnshaw and Edgar Linton give brief accounts of their journeys – to Liverpool and somewhere 'in the south' respectively – on their return; but theirs are brief journeys of a few days and three weeks respectively. Hindley, on the other hand, lives away from the area for an indefinite amount of time while at college, and returns with a wife; Heathcliff disappears for three crucial years; and Isabella goes to live the rest of her life 'in the south', staying there for twelve years and dying there.

Hindley's return for his father's funeral brings 'a thing that amazed us' (p. 45) – a wife – and their meeting is never explained. When Heathcliff returns after his three years' absence, his manners have been transformed and he has acquired both an education, and money. However, we are never told where he was nor what he did during that time. The story simply remains in its conflicting twin locations of Wuthering Heights and Thrushcross Grange, and Heathcliff is absent. In the same way, Isabella's life 'in the south' is treated as merely her absence from the story, until the new character Linton Heathcliff is brought back from the south by his uncle Edgar.

In this way, Emily Brontë preserves the sense that the two poles of the novel's world are the two houses and their two related attitudes to life: Wuthering Heights and Thrushcross Grange (we will look at the structure of the novel's setting in greater detail in Chapter 4). The characters who travel away simply disappear for the time of their absence, and the narrative makes no attempt to follow them or relate anything about their life. A vast amount of speculation has been written about Heathcliff's three years away; but all that we learn from the text is that he was not there, on the limited 'stage' of the novel itself. We can imagine Brontë saying that Heathcliff's experiences while he was away were not relevant – they are not part of the single 'complete' action of his passion for Cathy and its products, his revenge and death. Therefore, they have no place in the 'unity' of the novel's fable.

In these ways, *Wuthering Heights* can be likened to a play, and its narrative devices create the sense of a limited area within which all vital actions will occur, like a 'stage'. Messengers and characters run on and off this stage, bringing news and stories from elsewhere; and characters often reveal their inner selves dramatically, from their own mouths, rather than by means of the observation or omniscience of a novelist.

Conclusions

1. The two main narrators, Mr Lockwood and Mrs Dean, are in contrast to the story they tell and the characters involved in that story. This contrast is apparent in their attitudes and in the language.
2. The story and characters repeatedly 'break' the framework of the narrators. That is, events and characters exceed the emotional or moral range of the storytellers. This has the effect of emphasising the power of story and characters.
3. Both main narrators become characters whose unacknowledged thoughts, limitations and weaknesses are revealed to the reader.

The above three features of *Wuthering Heights* have the effect of shining a constant spotlight upon the act of storytelling, and insecurity about the truth or reality of the thing – the story – itself.

4. Other narrators are dramatically characterised by their individual patterns of speech, and they often provide different points of view on the same event. These points of view are ironically related to each other. We have noticed, for example, that

Heathcliff and Isabella are perceptive about each other, but reticent about themselves, when describing their married life.

5. A number of techniques, such as narratives of events that take place elsewhere, and long self-revealing speeches by the characters, suggest a comparison between Brontë's method in *Wuthering Heights*, and a dramatist's devices when setting his fable on a stage. In this sense, we have called the novel a 'dramatic' work, and we suggested that it has a quality of completeness and intensity that Aristotle called 'unity'.

Methods of Analysis

[a] **Approaches to the text.** In our analysis of extracts in this chapter, we have focused on various aspects of the text that are often revealing during prose analysis:

1. Narrative of events and actions; description; direct and indirect speech.
2. Variation in the length of sentences, and variation in the length and directness of constructions (we noticed, for example, that Heathcliff's sarcastic constructions are elaborate and long, but he contrasts these with blunt, short and direct statements).
3. The structure of sentences. Look at the clauses or groups of words, and describe how they are linked together. Find ways of describing the structure, and the effect it produces. Compare this with the progress of ideas in the sentence (we noticed, for example, that Isabella uses logical structures and conjunctions, while Heathcliff's diction is much more loosely connected and seems closer to the origin of thought and feeling in the character).
4. Other noticeable effects of diction such as verbs, repetition, or the use of particular words, which are noticeable in their context (in this connection, we noticed Lockwood's pompous latinism 'penetralium', or the blunt and active energy of Heathcliff's verbs, in our extract from Chapter 1).
5. Imagery, both of actual objects which are part of the narrative, and in figurative references to natural things and forces.

This amounts to observing **the way in which the passage is written** very closely, and involves an open-minded, detailed scrutiny. Whatever you *notice* about the writing is of interest, because it must be *noticeable*, i.e. a feature of the style. Describe the feature and its effect as accurately as you can.

[b] The specific question. In addition to describing **the way in which the passage is written** as closely as possible, we began with a specific question in our minds, and we pursued an answer to that question throughout our analysis. The question came from the subject of this chapter, and is: How and why does Emily Brontë introduce such complex relationships between the original story and the reader, and how does she play the narrators off against each other? In short, we kept the question of narration, of the act of story-telling, at the forefront of our minds as we analysed extracts from *Wuthering Heights*. This helped us, because we could look at the features we found in the text, and ask: What does this tell us *about the act of narration*? In other words, we had a **specific question** in mind, and this is an enormous help when searching for deductions and conclusions.

In later chapters, we will make use of different **specific questions** when approaching extracts from the novel. We will find ourselves asking about the setting, the characters, and the themes. When you become practised at analysing the text, you will find that your mind naturally pursues several questions about the text at the same time, as you analyse, so there is no need to go back and back over one passage, laboriously and repetitively. The important elements of a passage will seem to highlight themselves to you as you study – because you are used to approaching a text with specific, purposeful questions in your mind.

Suggested Work

We have found that the question of narrative is a constant and complex concern in *Wuthering Heights*. It would be helpful to add further details to your understanding of the way the narrative framework affects the novel, by studying further relevant passages in detail. We suggest one as a starting-point.

Study the final two paragraphs of Chapter 10 (X), beginning at 'From their tongues, they did dismiss it . . .' (p. 106); and the start of Chapter 11 (XI) as far as '. . . supposing it were a sign of death!' (p. 108). Look, in particular, at the relationship between Mrs Dean's character and the material she relates; and the experience she relates in comparison with others' experiences, narrated by her.

2

Characterisation

In Chapter 1 we found that the story in *Wuthering Heights* is often powerful enough to shatter or transcend the narrators' attempts to mediate between the action and the reader. On the other hand, Mrs Dean has a narrow morality and is often foolish in both thought and action; and Mr Lockwood is a self-centred ass, ignorant of his own character. So there is no mystery about the 'power' of the story: Emily Brontë enhances the effect by characterising narrators who are shallow and easily pushed aside.

As with the 'power' of the story, much is often made of the power of the principal characters in *Wuthering Heights*. Heathcliff in particular seems to earn wondering adjectives, as 'mesmerising', or 'demon-like'. In this chapter we will examine Brontë's characterisation, looking closely at the way she creates these personalities. Our job is to explain how the characters have been brought to life, and how they work. We want to gain insight, not mystery. By marshalling all the information available in the text, and analysing with care, we hope that any 'mystery' that remains at the end of our study will at least have well-defined boundaries.

We begin with a general discussion of secondary figures from the novel, in order to establish Brontë's methods of characterisation, before going on to consider extracts relating to each of Heathcliff and the elder Cathy, the two protagonists who are presented in the greatest depth.

Secondary Characters

Joseph

How does Brontë introduce a character? We will look at Joseph, who appears in the first chapter. We first see him through Lockwood's eyes, and the narrator is typically uncertain of his age: 'Joseph was an elderly, nay, an old man, very old, perhaps, though hale and sinewy.' Joseph's voice and expression are described in the next paragraph, the first as 'an undertone of peevish displeasure' and the second as 'looking . . . sourly' (all from p. 4). This is the sum total of description devoted to Joseph, but it is reinforced, strengthening the impression he makes. On page 6 Joseph's 'undertone' is mentioned again as he 'mumbled indistinctly', and his sour expression develops into 'vinegar-faced Joseph' on page 9.

Joseph's manner of speech begins with the common, intelligible phrase 'The Lord help us!' (p. 4), which establishes his voice as being laced with religious phrases and names. The next time he speaks, his dialect is fully represented: 'Whet are ye for? . . . T'maister's dahn i' t'fowld' (p. 9). Joseph's dialect curses and mumbles are a recurrent feature of the novel until his last appearance by Heathcliff's body, when he exclaims 'Th'divil's harried off his soul' (p. 332). He also frequently mumbles and mutters in his 'undertone', and looks bad-temperedly.

We have examined Joseph's first appearances, then, and found certain distinct features in the way this is done. First, Emily Brontë does not pause to introduce him: there is a minimum of description, and hardly any visual presentation of the character. The impression he makes appeals to the mind and emotions, and the ear. That is, the riddle of his age, his 'sour' expression, and the sound of his voice. These impressions are given immediately and strongly, and are reinforced, appearing like a *motif* each time we meet him again.

The absence of pictorial details is quite striking, and contributes to the emphasis on emotion: we do not know whether he was tall or short, thin or stocky, with a pudgy nose or a hooked beak. However, we are told the feeling that animates his expression – he looked 'sourly'. In the same way, we are not told that he had a high voice, or a rich deep tone; but we are told that it was full of 'peevish displeasure'. So we can say that Joseph is presented with an absence of conventional description: instead there is an emphasis on the mood he projects, and the impact of that on the feelings.

Hindley Earnshaw

We can now look at the introduction of another secondary character, Hindley Earnshaw. Does Emily Brontë follow the same method consistently, focusing on mood and emotional impact, and throwing her character into actions and speech as quickly as possible?

The suddenness of Hindley's arrival in the novel is accentuated because he is introduced in Catherine's journal, not in Lockwood's narrative. A strongly paradoxical effect is set up by the journal device: Hindley's name is mentioned without explanation, as if we already know his character, and his relationship to the narrator. On the other side of this narrative paradox, however, ignorance and doubt are heavily underscored. We do not know anything about Hindley at all. In fact, we know nothing about the person who is writing about him, our narrator for the moment, either. Lockwood's confusions emphasise uncertainty: this person seems to have many different handwritings, and three possible surnames: '. . . in all kinds of characters, large and small – *Catherine Earnshaw*, here and there varied to *Catherine Heathcliff*, and then again to *Catherine Linton*' (p. 19).

Hindley, then, arrives as an unexplainable name. On the other hand, he does appear attached to powerful feelings: he is immediately 'detestable', and his behaviour is 'atrocious'. This hostility is strongly marked throughout the short scene Catherine's journal relates. He is called 'the tyrant' and is physically aggressive ('seizing one of us by the collar, and the other by the arm, hurled both into the back-kitchen') before the end of the scene. Brontë slips in the fact that he is the writer's 'brother', unobtrusively, during the narration.

A second strong character-trait of Hindley is also established quickly. He and his wife 'basked' in front of the fire, and they were 'like two babies, kissing and talking nonsense by the hour'. When he threw the children out of the room, Hindley came from 'his paradise on the hearth'. The reader already has a strong impression of Hindley, then, created by his hostility and violence; and the repeated idea of childish gratification, his self-indulgence with his wife.

Catherine clearly uses the word 'paradise' sarcastically, when describing Hindley's happiness by the warm fire, with Frances on his knee. This word carries wider suggestion. Catherine would have been 'ashamed of' their 'foolish palaver', and she has earlier pointed out that they were not 'reading their Bibles' but indulging themselves. The contemptuous force of the word 'paradise' therefore implies that Hindley's feelings are so childish they are not even grounded in the real world – they are an impossible fantasy.

At the time of reading Chapter 3, this suggestion is subtle; but it grows in meaning and strength as the novel proceeds. So, when Mrs Dean relates Hindley's reaction to the broken violin, going back in time but forward in the novel, she describes his behaviour as younger than his years – he was 'a boy of fourteen' but he 'blubbered aloud' (p. 37); while the concept of a paradise so unreal as to make Catherine miserable is developed in the 'heaven' of her dream, when she tells Nelly 'heaven did not seem to be my home; and I broke my heart with weeping to come back to earth' (p. 80).

From looking at the way these two characters are introduced to the novel, we have learned that Brontë does not allow characterisation to interrupt the pace of her narrative. Details of Joseph and Hindley are given in occasional words and phrases while the action proceeds. We have also found that, in each case, a powerful emotional focus for the character is established immediately – Joseph's 'sour' expression and 'displeasure' are among the first words used of him, while Hindley is 'detestable' and 'atrocious' as soon as his name is mentioned. These strong emotional notes are enhanced by the absence of visual or other conventional stimuli in the language: the effect is as if the character were only an emotional energy, and nothing else.

We have also looked at the beginnings of character-development in each case. Emily Brontë uses a technique comparable to the Homeric 'epithet'. In *The Odyssey*, each mention of Odysseus's name is accompanied by an 'epithet', a word describing the most important element of his character. He is always mentioned as 'the *wily* Odysseus'. Brontë uses a technique developed from this by repeatedly emphasising the same aspect of character or behaviour, adding a recognisable 'epithet' of description each time that person is mentioned. In *Wuthering Heights*, the words used change and the situation alters; but the underlying element of character remains constant. It reappears at regular intervals, in different guises. So Joseph began with a 'sour' expression, and this is varied only pages later when he is called 'vinegar-faced Joseph'. In the same way, Hindley 'basked' by the fire, then later in the scene he and his wife are like 'two babies', and subsequently the hearth is called his 'paradise'. The words are different, but the fact of childish self-indulgence is constant.

We are struck by the extraordinary economy of the characterisation. We never read the thoughts or inner emotions of these people – yet we have an immediate emotional response to them, and they make a vivid impression on us. Analysis shows that this is all achieved within a few words and phrases.

One further point about Brontë's characterisation in general deserves noting, before we move on to consider Catherine and Heathcliff. The technique I have compared to Homer's 'epithets' has a further function. It provides the reader with an underlying understanding which guides interpretation of that character throughout the novel. So, even when events become more complex, and the character responds in a transformed situation, we can rely on our grasp of these basic traits to guide us in understanding how they work. An example will make this clear.

When Hindley is master of Wuthering Heights, and a father, he continues to deny reality. So, when we hear him asserting that his dying wife is well ('she's well – she does not want any more attendance from you! She never was in a consumption' – p. 64), we understand that he is furiously sustaining the illusion of a 'paradise' by the hearth, that we met on page 22. Equally, when he becomes irascible and takes to drink, and 'gave himself up to reckless dissipation' (p. 65), we understand that the same principles – a childish inability to confront reality, and indulgence of escapism – still rule his character. However, the simple character-trait is now enmeshed within complex development. It provides matter for sympathy, regret and fear, because the inadequate and immature boy now wields a man's power and holds an adult's responsibility.

In this way, even the minor characters in *Wuthering Heights* have a convincing quality. The simple 'epithet' or dominant trait of character, introduced at the start, enables us to imagine the inner developments of their feelings, and believe in their responses, even much later in their lives and in the story. It is this technique that enables us to see life from their point of view, even though they do not hold centre-stage, and are not as complex as the major figures. One of the clearest examples of this effect is to be seen in Isabella. We first see her when, at the age of eleven, she 'lay screaming . . . shrieking as if witches were running red hot needles into her', having cruelly hurt the lap-dog she and her brother 'had nearly pulled in two between them'. Heathcliff comments bitterly that 'That was their pleasure!' (all quotations are from p. 48). It is startling that the same combination of self-torture, cruelty and possessiveness marks Isabella's exit from the story, when she wishes to 'take an eye for an eye, a tooth for a tooth, for every wrench of agony, return a wrench, reduce him to my level' (p. 179). In the case of Isabella, the disturbing mix of her personality in Chapter 17 (Vol. 2, Chapter 3) includes hints of sado-masochism as she attempts to torture Heathcliff and attract his violence towards herself. Yet, within this very adult brew, the reader can still recognise an eleven-year-old girl quarrelling over a lap-dog.

Heathcliff

We can now consider the major characters. Young Cathy, Hareton, Mrs Dean herself, Edgar Linton and Linton Heathcliff are all characterised in greater detail and depth than those we have called 'secondary' in the previous section. However, in the remainder of this chapter we focus our attention on the two most famous figures from the novel – Heathcliff and Cathy. There are two distinct stages in our investigation. First, we look closely at crucial extracts, hoping to gain further insight into Brontë's methods and intentions in creating the people in *Wuthering Heights*. Subsequently, we will discuss the role each character plays in the scheme and meaning of the novel as a whole.

* * *

Here is an extract focusing on Heathcliff, from his account of opening Catherine's grave:

> He turned abruptly to the fire, and continued, with what, for lack of a better word, I must call a smile –
>
> 'I'll tell you what I did yesterday! I got the sexton, who was digging Linton's grave, to remove the earth off her coffin lid, and I opened it. I thought, once, I would have stayed there, when I saw her face again – it is hers yet – he had hard work to stir me; but he said it would change, if the air blew on it, and so I struck one side of the coffin loose – and covered it up – not Linton's side, damn him! I wish he'd been soldered in lead – and I bribed the sexton to pull it away, when I'm laid there, and slide mine out too. I'll have it made so, and then, by the time Linton gets to us, he'll not know which is which!'
>
> 'You were very wicked, Mr Heathcliff!' I exclaimed; 'were you not ashamed to disturb the dead?'
>
> 'I disturbed nobody, Nelly,' he replied; 'and I gave some ease to myself. I shall be a great deal more comfortable now; and you'll have a better chance of keeping me underground, when I get there. Disturbed her? No! she has disturbed me, night and day, through eighteen years – incessantly – remorselessly – till yesternight – and yesternight, I was tranquil. I dreamt I was sleeping the last sleep, by that sleeper, with my heart stopped, and my cheek frozen against hers.'
>
> 'And if she had been dissolved into earth, or worse, what would you have dreamt of then?' I said.
>
> 'Of dissolving with her, and being more happy still!' he answered. 'Do you suppose I dread any change of that sort? I expected such a transformation on raising the lid, but I'm better pleased that it should not commence till I share it. Besides, unless I had received a distinct impression of her passionless features, that strange feeling would hardly have been removed. It began oddly. You know, I was wild after she died, and eternally, from dawn to dawn, praying her to

return to me – her spirit – I have a strong faith in ghosts; I have a conviction that they can, and do exist, among us!

'The day she was buried there came a fall of snow. In the evening I went to the churchyard. It blew bleak as winter – all round was solitary: I didn't fear that her fool of a husband would wander up the den so late – and no one else had business to bring them there.

'Being alone, and conscious two yards of loose earth was the sole barrier between us, I said to myself. –

'"I'll have her in my arms again! If she be cold, I'll think it is this north wind that chills *me*; and if she be motionless, it is sleep."

'I got a spade from the toolhouse, and began to delve with all my might – it scraped the coffin; I fell to work with my hands; the wood commenced cracking about the screws, I was on the point of attaining my object, when it seemed that I heard a sigh from some one above, close at the edge of the grave, and bending down. – "If I can only get this off," I muttered, "I wish they may shovel in the earth over us both!" and I wrenched at it more desperately still. There was another sigh, close at my ear. I appeared to feel the warm breath of it displacing the sleet-laden wind. I knew no living thing in flesh and blood was by – but as certainly as you perceive the approach to some substantial body in the dark, though it cannot be discerned, so certainly I felt that Cathy was there, not under me, but on the earth.

'A sudden sense of relief flowed, from my heart, through every limb. I relinquished my labour of agony, and turned consoled at once, unspeakably consoled. Her presence was with me; it remained while I re-filled the grave, and led me home. You may laugh, if you will, but I was sure I should see her there. I was sure she was with me, and I could not help talking to her.

'Having reached the Heights, I rushed eagerly to the door. It was fastened; and, I remember, that accursed Earnshaw and my wife opposed my entrance. I remember stopping to kick the breath out of him, and then hurrying upstairs, to my room, and hers – I looked round impatiently – I felt her by me – I could *almost* see her, and yet I *could not*! I ought to have sweat blood then, from the anguish of my yearning, from the fervour of my supplications to have but one glimpse! I had not one. She showed herself, as she often was in life, a devil to me! And, since then, sometimes more, and sometimes less, I've been the sport of that intolerable torture! Infernal – keeping my nerves at such a stretch, that, if they had not resembled catgut, they would, long ago, have relaxed to the feebleness of Linton's.

'When I sat in the house with Hareton, it seemed that on going out, I should meet her; when I walked on the moors I should meet her coming in. When I went from home, I hastened to return, she *must* be somewhere at the Heights, I was certain! And when I slept in her chamber – I was beaten out of that – I couldn't lie there; for the moment I closed my eyes, she was either outside the window, or sliding back the panels, or entering the room, or even resting her darling head on the same pillow as she did when a child. And I must open my lids to see. And so I opened and closed them a hundred times a-night – to be always disappointed! It racked me! I've often groaned aloud, till that old rascal Joseph, no doubt, believed that my conscience was playing the fiend inside of me.

'Now since I've seen her, I'm pacified – a little. It was a strange way of killing, not by inches, but by fractions of hair-breadths, to beguile me with the spectre of a hope, through eighteen years!'

Mr Heathcliff paused and wiped his forehead – his hair clung to it, wet with perspiration; his eyes were fixed on the red embers of the fire; the brows not contracted, but raised next the temples, diminishing the grim aspect of his countenance, but imparting a peculiar look of trouble, and a painful appearance of mental tension towards one absorbing subject. He only half addressed me, and I maintained silence – I didn't like to hear him talk!

(pp. 285–8)

This extract is Heathcliff's account of his feelings over the eighteen years between Catherine's death and that of Edgar Linton. It is a crucial passage that explains elements of Heathcliff's behaviour that we have only partly understood, earlier in the novel. For example, in Chapter 3, Heathcliff 'got on to the bed, and wrenched open the lattice, bursting, as he pulled at it, into an uncontrollable passion of tears' (p. 28). Heathcliff sobs 'Come in! come in!' through the opened window. The present extract tells us that Heathcliff has expected to meet Catherine at every moment, for eighteen years.

We should start by making use of what we have already discovered about *Wuthering Heights*. Our first chapter focused on the narrative framework, and the varieties of narrative which are woven into the novel. We observed that the power of the story is enhanced by being set in contrast to flimsy narrators (Mrs Dean, Lockwood). That power is most apparent when the story exceeds, or brushes aside, the limited 'filter' of a narrator, and speaks straight to the reader without intermediary.

Clearly, this happens in our chosen extract. After Heathcliff's first paragraph, Mrs Dean interrupts to call him 'very wicked' for trying to 'disturb the dead'. His reply makes light of her conventional horror ('I disturbed nobody, Nelly'). Her next attempt to stop him tries to shock him with the harsh fact that corpses rot: 'And if she had been dissolved into earth, or worse, what would you have dreamt of then?' Heathcliff is equal to this, and turns the question back upon Nelly, discussing 'such a transformation' easily and asking 'Do you suppose I dread any change of that sort?' In Nelly's view, then, opening coffins is beyond the pale, and she is shocked in her respectable soul. She makes an effort to shame Heathcliff, then she challenges him, trying to shock him into silence. Heathcliff brushes aside her efforts. The narrator is left broken and ineffectual, and from this point onward we listen to the character giving a direct account of his experience, unimpeded by Mrs Dean's viewpoint.

When we looked at the narrative method, we found that Brontë insistently reminds us how unreliable our perceptions are. In Chapter 1, we came across Lockwood's guesswork, Mrs Dean's misinterpretations, and even Heathcliff's and Isabella's differing, subjective views of the same events. We are therefore constantly engaged in an attempt to reach a reliable understanding of the story itself. The reader sifts the various narratives, making allowances for the blindnesses and distortions of different viewpoints, constantly seeking a definitive version of what is happening.

The extract we are looking at is of the kind we likened to a 'soliloquy', in the last chapter. Nelly observes that 'He only half addressed me, and I maintained silence', because Heathcliff's mind is filled with 'mental tension towards one absorbing subject'. So, we can expect that this extract speaks directly to the reader: here, we are dealing with evidence from the core of Heathcliff's nature. This extract is therefore at the top of the scale of authenticity in the novel. Heathcliff's 'soliloquy' is as reliable a guide to the truth as the reader can find anywhere.

So far, we have used our understanding of Brontë's narrative method to define the kind of extract we are faced with. Clearly, this is a crucial and authoritative passage: we are meeting the enigma of Heathcliff's character head-on. However, before we do so, we should consider Heathcliff in the light of what we learned from Joseph and Hindley: What are his prominent characteristics when he first arrives at Wuthering Heights? Can we find a clear, consistent character-trait in the young Heathcliff, comparable to Hindley's childish escapism, that will help to explain his actions later in the story?

Soon after Heathcliff's first appearance at the Heights, Nelly observes that he seems willing to endure anything, in order to gain his desire. She begins by calling him 'sullen, patient' and comments on his 'endurance' (p. 38). She elaborates in the anecdote of the colts, when Heathcliff submits to Hindley's brutal attack: he had the lame colt, and in order to change this he suffers having an iron weight thrown at him, and being knocked under a horse's hooves. Mrs Dean 'was surprised to witness how coolly the child gathered himself up, and went on with his intention' (p. 40). It seems, then, that if something about his situation is not to Heathcliff's liking, he is prepared to endure any suffering and privation in order to change it. He will make things be the way he wants them to be, or die in the attempt.

Does this understanding of Heathcliff's character help us later in the story? Clearly, the answer is yes. In Chapter 9, Heathcliff over-hears Cathy's view of him: that Hindley has 'brought Heathcliff so low . . . It would degrade me to marry Heathcliff, now' (p. 80). Characteristically, Heathcliff says nothing, but singlemindedly sets about changing the situation. When he returns to the area three years later, he has acquired education, gentlemanly manners, and money. That is, he has cleared away the obstacles that stood between him and Cathy. So the prominent 'motif' in Heathcliff's character, that was apparent when he was a child, helps us to understand him when he mysteriously disappears and returns transformed. We will keep this knowledge in mind as we analyse our chosen extract.

We now turn to the extract itself, and look closely at the way in which Heathcliff tells his story. First, we are struck by his distinctive voice. In Chapter 1 we remarked on his loosely-constructed sen-tences, which seem to convey experience at the moment when it is lived. This quality is quickly apparent again, marking the style out as Heathcliff's own. Look at this sentence from his first paragraph:

'I thought, once, I would have stayed there, when I saw her face again – it is hers yet – he had hard work to stir me; but he said it would change, if the air blew on it, and so I struck one side of the coffin loose – and covered it up – not Linton's side, damn him!'

There are twelve phrases in this sentence, all short. Heathcliff begins with the thought he had before opening the grave, but the sentence is interrupted at the moment when he sees Cathy's face. He conveys that moment by interjecting 'it is hers yet', but in the background he is also aware of the sexton's worries ('he had hard work to stir me'). The sexton's words finally penetrate to Heathcliff, and the result is immediate action: 'so I struck one side of the coffin loose'. Notice that the action follows Heathcliff's hidden intention, not logic. The sexton *says* the body should be covered; '*so*' Heathcliff loosened the side of the coffin. This does not follow. The logical action would be to cover her, but he does not do this until afterwards. Even then, covering her only occupies his mind for a moment: it is the side of the coffin away from Linton's side which absorbs Heathcliff's attention. The effect of this writing is to convey Heathcliff's feelings, thoughts and actions as if they are happening at the moment. The sentence-structure seems to move, stop, look, listen and act, as if it were re-living the event. Typically, Heathcliff begins the sentence focusing on one aspect of the situation, and ends it having transferred his attention to something else. In this case, his first idea is to stay with Cathy's body for ever; but by the end of the sentence Heathcliff's emotional energy is focused on hating Linton: 'damn him!'

Heathcliff's style, then, emphasises immediate experience in which actions, emotions and thoughts seem to spring directly from each other. This enables the reader to re-live the story vividly; but it also gives us the opportunity to follow the workings of Heathcliff's character very closely. His state seems to alter during this sentence, and this naturally leads us to ask why? A technique based on summary can often help us understand a character's changes. First, summarise his state before the pivotal moment; then summarise his state after. Here are my summaries of Heathcliff either side of seeing Cathy's dead face:

1. Heathcliff intends to see Cathy's face, and intends to stay with her (i.e. to die there).
2. Heathcliff hates Linton, and makes an elaborate plan to enable him and Cathy to rot together without Linton.

The change between these two states is startling. By the end of the sentence, Heathcliff has forgotten his need to stay with Cathy, and has deferred his own death to some future date. His love for Cathy has left his mind, which is now filled with jealousy of Linton. This is a major change, and we are provoked to ask: Why has he changed so radically? What has brought this about?

The text provides one answer, in the form of Heathcliff's plan to doctor the coffins: he can look forward to being with Cathy after death, because of the coffin-sides. So, this plan is a substitute for staying with her now. This would seem to be the answer Heathcliff gives to himself, but are we convinced? If we think about it in practical terms, the answer has to be no. Heathcliff's plan is elaborate, because it involves ordering a special coffin for himself, and bribing the sexton. The plan is very uncertain, because it depends on Heathcliff being obeyed after his own death.

It seems odd that a man whose plots are successful elsewhere should be satisfied with such a rickety plan. We remember Heathcliff hastening young Cathy's marriage to his son, and bribing the lawyer to delay his visit to Thrushcross Grange, just before Edgar's death. Is this the same man, who now relies on bribing a sexton to do something after he is dead?

If, then, the coffin-plan is not a satisfying answer to our question, we have to ask the question again. This time, we look at the story itself for any clue we can find. Heathcliff seems completely absorbed by Cathy, despite the sexton's efforts to move him, until the semi-colon. The first words that strike him say that 'it [Cathy's face] would change'. This galvanises Heathcliff into action, he strikes out the side of the coffin, and curses Linton.

This is our only evidence, so we must conclude that the thought of Cathy's face changing causes a deep disturbance in Heathcliff and brings about his startling change of tack. The emotions Heathcliff is driven by at this moment are shadowy and ambiguous. He has kept an 'image' of Cathy in his mind. He confirms this by seeing her face. Would he rather put her back underground and preserve his mind-image of her? Does he react against the threat of change itself, and cling to his disembodied ideal of Cathy? Or, does Heathcliff really shy away from the thought of his own death? Is he – despite his bravado – frightened, not ready to die yet? These are two possible explanations of his reaction. Notice that both of them include the idea that Heathcliff is running away, not facing the challenge.

We cannot expect clear answers to such subtle shifts of mood, but our exhaustive analysis of one sentence has revealed a number of important points. First, we have been able to follow the vagaries of Heathcliff's character by using a summary technique which helps to highlight the crucial questions about him. Secondly, we caught this most outspoken and honest of characters, in the act of deceiving himself. Thirdly, whatever the answer to our final question, it does seem that the idea of 'change' is pivotal: it pushes Heathcliff into a different direction. Fourthly, Heathcliff does seem to end more weakly than he began, in a more confused, less purposeful state of mind; so, we seem to be looking at a process where he avoids something. Heathcliff is not confronting whatever he faces, in this sentence. Instead, he rationalises an absurd plan, and his feelings and mind veer away from Cathy to focus on cursing Linton.

We have spent a long time analysing one sentence, but it has provided us with a rich reward. Our next task is to look for other times when Heathcliff's emotional state seems to develop or change direction.

The second story Heathcliff tells about Cathy's grave goes back eighteen years to the day of her funeral. Heathcliff abandons his plan on the earlier occasion, as well. As he is breaking open the coffin, he clearly wishes to die then and there: 'I wish they may shovel in the earth over us both!' But he turns, re-fills the grave and goes home. What made him change, and do the opposite of what he originally intended?

The extract gives us an answer: Heathcliff hears several sighs and 'appeared' to feel warm breath by his ear. He becomes convinced that Cathy is above the ground with him: 'as certainly as you perceive the approach to some substantial body in the dark, though it cannot be discerned, so certainly I felt that Cathy was there, not under me, but on the earth'. This part of the passage conveys a powerful conflict in Heathcliff. At first he works methodically and there is no doubt that he will open the coffin: 'the wood commenced cracking' and he was 'on the point of attaining my object'. At this moment he hears the first sigh. Heathcliff's behaviour changes immediately. First, he stoops lower ('and bending down') as if to shut out and deny the 'sigh'. Then he begins to talk to himself, and what he says reveals that he is now doubtful of his ability to open the coffin ('If I can only get this off'). He no longer works methodically or calmly ('I wrenched at it more desperately still'). What is Heathcliff struggling against? He knows he is strong enough to open the coffin, so the only possible answer is the sigh itself. This causes him to reinforce his resolve with muttered words, doubt his own power to continue, and work frenetically, in a hurry.

A second sigh decides the conflict, and causes a radical change in his feelings. He is overwhelmed by a 'sudden sense of relief' and is 'consoled at once, unspeakably consoled' as he turns away from the grave. The labour he was so desperate to complete now appears different also: he describes it as 'my labour of agony'.

This passage, however, presents us with a perplexing difficulty. Just like the story of his second attempt on the grave, the force which decisively acts upon Heathcliff is full of suggestion, but ambiguous. Turning from a clear physical act with a physical goal, Heathcliff follows some metaphysical 'presence' that he never sees, but *feels* as 'substantial' as if it were a real thing. At the same time, he is overcome by a powerful feeling of 'relief'. We asked why he ends by doing the opposite of what he intended. The answer given in the passage is rather like his plan of removing the coffin-sides: it is ambiguous, and, in itself, it is rather unsatisfactory. In these circumstances we can try the summary technique again, to clarify what happens.

1. Before the crucial moment Heathcliff is in intolerable grief. The frightening depth of his loss is conveyed to us by Nelly's description of him tearing at the bark of a tree (see p. 167).

Heathcliff needs to join Cathy's physical body, and wishes to die.

2. Afterwards, Heathcliff is suffused with 'relief' and 'consoled'. He rushes to every place, convinced that he will meet Cathy wherever he goes, yet never meeting her.

What answers can we suggest for what has happened at the grave? One possibility is that Cathy's ghost haunts Heathcliff for eighteen years. The other possibility is that Heathcliff's mind creates the illusion that Cathy's ghost is near, and he lives with this delusion for eighteen years.

On reflection, this ambiguity should not surprise us. As we study *Wuthering Heights* in increasing detail, we realise that Emily Brontë treats the 'supernatural' elements of her tale with great care. Whenever the question of ghosts or the supernatural enters, Brontë is careful to provide a natural explanation that is true to the characters and situation, which explains the extraordinary phenomenon. The present extract is no exception, and our summaries point to an understanding of Heathcliff that explains the event.

His state before trying to open the grave emphasises that Cathy's death is unbearable for him. He has suicidal wishes, and his grief is intolerable. He bears witness to these feelings himself in the final meeting with Cathy (see pages 157–161), and after her death he seems incapable of believing that she is gone: 'Where is she? Not *there* – not in heaven – not perished – where?' It is significant that he includes the words 'not perished'; and he goes on to express his desire for her to haunt him: 'may you not rest, as long as I live' (both from p. 167). In our extract, Heathcliff recapitulates these feelings:

'I was wild after she died, and eternally, from dawn to dawn, praying her to return to me – her spirit – I have a strong faith in ghosts; I have a conviction that they can, and do exist, among us!'

To sum up, we have found abundant evidence for the fact that Heathcliff could not bear Cathy's death, and could not accept it; and that he was both predisposed to believe in ghosts and longing for Cathy's ghost to haunt him. So, he can only escape from intolerable emotional pain by believing in a ghost. The two motives driving him are, first, to die and join Cathy physically; and second, to escape pain and death by creating the delusion of a ghost. Both are powerful desires, and their conflict is violent. Notice that Heathcliff describes himself as 'consoled' when he senses the 'ghost' – that is, its presence does what he desired it to do: it erases the physical fact of her death, that he cannot accept.

Our analysis, then, suggests that Heathcliff's emotions are so powerful that they create an illusion in his brain. The 'ghost' is a psychological phenomenon in Heathcliff, not a supernatural event. This explanation has the virtue that it chimes with the central trait of Heathcliff's character, as we have come to know him. He repeatedly goes to extraordinary lengths in order to change reality so that it will conform to his wishes. This time, he manages (but only in his mind) to change the facts of life and death, and make them conform to his desires.

We have found, then, a central conflict within Heathcliff. On the one hand, he has a powerful grasp of reality. On the other hand, his emotions cannot accept the pain they experience in living through change – in particular the most fundamental change human beings encounter: death. Can we find corroborative evidence elsewhere, to add weight to our theory of conflict in Heathcliff?

The conflict is not resolved by his illusion of Cathy's ghost, and we can trace it through his account of the next eighteen years. It has a cumulative effect on him. He calls it 'a strange way of killing', and it has 'racked' him until he 'groaned aloud'. The nervous tension of his state has been 'intolerable torture! Infernal' and 'keeping my nerves at such a stretch' that only his unusual powers of endurance have kept him from collapse. His second visit to the grave is presaged by some fiercely practical expectations, for he tells Nelly that he 'expected . . . a transformation on raising the lid'. On the second occasion, however, the conflict swings in the other direction: the event seems to work the other way around. The first time, he obtained 'relief' by feeling that Cathy was *not* in her grave. On the second occasion, he says 'I gave some ease to myself' and became 'tranquil' for the first time in eighteen years, after making sure that she *was* in her grave. He obtained further reassurance by discovering that her face was 'hers yet': it had not changed as much as his realistic side had schooled him to expect.

Finally, we must notice elements within the extract which warn us against being too credulous of the supernatural. Brontë carefully writes in such a way as to remind us that Cathy's ghost was not really there. Notice that Heathcliff 'appeared' to 'feel' warm breath. The mixture of verbs associated with different senses (sight, touch) highlights the incongruous statement; and Heathcliff's repeated insistence that 'I had not one [glimpse]', and that he was 'always disappointed' leads up to his final summary of what had happened. He says, clearly, that the illusion's effect was to 'beguile me with the spectre of a hope'. Earlier, Heathcliff has commented on the new calmness he now feels, describing it as a return to realism after delusion: 'unless I had received a distinct impression of her passionless features, that strange feeling would hardly have been removed'. Brontë implies that Heathcliff's faith in ghosts is his belief – but it is not a reason for us to believe in them as well.

Two further features of this extract deserve remark before we move on. First, we should look at the imagery. Heathcliff refers to death as 'the last sleep', and Cathy's death as 'sleep'; and he compares his sense of Cathy's presence to being aware of a solid object in the dark. His relief 'flowed', but when he could not find her at the Heights, he should have 'sweat blood' but she was a 'devil' to him. There are four images of torture: he is the 'sport of that intolerable torture', is 'beaten' from sleeping in Cathy's bed, and 'racked'; and he is being killed 'not by inches, but by fractions of hair-breadths'. Meanwhile, his nerves 'resembled catgut', being strong and tightly stretched.

When we analyse imagery, it is often helpful to arrange the image-ideas in groups. In this extract there is one clear group of images which have violence and horror in common: the images of torture and stretched nerves go together with 'sweat blood' and 'devil'. The other images in the extract are much softer and more natural, for his feelings 'flowed' and death is likened to 'sleep' twice. So, there is a contrast in the imagery, which highlights the extremes of Heathcliff's emotions between relaxation and relief, and intolerable pain. When we think of the story these image-ideas are related to, it appears that they reinforce the idea that death is restful, and life is intolerable suffering.

The final feature of this extract for us to remark, is the way Brontë organises the plot. We have focused on two particular parts of Heathcliff's account, his two visits to Cathy's grave. However, they are not told in chronological order. Heathcliff begins with the most recent event that occurred 'yesterday', and leads us back into the past. Towards the end of his speech, he returns us to the present. So the shape of the speech as a whole resembles an excursion in time.

We can appreciate the care and density of Brontë's plotting of the novel, also; as Heathcliff's speech travels through time, it touches two other events that we recognise: we are taken back to Heathcliff 'like a savage beast getting goaded to death' by his grief (p. 167), when he remarks 'You know, I was wild after she died'; and we go back more than a hundred pages to Isabella's narrative, when Heathcliff comments that 'that accursed Earnshaw and my wife opposed my entrance' and remembers stopping 'to kick the breath out of him'. Heathcliff's narrative, then, has been constructed to have its own complete shape as an excursion into his experience; and it makes one unit in a series of accounts that interlock with each other elaborately, touching other events but from a new point of view.

The effect of re-visiting Heathcliff's fight with Earnshaw, for example, is to change our perception of that event. All that seemed so important to Isabella and Hindley on that evening, and their debate about the possible murder of Heathcliff, now suddenly seems trivial: his preoccupation with 'one absorbing subject' puts their desperation into perspective and he narrates the event in eighteen words. In this way, Brontë enhances our impression of a difference in scale – Heathcliff's and Cathy's emotions seem to be larger, more powerful than those of other characters. So much so that Heathcliff barely notices kicking Hindley almost to death.

*   *   *

We now turn our attention to a second extract focusing on Heathcliff. Here is another of his 'soliloquies' – a speech in which he relieves himself by describing his feelings to Nelly; but again, he treats her almost as if she is not there:

'Nelly, there is a strange change approaching – I'm in its shadow at present – I take so little interest in my daily life, that I hardly remember to eat, and drink – Those two, who have left the room, are the only objects which retain a distinct material appearance to me; and, that appearance causes me pain, amounting to agony. About *her* I won't speak; and I don't desire to think; but I earnestly wish she were invisible – her presence invokes only maddening sensations. *He* moves me differently; and yet if I could do it without seeming insane, I'd never see him again! You'll perhaps think me rather inclined to become so,' he added, making an effort to smile, 'if I try to describe the thousand forms of past associations, and ideas he awakens, or embodies – But you'll not talk of what I tell you, and my mind is so eternally secluded in itself, it is tempting, at last, to turn it out to another.

'Five minutes ago, Hareton seemed a personification of my youth, not a human being – I felt him in such a variety of ways, that it would have been impossible to have accosted him rationally.

'In the first place, his startling likeness to Catherine connected him fearfully with her – That, however, which you may suppose the most potent to arrest my imagination, is actually the least – for what is not connected with her to me? and what does not recall her? I cannot look down to this floor, but her features are shaped on the flags! In every cloud, in every tree – filling the air at night, and caught by glimpses in every object, by day – I am surrounded with her image! The most ordinary faces of men, and women – my own features – mock me with a resemblance. The entire world is a dreadful collection of memoranda that she did exist, and that I have lost her!

'Well, Hareton's aspect was the ghost of my immortal love, of my wild endeavours to hold my right, my degradation, my pride, my happiness, and my anguish –

'But it is frenzy to repeat these thoughts to you, only it will let you know why, with a reluctance to be always alone, his society is no benefit, rather an aggravation of the constant torment I suffer – and it partly contributes to render me regardless how he and his cousin go on together. I can give them no attention, any more.'

'But what do you mean by a *change*, Mr Heathcliff?' I said, alarmed at his manner, though he was neither in danger of losing his senses, nor dying, according to my judgment he was quite strong and healthy; and, as to his reason, from childhood, he had a delight in dwelling on dark things, and entertaining odd fancies – he might have had a monomania on the subject of his departed idol; but on every other point his wits were as sound as mine.

'I shall not know that, till it comes,' he said, 'I'm only half conscious of it now.'

'You have no feeling of illness, have you?' I asked.

'No, Nelly, I have not,' he answered.

'Then, you are not afraid of death?' I pursued.

'Afraid? No!' he replied. 'I have neither a fear, nor a presentiment, nor a hope of death – Why should I? With my hard constitution, and temperate mode of living, and unperilous occupations, I ought to, and probably *shall*, remain above ground, till there is scarcely a black hair on my head – And yet I cannot continue in this condition! – I have to remind myself to breathe – almost to remind my heart to beat! And it is like bending back a stiff spring . . . it is by compulsion, that I do the slightest act, not prompted by one thought, and by compulsion, that I notice anything alive, or dead, which is not associated with one universal idea. . . . I have a single wish, and my whole being, and faculties are yearning to attain it. They have yearned towards it so long, and so unwaveringly, that I'm convinced it *will* be reached – and *soon* – because it has devoured my existence – I am swallowed in the anticipation of its fulfilment.

'My confessions have not relieved me – but, they may account for some, otherwise unaccountable phases of humour which I show. O, God! It is a long fight, I wish it were over!'   (pp. 320–2)

We are familiar with the loose stream of Heathcliff's thoughts, from the previous extract. Here, we recognise the characteristics of his sentence-structure. First, there are sudden breaks where he does not complete the idea he was originally expressing. This happens several times, beginning with 'a strange change approaching – I'm in its shadow', where the new thought changes the viewpoint from him watching something approach, to another where he seems to watch himself from outside. Later, he begins by talking of Hareton ('ideas he awakens; or embodies') and breaks off with the idea that he can confide in Nelly ('But you'll not talk'). The most noticeable sudden break in Heathcliff's train of thought, in this extract, comes when he struggles to describe his battle with the vision of Catherine: 'my degradation, my pride, my happiness, my anguish –'. At this interesting point he breaks off, and comments on the wildness of his ideas: 'But it is frenzy to repeat these thoughts to you.' All three of these breaks share one feature: that Heathcliff is enlarging on his inner feelings, but suddenly stops and adopts a more objective viewpoint, seeming to check himself by returning to an outside awareness. On the first occasion, he turns the viewpoint to watch himself from somewhere else. The second and third times, he emphasises the gulf between himself and Nelly, his audience.

Secondly, most of Heathcliff's sentences incorporate complex situations, so that their loose, wandering structure takes our minds all around conflicts of feelings and desires, or relationships which have three focuses. Analysing one example will clarify this point. Look at the sentence which begins the third paragraph. Here is a list of the ideas it contains, in the order Heathcliff expresses them:

1. Hareton resembles the elder Catherine
2. This aspect of Hareton is foremost in Heathcliff's mind (other people's view)
3. This is the most minor aspect of Hareton, to Heathcliff (Heathcliff's view)
4. The whole world resembles Catherine.

In this sentence, the relationship with Hareton is part of the relationship with Cathy, and vice versa; and this complex of feelings and ideas is seen through Heathcliff's eyes, and imaginatively through the eyes of others. However, we cannot understand this sentence by analysing Heathcliff's logic: it is obscure, if not self-contradictory. If everything reminds him of Catherine, and Hareton's 'aspect' is the 'ghost' of his love, which he eventually says causes 'an aggravation' of his torment, then Hareton's resemblance to Catherine *is* the foremost thing about him in Heathcliff's mind. Yet he denies this. So, the sentence is not logical. We will understand such sentences better if we think of them as journeys, where we travel with Heathcliff's mind on a ride through associated knots of ideas. This involves reading and analysing in an unconventional way: Heathcliff's sentences do not *explain*, so simple analysis of meaning will only confuse us. Instead, his sentences travel, and our understanding must go with them, noticing when they hit rough patches, or bump into things which stop them or force them to change direction. If we look at this particular sentence as a journey, then, what can we say about it? The answer to this question is much more revealing: the sentence begins with Hareton and travels to Catherine, via everything else in the world. Clearly, the next question to ask is: Does this journey happen elsewhere? No, this is the only time Heathcliff's thoughts journey from Hareton to Catherine, but there are three other times when the journey is similar because it is away from Hareton. So, we can say that Heathcliff repeatedly thinks of Hareton and then his ideas travel away from the young man. First, he says that Hareton moves him 'differently'; then he comments on a 'thousand forms . . . ideas he awakens, or embodies'; next, he calls him 'a personification of my youth' and feels him 'in such a variety of ways', and, finally, after the sentence we looked at, he calls Hareton the 'ghost of my immortal love'. Each of these attempts to describe Hareton's effect upon him bumps up against something that stops Heathcliff, and then travels off in another direction. Our most abiding impression is Heathcliff's inability to describe his feeling in words.

It is clear, then, that Emily Brontë is using Heathcliff's monologue to convey him as a character with repressed or denied feelings. His feelings about Hareton are shown, in the repeated forms of these 'journeying' sentences, as an area in his own heart that he is unable to enter, or at least unable to put into words. Heathcliff cannot tell us what is in this unreachable area of his mind, then; so we can only look around for other clues which might help us to understand. We know that he says little about his feelings for Hareton except that they are powerful. What else does he say about Hareton?

First, we notice that Heathcliff identifies the boy with himself ('a personification of my youth') and Catherine ('the ghost of my immortal love'). Secondly, we notice that it is not only his ideas that shy away from the disturbance Hareton arouses in him: Heathcliff physically withdraws, as well. He fervently desires to 'never see him again', feels him as 'an aggravation of the constant torment I suffer' and has therefore become 'regardless' about Hareton and young Cathy. He finds he 'can give them no attention, any more'. We can construct a theory based on these snippets of information. First, Heathcliff's problem seems to be that Hareton reminds him of *both* himself *and* Catherine. To put this another way, Hareton represents *Heathcliff and Catherine together*. We have seen that Heathcliff instinctively sheers away from this experience: his mind runs away from the idea, and he feels like physically turning his back on Hareton, never seeing him again. He has actually gone as far as no longer noticing what Hareton does. We are left asking: Why is it that Heathcliff cannot bear the embodiment of what he has so long desired?

There are, of course, obvious parallels between Hareton's situation now, and Heathcliff's when he was a boy. It is therefore easy for us to understand Heathcliff's feelings as the romance blossoms between this degraded, uneducated young man and his Cathy: Hareton is succeeding where Heathcliff failed. This is clearly disturbing for Heathcliff as it presents the real prospect of union in a similar form to that he compulsively seeks with the dead Catherine. However, his speech indicates something less conscious, something deeper. His speech suggests that Hareton alone already embodies that union: his mind identifies the young man with both himself and Catherine, simultaneously. Hareton, then, is the 'one universal idea' Heathcliff yearns for.

After Nelly's interruption, Heathcliff enters a final section of his monologue, in which some of the questions we have raised about his inner conflicts, and the unapproachable area in his mind, are answered. It is inner conflict that he describes. On the one hand, he is swept up in 'one universal idea', 'a single wish' which he is 'yearning' to attain with his 'whole being'. This is clearly his preoccupation with the illusion of Catherine, and his overwhelming desire to join her. On the other hand, there are the actions which keep him alive, such as breathing and forcing his heart to beat. These are reflex actions: it would be difficult for the rest of us to *stop* breathing, or to *stop* our hearts from beating. However, here they are set in opposition to the desire for Catherine, so that he achieves them by 'compulsion' and with a great effort 'like bending back a stiff spring'.

Heathcliff's state during these final chapters of the novel is the culmination of various elements in an extraordinary character. How can we understand what happens to him during the final eighteen years of his life? How make sense of his long-prosecuted revenge on Linton, and the final lack of will-power which allows him to fail in the end? How make sense of his two attempts to open Catherine's grave, his long torment, and the enigmatic nature of his eventual death? In this extract, as in the previous one, we have been able to analyse a character at war within himself. In both cases he is driven by powerful desires, yet in each case something hidden within him seems to thwart these desires, and forces him to work against his own wishes. Brontë has characterised Heathcliff with a powerful unconscious block of some kind, yet it appears in different guises each time we come across it.

In this perplexity, we can turn back to the prominent character-trait apparent from the start. We said that Heathcliff has unusually powerful desires, and is willing to undergo extremes of endurance and suffering in order to alter the world so that it fulfils his wishes. We noticed, for example, that he stoically allowed Hindley to attempt his murder, in order to gain the pony he desired. Later, he transformed himself from a rural clown into a gentleman of manners and means, in order to change the context for Catherine's marriage-choice. Let us follow this characteristic through the remainder of the story.

Following Catherine's death, Heathcliff's overwhelming desire is to join her. The barrier between them is death. Only deterred by his firm grasp on reality – his sanity – Heathcliff sets about destroying this barrier with all his will. There are two ways to do this: either he must die, and join Catherine on the other side of death; or she must come back, and join him on this side of it. His first visit to the grave shows the first resolution of this dilemma: as we have seen, Heathcliff is diverted from his planned suicide, and in his vivid imagination he creates the impression that Catherine's ghost has returned to join him on earth. For eighteen years Heathcliff strains to bring about this outcome: Catherine will return from death and join him in life. However, although all the power of his desires persuades him that she is *almost* in sight, Catherine never actually appears to him. This is what he calls a 'strange way of killing', to 'beguile me with a spectre of a hope'.

Heathcliff's second visit to the grave, when he opens the coffin, marks a turning-point. He now knows that she is underground. Compared with his previous state of 'intolerable torture', he becomes 'pacified'. On the other hand, his desires now present him with the original challenge. Heathcliff has failed to bring Catherine back across the barrier of death, so now, to fulfil his desires, he must strain every iota of his being to make himself die – to cross that barrier and join her on the other side.

This sets Heathcliff's deepest will in opposition to his revenge, which can only be completed if he survives, and in conflict with the instinct of survival itself: to succeed, his desire will have to achieve a victory over the very reflexes of living. This is the conflict described in the final long paragraph of our extract. He tells Nelly that his 'whole being, and faculties' yearn for union with Catherine, and the stubborn strength of his physical existence fights back: 'With my hard constitution, and temperate mode of living, . . . I ought to, and probably *shall*, remain above ground'; yet against the power of his single obsession, the involuntary actions of survival – like breathing, and his heartbeat – feel like 'compulsion' and a tremendous effort to him. The oddness that strikes the reader at this point is largely due to the way effort is associated with life, not death. The words for his death-longing are natural and do not imply effort ('wish', 'yearning'); he does not fight for it since he is sure that it '*will* be reached', and its power is from itself, expressed in constructions which cast Heathcliff in a passive role: 'it has devoured my existence – I am swallowed'. By contrast, the natural actions of living are expressed as 'compulsion' and 'like bending back a stiff spring'. Brontë creates the opposite impression from the normal one – that survival reflexes are natural and involuntary – and this in turn emphasises the utter depth of Heathcliff's identity with Catherine. This effect reminds us of her bald statement 'I *am* Heathcliff' (p. 82), and Heathcliff's 'nothing that God or Satan could inflict would have parted us' (pp. 160–1). So Brontë creates the effect that, for Heathcliff, union with Catherine is more natural than breathing, or his heartbeat.

The interpretation we have put forward is based on Heathcliff's prominent characteristic: his determination, and his fixed belief that he can change the world to suit his desires. Our interpretation simply takes this characteristic beyond his youthful victories, when he braved Hindley's violence, or transformed himself into a gentleman. In the final phase of the novel, Heathcliff is no longer attempting to change a part of the world, or adjust reality. Now, he is at war with the very facts of life and death, and seeks to change them. Our interpretation appears to be borne out by analysis of the two extracts we have focused on in this chapter. It fits, and clarifies, the experiences he undergoes on his two visits to Catherine's grave; and it helps to explain the 'change' he refers to, when he finally sets off on his last course towards death. Near to the end of the present extract, Heathcliff reiterates the belief in his power to change the world by a simple act of will, that has been his consistent faith:

'I have a single wish, and my whole being, and faculties are yearning to attain it. They have yearned towards it so long, and so unwaveringly, that I'm convinced it *will* be reached – and *soon* – because it has devoured my existence – I am swallowed in the anticipation of its fulfilment.'

We have, then, arrived at an understanding of Heathcliff's character from analysing our two extracts. In order to confirm our understanding, we can look more widely in the text for corroborative evidence. We do not have the space to pursue further analysis of Heathcliff in the present chapter; however, we can indicate a start to this work, briefly, before moving on to study Catherine.

First, the idea of Heathcliff joining Catherine in death is a consistent part of the novel. After her illness, Catherine's speech appears to wander, and she apostrophises the absent Heathcliff:

'. . . we must pass by Gimmerton Kirk, to go that journey! We've braved its ghosts often together, and dared each other to stand among the graves and ask them to come. . . . But Heathcliff, if I dare you now, will you venture? If you do, I'll keep you. I'll not lie there by myself; they may bury me twelve feet deep, and throw the church down over me; but I won't rest till you are with me. . . . I never will!'

(p. 125)

Catherine's death, then, is a challenge: in separating her from Heathcliff, it is a challenge to the unity they have both asserted so forcefully. It is therefore a challenge to Heathcliff, whether he has the courage and firmness of will to follow her, or whether death will finally divide them. Having studied Heathcliff's two speeches, which chronicle his attempts to meet this challenge either by bringing Catherine back, or by dying himself, we now notice the prophetic significance in Catherine's words when she imagines Heathcliff's response to her appeal: 'He's considering . . . he'd rather I'd come to him! Find a way, then! not through that Kirkyard. . . . You are slow! Be content, you always followed me!' (p. 125). Here, Catherine seems to foretell the stages of Heathcliff's development for eighteen years after her death.

Secondly, we should notice that Heathcliff's revenge is regularly portrayed as a secondary, more superficial motive in him. Remember how he casts new light on the fight with Earnshaw: to others, he seems to concentrate on revenge; but in his own experience, kicking Earnshaw almost to death is only a momentary pause before he leaps upstairs to pursue the consuming illusion of Catherine's 'ghost'. There is a hierarchy in Heathcliff's mind, then, and revenge against others is on a lower level than anything to do with Catherine. He makes this clear to us during the quarrel about Isabella, using the image of a tyrant and slaves: 'The tyrant grinds down his slaves and they don't turn against him, they crush those beneath them – You are welcome to torture me to death for your amusement, only, allow me to amuse myself a little in the same style' (p. 111). Clearly, torturing others does not interfere with the higher relationship between him and Catherine. So we should not be surprised when Heathcliff loses interest in completing his revenge, towards the end of the novel, when he is moving closer and closer to death and Catherine.

In this chapter, we have considered Heathcliff as a character, hoping to explain his feelings and motives. It is already clear, however, that there are numerous themes to which he contributes, or even which he embodies. Additionally, his arrival at Wuthering Heights, his supposed gipsy parentage and the recurrent imagery of demons and devils that surrounds him, make him a figure of larger and more shadowy significance in the novel as a whole. We will return to discussion of Heathcliff, then, for various reasons, in later chapters.

Catherine

We now turn to Catherine. When Nelly enters her room, where she has starved herself for three days, Catherine's wits appear to wander and she imagines that she is still at Wuthering Heights. She describes Nelly 'dreamily' as an aged witch:

> 'That's what you'll come to fifty years hence; I know you are not so now. I'm not wandering, you're mistaken, or else I should believe you really *were* that withered hag, and I should think I *was* under Penistone Crag, and I'm conscious it's night, and there are two candles burning on the table making the black press shine like jet.'
>
> 'The black press? where is that?' I asked. 'You are talking in your sleep!'
>
> 'It's against the wall, as it always is,' she replied. 'It does appear odd – I see a face in it!'
>
> 'There is no press in the room, and never was,' said I, resuming my seat, and looping up the curtain that I might watch her.
>
> 'Don't *you* see that face?' she enquired, gazing earnestly at the mirror.
>
> And say what I could, I was incapable of making her comprehend it to be her own; so I rose and covered it with a shawl.
>
> 'It's behind there still!' she pursued, anxiously. 'And it stirred. Who is it? I hope it will not come out when you are gone! Oh! Nelly, the room is haunted! I'm afraid of being alone!'
>
> I took her hand in mine, and bid her be composed, for a succession of shudders convulsed her frame, and she *would* keep straining her gaze towards the glass.
>
> 'There's nobody here!' I insisted. 'It was *yourself*, Mrs Linton; you knew it a while since!'
>
> 'Myself,' she gasped, 'and the clock is striking twelve! It's true, then; that's dreadful!'
>
> Her fingers clutched the clothes, and gathered them over her eyes. I attempted to steal to the door with an intention of calling her

husband; but I was summoned back by a piercing shriek. The shawl had dropped from the frame.

'Why, what *is* the matter?' cried I. 'Who is coward now? Wake up! That is the glass – the mirror, Mrs Linton; and you see yourself in it, and there am I too by your side.'

Trembling and bewildered, she held me fast, but the horror gradually passed from her countenance; its paleness gave place to a glow of shame.

'Oh, dear! I thought I was at home,' she sighed. 'I thought I was lying in my chamber at Wuthering Heights. Because I'm weak, my brain got confused, and I screamed unconsciously. Don't say anything, but stay with me. I dread sleeping, my dreams appal me.'

'A sound sleep would do you good, ma'am,' I answered; 'and I hope this suffering will prevent your trying starving again.'

'Oh, if I were but in my own bed in the old house!' she went on bitterly, wringing her hands. 'And that wind sounding in the firs by the lattice. Do let me feel it – it comes straight down the moor – do let me have one breath!'

To pacify her, I held the casement ajar, a few seconds. A cold blast rushed through, I closed it, and returned to my post.

She lay still, now: her face bathed in tears – Exhaustion of body had entirely subdued her spirit; our fiery Catherine was no better than a wailing child!

'How long is it since I shut myself in here?' she asked, suddenly reviving.

'It was Monday evening,' I replied, 'and this is Thursday night, or rather Friday morning, at present.'

'What! of the same week?' she exclaimed. 'Only that brief time?'

'Long enough to live on nothing but cold water, and ill-temper,' observed I.

'Well, it seems a weary number of hours,' she muttered doubtfully, 'it must be more – I remember being in the parlour, after they had quarrelled; and Edgar being cruelly provoking, and me running into this room desperate – As soon as ever I had barred the door, utter blackness overwhelmed me, and I fell on the floor – I couldn't explain to Edgar how certain I felt of having a fit, or going raging mad, if he persisted in teasing me! I had no command of tongue, or brain, and he did not guess my agony, perhaps; it barely left me sense to try to escape from him and his voice – Before I recovered sufficiently to see and hear, it began to be dawn; and Nelly, I'll tell you what I thought, and what has kept recurring and recurring till I feared for my reason – I thought as I lay there with my head against that table leg, and my eyes dimly discerning the grey square of the window, that I was enclosed in the oak-panelled bed at home; and my heart ached with some great grief which, just waking, I could not recollect – I pondered, and worried myself to discover what it could be; and most strangely, the whole last seven years of my life grew a blank! I did not recall that they had been at all. I was a child; my father was just buried, and my misery arose from the separation that Hindley had ordered between me and Heathcliff – I was laid alone, for the first time, and rousing from a dismal doze after a night of weeping – I lifted my hand to push the panels aside, it struck the table-top! I swept it along the carpet, and then, memory burst in – my late anguish was swallowed in a paroxysm of despair – I cannot say why I felt so wildly wretched – it must have been temporary derangement for there is scarcely cause – But, supposing at twelve years old, I had been wrenched from the Heights, and every early association, and my all in all, as Heathcliff was at that time, and been converted at a stroke into Mrs Linton, the lady of Thrushcross Grange, and the wife of a stranger; an exile, and outcast, thenceforth, from what had been my world – You may fancy a glimpse of the abyss where I grovelled! Shake your head, as you will, Nelly, *you* have helped to unsettle me! You should have spoken to Edgar, indeed you should, and compelled him to leave me quiet! Oh, I'm burning! I wish I were out of doors – I wish I were a girl again, half savage and hardy, and free . . . and laughing at injuries, not maddening under them! Why am I so changed? Why does my blood rush into a hell of tumult at a few words? I'm sure I should be myself were I once among the heather on those hills . . . Open the window again wide, fasten it open! Quick, why don't you move?'

(pp. 122–4)

It is clear that Catherine is in a state of extreme and confused emotions at this point of the story. Our task is to study Emily Brontë's methods and aims in portraying such a complex state of mind in her character.

The extract begins with a series of statements about Catherine's state of mind. She begins this with 'I'm not wandering' and 'I'm conscious'; but when she mentions the black press, Nelly takes alarm and comments 'You are talking in your sleep!' In the ensuing exchanges, Catherine feels that the press '*does* appear odd', then concludes that 'the room is haunted!' These transitions display different levels of illusion. Catherine begins with what might have been a dream about Nelly (she describes her as an old hag 'dreamily'); but she is aware that this vision is not real in the normal sense and claims that her wits are not 'wandering'. The next level of illusion is Catherine's conviction that she is at Wuthering Heights, not Thrushcross Grange. She sees her present dressing-table and mirror as the old 'black press'. This illusion stands in the place of reality in her mind: indeed, she refers to it as part of the evidence that she is not losing her wits. The element that makes it appear 'odd' to Catherine, is that she sees a face in it. Of course, if she sees the black press, seeing a face is 'odd'; if it is the mirror, on the other hand, it is not odd at all. Catherine does not question her sense of reality, however: instead of realising that it is *not* the black press, her mind draws the unlikely, supernatural conclusion that the room is 'haunted'.

Why does Brontë construct such an elaborate set of statements about reality and illusion? If we go through these mental events in turn, we notice that they have the effect of excluding several of the assumptions we might casually make about Catherine's state. Here is a summary-list of what happens, showing how Brontë eliminates the easier explanations, one after another:

[i] Cathy sees Nelly as an old hag 'gathering elf-bolts to hurt our heifers'. In other words, she sees Nelly as hostile and working deviously (using witchcraft) to harm her. Since her imagined setting is 'under Penistone Crag', the possessive 'our [heifers]' must refer to Catherine as an Earnshaw of Wuthering Heights, not as a Linton of Thrushcross Grange.

There is an essential truth in Catherine's insight here. Nelly persuaded Edgar to ignore his wife's headstrong fit (see p. 117), and did not alert him to her starving for a further three days. When this is revealed, Catherine confirms that she 'saw' the truth about Nelly: '"Ah! Nelly has played traitor," she exclaimed, passionately. "Nelly is my hidden enemy – you witch! So you do seek elf-bolts to hurt us!"'

(p. 127). So, Brontë presents this as a sort of dreamlike or symbolic perception; but Catherine fully understands the distinction between this kind of 'seeing' and objective reality: she says 'I'm not wandering' because 'I know you are not so now.'

[ii] Nelly tells Catherine 'You are talking in your sleep.' This introduces a question about Catherine's physical state: awake or asleep? The question is never fully answered, but several further details are contributed. Her eyes are open, as she is 'gazing earnestly at the mirror', and Nelly finds it impossible to persuade her that she is seeing her own face. Whatever word we use to describe this state, then, it is prolonged well beyond the normal stuporous transition between drowsiness and sleep. After her scream, Nelly again treats her as if she were asleep, shouting 'Wake up!' Next, we hear that she is 'bewildered', and she describes herself as 'weak' leading to 'my brain got confused' and the extraordinary phrase 'and I screamed unconsciously'. Nelly picks up Catherine's idea of weakness, and comments: 'I hope this suffering will prevent your trying starving again.'

This leaves us with suggestions of exhaustion brought on by starvation, and a state which might be likened to sleep but is not sleep. As a final note on this discussion, Catherine says 'I dread sleeping, my dreams appal me.' We will return to this remark after looking at the actual hallucination of the black press.

[iii] Catherine's belief that she is in her old room at Wuthering Heights occupies a persistent place in her mind. She first introduces it as firm reality in contrast to her symbolic vision of Nelly. Catherine's senses contradict this belief, when she sees a face in the press where no reflection should be. She rejects the evidence of her senses and clings to the belief that the press is there, inventing the bizarre idea of a 'haunted' room and a disembodied face behind the shawl, which 'stirred', to explain the contradiction.

Catherine appears to realise the truth when she says 'Myself . . . and the clock is striking twelve! It's true, then; that's dreadful!' We assume that the 'dreadful' thing that is 'true' is that she is Mrs Linton and lives at Thrushcross Grange. Following this apparent realisation, however, there is a further crisis in Catherine. She covers her eyes, and a moment later, screams.

It is noticeable that Catherine's first question when she is fully herself again concerns time. Clearly, the time Catherine has experienced seems to have been much longer than objective time, so that she comments 'Only that brief time?' and when she begins to remember what she has been through, she is still convinced that it must have taken longer ('it must be more').

This summary excludes several straightforward explanations. Catherine is not asleep – at least not in any normal sleep. What she sees is not a 'dream' either, since she is aware of the contradiction between her senses and her belief. Nor is there any 'supernatural' vision: the idea of haunting is only mentioned as part of her fierce resistance against the truth. In conclusion, then, we are left with only one outstanding fact: Catherine has a powerful belief, and it is so strong that she will not give it up – even despite the evidence of her eyes.

This is an important point to realise, as it makes all ideas of sleep, dream, weakness and delirium irrelevant. Catherine does not suffer from random or successive hallucinations, but has a single fixed idea. Why? Clearly, Catherine wishes to be at Wuthering Heights; and she sees her true situation as 'dreadful'. She desires to see the 'black press' and feel the wind from the moors; and her desire is so powerful that her brain both creates the illusion of being there and fights hard to maintain this illusion. Her weakness, or delirium, or whatever we may call it, has only served to bring this desire to the surface.

Now we can turn to the final part of the extract, in which Catherine gives an account of her inner experiences since locking herself into her room. The story she tells is straightforward. Catherine has regressed in her memory, going back to the major trauma in her childhood, when she was separated from Heathcliff and 'laid alone, for the first time' at Hindley's orders. In her mind, she becomes twelve years old again. When she wakes into the present, realising that she is now nineteen and Mrs Linton, she is 'in a paroxysm of despair'.

This is a simple story of exhaustion and dreams, and we have no excuse for being surprised at what it tells us about Catherine. The major emotional event of her life has been separation from Heathcliff; and she is miserable and regretful about everything she has done for the past seven years – the entire story of her friendship with Linton, and his courtship, Heathcliff's absence and her marriage, and Heathcliff's recent return. Catherine's difficulty in remembering her life since she was separated from Heathcliff reminds us of what she told Nelly years before:

> 'My love for Linton is like the foliage in the woods. Time will change it, I'm well aware, as winter changes the trees – my love for Heathcliff resembles the eternal rocks beneath – a source of little visible delight, but necessary.'
>
> (p. 82)

Everything to do with Linton is superficial, unimportant to her; and her real, underlying life is permanently fixed to Heathcliff's. The image-contrast between 'foliage' and 'rocks' helps to explain how she can forget seven years of her life and believe herself to be back at Wuthering Heights. In her heart, *nothing memorable has happened* in the last seven years.

This emotional story is simple, then, and its most outstanding quality is the sweeping way in which it disposes of any supposed conflict between Linton's and Heathcliff's influences over Catherine: seven years becoming closer and closer to Linton is 'a blank!'; while by contrast, one night away from Heathcliff is a 'great grief'. In the deeper part of Catherine, then, we now know that there is no conflict, no competition at all: Heathcliff is, and always has been, her 'all in all'. However, there are other elements in this speech which tell us more about Catherine's psychological state both now and in the past.

First, there are several references to forgetting and remembering. These apply to both the separation from Heathcliff and her more recent life with Linton. She begins by feeling 'some great grief' which 'just waking, I could not recollect'. Then she remembers being separated from Heathcliff, which she describes as 'misery' and 'anguish'. However, as she remembers this grief, she simultaneously forgets the last seven years. These two mental events happen simultaneously: as she struggles to remember the nameless 'great grief', she says, 'most strangely, the whole last seven years of my life grew a blank! I did not recall that they had been at all. I was a child.' Now Catherine remembers being separated from Heathcliff, but has forgotten being Mrs Linton. This memory returns suddenly ('memory burst in') and causes such intense pain that it blots out the other: 'my late anguish was swallowed in a paroxysm of despair'. Brontë carefully balances these two states. Just as Catherine felt her twelve-year-old anguish but 'could not recollect' its cause, now she feels her nineteen-year-old despair, and is again unsure of the reasons for her feeling: 'I cannot say why I felt so wildly wretched – it must have been temporary derangement for there is scarcely cause.'

The changes in Catherine's mind and heart, then, mirror each other: she is unable to remember Heathcliff's importance to her and be Mrs Linton at the same time. Forgetting and remembering occur simultaneously as she changes between her two states – as a twelve-year-old at Wuthering Heights, and as a nineteen-year-old at Thrushcross Grange. Two further points intensify Catherine's suffering. First, these changes have 'kept recurring and recurring till I feared for my reason'. Secondly, as she changes, seven years seem to pass in a moment and she is taken from all her childhood associations 'at a stroke'. This effect of suddenness is built into the passage. We already noticed Catherine's conviction that it should have taken longer. Notice also the violent suddenness of 'memory *burst* in' and 'swallowed'.

The oscillations of Catherine's feelings and memories are symmetrical, as we have said. In addition, they match each other in that both states are founded on 'misery', 'anguish', 'a paroxysm of despair' and an 'abyss where I grovelled'. In both cases, Catherine feels intolerable emotional pain, yet when she attempts to escape this pain, she can only do so by running directly into the other pain. These two states, then, are inescapable painful alternatives for Catherine. In the final part of her speech, Catherine discusses how she might cope with life. Her desire to return to Wuthering Heights and her childhood, is expressed again in 'I wish I were a girl again' and 'were I once among the heather on those hills'. Also, she regrets the fact that

Edgar did not 'leave me quiet': his attempt to make her choose himself or Heathcliff precipitated this outburst of unstable memories and agonies. Catherine is clearly rationalising here, hoping that her agonies will subside if they are left alone; and yearning for an unattainable return to childhood.

Concluding Discussion

Psychology and character in *Wuthering Heights*

The last extract reveals a clear understanding of repression, denial, unconscious mental events and rationalisation. Emily Brontë highlights features of Catherine's mind that would be familiar to modern psychoanalysis. In our analysis of Heathcliff, we found a similar insight into mental processes: both of these characters are driven by powerful desires, and the unconscious need to escape from emotional pain. Brontë portrays the strength of compulsive forces in the mind, also: in her characters, beliefs and desires are so powerful that they create illusions. In Heathcliff, his desire brought the conviction that Catherine was haunting him, and was above ground; and sustained this irrational belief through eighteen years. In Catherine, desire made her see the hallucination of the 'black press'. Both of these characters display an extraordinary strength of denial, also. Heathcliff used his revenge as an activity that diverted him from suicide: an activity that helped him repress Catherine's challenge to follow her through death. Now we know that Catherine's entire friendship, courtship and marriage to Edgar was a seven-year-long diversion. It enabled her to repress the pain of separation from Heathcliff, which was otherwise intolerable.

We have found that Emily Brontë builds these central characters with dynamic mental and emotional life, in a way that shows a grasp of psychology we would normally expect to find in a post-Freudian writer. Two small points from the present extract deserve comment before we move on. First, we said that we would return to consider Catherine's remark that 'I dread sleeping, my dreams appal me.' We can now consider this comment in the light of her explanatory speech. Catherine oscillates between being twelve at Wuthering Heights, and being nineteen at Thrushcross Grange. The 'dream' state that 'appals' her must refer to Wuthering Heights and being twelve. Several elements in the extract seem to contradict this idea, however: Catherine expresses horror at leaving her dreams, and 'screamed unconsciously' on returning to present reality, which she describes as swallowing other anguish in 'a paroxysm of despair'. While still half-aware, she truthfully describes her present situation as 'dreadful', and elaborates on this feeling later when she calls herself 'the wife of a stranger; an exile, and outcast, thenceforth, from what had been my world'. Not only is it painful for her to wake from her 'dream' state, she also wishes to return to it, begging Nelly to open the window, longing to be 'a girl again, half savage and hardy, and free' and convinced that she would be 'myself' again if she could return 'among the heather on those hills'. The statement 'my dreams appal me' does not seem to fit Catherine's feelings, then. When we find a character making a statement at variance with her obvious emotions and behaviour, we need to ask: Where *does* this statement belong? The answer seems to be that it belongs with Catherine's continuing hope that she can escape from the trap her past has closed around her. The feeble rationalisation we notice at the end of her long speech – the idea that everything would have gone on happily if Nelly had 'compelled' Edgar to leave Catherine 'quiet'; and the hope of being cured by a return to the open moors – these come from the same part of Catherine as the idea that her dreams 'appal' her. This part of Catherine still, despite her recent experience, tries to suppress her childhood suffering and cling to the superficial marriage to Edgar. So, the two fundamental states of emotion and belief we have analysed in Catherine in this extract, are still 'overlaid' by a thin, superficial layer of her present life – the fiction of harmony with Edgar, the attempt to be friends with both her husband and Heathcliff, the vague hope that all the problems will go away if she ignores them.

The second detail we should remark belongs in the same subtle overlay. Catherine says that she 'screamed unconsciously'. This is a surprising phrase, since she screamed aloud and is now aware of it. Yet, the phrase aptly describes her pain at waking from childhood into the despair of her pointless adult life. She feels the pain sharply at the time, and screams – yet this scream is forced from her involuntarily, against her will; and she struggles to forget the pain as soon as possible afterwards. Again, this subtle and surprising touch conveys Catherine's continuing effort at repression of the truth.

We have analysed Heathcliff and Catherine, looking at the way Brontë builds their characters to reveal their psychological and emotional complexity. So far we have examined them as if they are real personalities, discussing their feelings, thoughts, desires and fears. Having looked at them in this way, we should now consider their place in the novel as a whole. The final discussion in this chapter considers the significance of what we have learned about Heathcliff and Catherine, in relation to the wider themes and 'meaning' of *Wuthering Heights*.

Heathcliff, Catherine and *Wuthering Heights*

This discussion is like a bridge, connecting this chapter's detailed analysis of Heathcliff and Catherine, with interpretation of the novel's significance through its symbols, structure and themes – which will be the focus of the next three chapters. The present section therefore only briefly relates the characters to various prominent themes; it does not pursue the points raised to their conclusion.

[1] **Love.** *Wuthering Heights* is a love story, so what does our analysis of characters contribute to the theme of love in the novel? In both Catherine and Heathcliff, we have found that the underlying force which compels their characters is a desire to be together, to be joined or unified. Both characters found themselves in situations where joining the other was impractical: in Heathcliff's case, he could only join Catherine by passing through the barrier of death, and she challenged him to do this: 'But Heathcliff, if I dare you now, will you venture?' (p. 115). In Catherine's case, Hindley ordered a separation between her and Heathcliff and 'brought Heathcliff so low' that marriage between them was out of the question, despite him being 'more myself than I am' (p. 80). This compelling, basic need to be together is frustrated by circumstances,

then. In both of their characters, we have found that this underlying force and its frustration throw up a conflict which rages throughout the remainder of their lives, and which ultimately leads to their deaths. For both Heathcliff and Catherine, the conflict takes the form of denial, repression and avoidance pitted against the deep force of their desire to be joined. In Catherine's case, she forgets the heartache of separation, rationalises her ability to help Heathcliff by marrying Linton, and devotes seven years of her life to creating a superficial existence at Thrushcross Grange. However, her underlying need for Heathcliff is so strong that when it reasserts itself, her new life seems like that of 'an exile, and outcast', 'the wife of a stranger'. She tells her husband 'I don't want you, Edgar; I'm past wanting you' (pp. 126–7). Eventually, then, it seems that Catherine's underlying need for Heathcliff reasserts itself and her resistance to it breaks down. In Heathcliff's case, we found that his eighteen years of being haunted and pursuing revenge were a diversion, a denial of the fact of Catherine's death and a distraction from the challenge her death presented to him. The conflict in Heathcliff is a 'long fight' (p. 322), but eventually his interest in revenge seems to fade, and living, rather than dying, seems to require an effort from him (breathing 'is like bending back a stiff spring' – p. 321). At the end, Heathcliff has 'one universal idea . . . I have a single wish' (p. 321), which is to re-join Catherine via the grave.

Both of these characters, then, display an underlying and ultimately decisive need for each other, and this need is the force that drives both their lives and their deaths. We have also noticed that Brontë presents this need as so powerful that it can alter objective reality to the lover: Heathcliff 'appeared to feel the warm breath' of Catherine's ghost (p. 287), and the conviction of its existence remained with him for eighteen years; Catherine believes herself to be a girl at Wuthering Heights, and sees the 'black press' (p. 122). Love, then, is presented as a need to join the beloved; it is the fundamental driving force of character, can distort objective reality, and is ultimately victorious over even involuntary survival instincts.

[2] **Reality and perception.** In Chapter 1 we discussed the complex nature of reality and perception, shown in the elaborate interplay

between story and narrative framework. We have found that Emily Brontë presents reality as a flexible, changeable thing, differing between different subjective points of view. For example, the crisis in Isabella's story, when Heathcliff assaults Hindley, is only a momentary pause in Heathcliff's account. Our study of characters has taken this insight further, in the form of the hallucinations both Heathcliff and Catherine experience, which are created by the power of their desires. We may be reminded of other famous lovers who have asserted love's subjective reality against the rest of the world. Romeo felt that banishment was death because 'There is no world without Verona walls' (*Romeo and Juliet*, III, iii, line 17); and John Donne, having declared that the entire world is in his bed with him and his mistress, concludes that they also embody the sun itself: 'This bed thy center is, these walls, thy sphear' (*The Sunne Rising*, line 30). These references show that Emily Brontë's lovers are part of a vigorous literary tradition; but it is possible that *Wuthering Heights* considers a further question: how far is reality actually made by the power of desire? Is reality not a separate thing at all, but only created out of human will, and subjective perceptions driven by emotion? In this connection, we should remember that our early 'character-note' on Heathcliff revealed his persistent belief that he could alter reality to align it with his desires: as a boy, and later, as a man, Heathcliff consistently strove to change reality by means of determination and endurance.

[3] **Childhood: a paradise of the undivided self.** Our discussion of characters suggests a theme of human development, also. Catherine's trauma occurred following her separation from Heathcliff, and this implies their unity before that event. We have seen that Catherine longs to re-create her original state of harmony and simplicity: she wants to be 'half savage and hardy, and free' again, and bemoans the confusion of adult life: 'Why am I so changed? Why does my blood rush into a hell of tumult at a few words?' Catherine's vision of harmony includes living in her original, natural surroundings 'among the heather on those hills'.

Heathcliff describes a similar moment of division during childhood, and he comments to Catherine '*Why* did you betray your own

heart' (p. 160). He remembers a time when: 'misery, and degradation, and death, and nothing that God or satan could inflict would
have parted us', but now finds division intolerable: 'oh God! would
you like to live with your soul in the grave?' (both from pp. 160–1).
Both of these characters, then, seem to remember a time in childhood when they had a unitary self and were in harmony with each
other and the surrounding world. The suggestion of a childhood
paradise is stronger in Catherine than in Heathcliff, but both of
them, as children, express the view that Heaven is a miserable exile
compared with their childish life together (Heathcliff indirectly
rejects the 'heaven' of Thrushcross Grange – p. 48; and Catherine
dreams of misery in Heaven – p. 80). The traumatic destruction of
childhood's paradise, and the ensuing division of the self, is clearly
part of the developmental story Emily Brontë tells. It could be
argued that much of the characterisation of Heathcliff and
Catherine hinges on the agonies of a divided self – or a divided
couple which they feel as a divided self – and their struggles to
re-attain a harmonious, unitary state.

[4] **Wuthering Heights and Thrushcross Grange.** In Chapter 4 we
will discuss the structure of *Wuthering Heights*. One outstanding
feature of this novel is the duality Brontë establishes – on many
levels – between the two houses Wuthering Heights and Thrushcross
Grange. We will look at contrasts between them in terms of their
settings, weathers, moral attitudes, and religions. In studying
Catherine, we have found that Brontë explores this duality through
her characterisation as well. Catherine's 'recurring' experience of forgetting and remembering, during her illness, heightens the sense
that Wuthering Heights and Thrushcross Grange represent opposing
states that cannot be reconciled. In the extract we studied, we see
Catherine's personality being torn apart between the two houses and
the contrasting lives she has lived in them. The author seems to hint
that Catherine's madness is bound up in the attempt to fuse these
two places, the two 'sides' of the novel, when she describes the hallucination of a 'black press' superimposed upon a dressing-table – each
piece of furniture emblematic of the place where it belongs.

Methods of Analysis

1. We remarked that Emily Brontë surrounds the introduction of characters with an emphasis on uncertainty about their identity and where they come from. The effect is to enhance mystery and excite but frustrate the reader's questioning and curiosity.

2. In analysing character, we looked for an early pattern of behaviour or repetition of ideas and qualities, which Emily Brontë establishes quickly, and which can become like the hallmark of a character. This dominant trait or quality often helps to explain the character's behaviour in later, more complicated situations. For example, we found that Hindley typically strove to preserve a simplified and false 'paradise', and did not confront unpalatable realities; or that Isabella's involvement in a self-centred cruelty and pain is consistent between her first and last appearances in the novel.

3. Look for the emotional content of significant or repeated words attached to the character you are studying. Consider the emotional relationship established with the reader, and at the same time notice Emily Brontë's economy: the few words that establish character, and the absence of external description or novelistic accounts of thought and feeling.

4. Analyse the character's 'voice', using various techniques as appropriate, including describing sentences, diction, or any typical recurrent patterns in their speech (such as Joseph's recurrently 'peevish' tone of voice).

5. When analysing crucial experiences involving Heathcliff and Catherine, we used various approaches to prose, including noticing sentence-structures, prominent diction, and imagery.

6. However, our understanding of these characters' psychology arose from noticing and carefully defining exactly what they do and say. Emily Brontë's characters are not oblique or obscure in what they say about themselves, but they have been sadly misread by many critics. Therefore, a careful reading, and clear, direct summary of what they do and say, is an important first stage.

7. The direct, accurate summary mentioned in (6) provides material which can be analysed by asking questions about the character's

motives, desires and fears. The answers to these questions both explain how the character's personality works, and suggest Emily Brontë's thematic concerns.

8. We found that we could apply a number of terms from modern psychological theory, to the characters of Heathcliff and Catherine. These include **repression, denial, unconscious, regression, hallucination;** and the broad terms **superficial** and **underlying** or **fundamental** were useful to describe aspects of Catherine's and Heathcliff's personalities.

Suggested Work

1. The analysis of Catherine and Heathcliff carried out in this chapter focuses on three extracts, and is far from complete. In studying *Wuthering Heights* you will undoubtedly want to pursue both of these characters further. Two important scenes involving both of them are the quarrel on pp. 110–16 (in Chapter 11), and their final meeting in Chapter 1 of Volume 2 (pp. 157–63).

2. However, a fascinating further study of Emily Brontë's development and revelation of characters in relation to each other can be found on pp. 73–6, which narrates Hindley's drunkenness, the baby Hareton's fall and Heathcliff's reflex catch which unintentionally saves the baby's life.

3

Imagery and Symbols

Imagery

Images are comparisons between something the author describes, and an idea the author imagines for the sake of the comparison. For example, in Chapter 2 we quoted Catherine's description of her love for Linton: 'My love for Linton is like the foliage in the woods. Time will change it, I'm well aware, as winter changes the trees' (p. 82). This describes Catherine's affection for Edgar by comparing it to 'the foliage in the woods'. The attraction she feels towards Edgar is there in the story, it really exists: that is the **literal** side of the comparison. The foliage in the woods is not there, it is an image-idea Brontë makes Catherine imagine as a comparison for her feeling: that is the **figurative** side of the comparison. In this example, Catherine explains that her feeling is '*like* the foliage in the woods'. The word 'like' tells us that there is a comparison, so we call this image a **simile**. One page before this example, Catherine imagines that 'every Linton on the face of the earth might melt into nothing' (p. 81). This time the insignificance of the Lintons (the **literal** side of the comparison) is compared to a vision of them as they 'melt into nothing' (the **figurative** side); but none of the words tell us that it feels 'as if' they might melt, Brontë simply writes that the Lintons *are* soft and likely to melt. This kind of image is called a **metaphor**.

When we analyse Emily Brontë's imagery, we think of the figurative ideas as elements that are added to, or contribute to, the literal story. In our first example, above, the reader is encouraged to think about 'foliage in the woods', the vulnerability and brief seasonal life of leaves, and bare winter trees, at the same time as we struggle to understand Catherine's feelings about Edgar Linton. This figurative idea is part of our experience as we read. Like any other element of the novel, it helps us to understand the book's effect, and Emily Brontë's aims and concerns in writing.

This first example has an obvious explanatory purpose, which Catherine tells us: her love is compared to foliage because 'Time will change it', she says. She highlights the ephemerality of foliage, to explain that her love is of a kind that will not last. Notice, however, that the reader's mind has taken in something more than the mechanical point that leaves only last until winter. 'Foliage in the woods' sounds plentiful and colourful, and we associate it with summer. 'Winter changes the trees', on the other hand, gives us a picture of dark bare sticks in a colourless landscape. The image does much more to us than is required by its simple explanatory purpose, so we are justified in examining these further effects, and looking more widely through the novel to study how imagery contributes to Brontë's whole creation. In this chapter, we will look at a selection of examples, building our understanding systematically. We begin with Catherine's description of her feelings about Edgar Linton and Heathcliff, already quoted in part.

Example: 'foliage' and 'rocks'

> 'My love for Linton is like the foliage in the woods. Time will change it, I'm well aware, as winter changes the trees – my love for Heathcliff resembles the eternal rocks beneath – a source of little visible delight, but necessary.'
>
> (Catherine, from p. 82)

The first stage in analysing imagery is to define both sides of the comparison. In the present example there are two comparisons to define: Catherine first compares her love for Linton with foliage; then she compares her love for Heathcliff to the rocks underneath the ground. The **literal** side of these comparisons is Catherine's feelings for the two men. The **figurative** side is foliage and rocks respectively. In this example, the first stage is straightforward, and is now done.

The second stage is to build up a full picture of the attributes or prominent qualities of the figurative idea. Here are notes about the attributes of 'foliage' and 'rocks'. Notice that I have not merely mentioned what Catherine draws to our attention. I have also allowed myself to think more widely about leaves and rocks, although I have only included reasonable ideas with which most people would agree.

[i] *Attributes of foliage.* Foliage is made up of thousands of leaves, but only lasts between spring and autumn, when it dies (as Catherine points out). It is colourful, bright, and light in weight. It is high, existing in the air above the ground and above a person if they are in the woods. It hides the tree itself, but when it falls and dies in winter, the tree is left bare.

[ii] *Attributes of rocks.* Rocks, when they show through the soil, may be impressive but do not bring a light-hearted feeling like 'delight' (as Catherine points out). She also comments that they are 'necessary', and seems to mean that they are part of the strength of the Earth itself – they are basic and structural in the sense that they hold everything together and keep everything in place. Particularly, she implies that trees would not stand or grow without the security of the rocks to hold them up. Catherine draws our attention to the fact that they last – they are 'eternal'. Rocks are generally dark, in shades of brown and grey. They are heavy in weight. They are often hidden under the ground and so unseen, and they are beneath people who, whether they think about it or not, stand upon rock. They are large, and strong.

These two sets of notes define the contrast Catherine points out, which is about endurance (brief life in contrast to 'eternal') and the kind of emotion produced ('delight' in contrast to 'necessary'). We have gone further than this, however. The contrast also suggests ideas of lightness, fragility, smallness, and height for the 'foliage', and heaviness, strength, large size and depth for the 'rocks'. This full sense of the attributes in the figurative ideas will be useful in the next stage, when we look for similar or comparable images elsewhere in the text. Now that we have analysed the attributes, we can look for images of things hidden beneath the earth, for Heathcliff; or images of fragility, for Linton.

Our close look at the figurative ideas has thrown up another odd point, however. We notice that Catherine's idea of 'foliage' becomes rather confusing when she imagines winter. The fact is that leaves die in winter – it does not 'change' them, it kills them. Yet at this point Catherine seems to move her ground. She does not show winter changing the 'foliage' but instead says that it changes 'the trees'. We must remember, also, that *her love for Edgar*, not Edgar himself, is compared to the foliage. For the present, we can comment that Catherine seems to forget her own figurative idea half-way through, and she avoids saying that her love for Linton will die. At this point in the story, she is telling Nelly of her decision to marry Edgar, so it is reasonable to suggest that she shies away from the idea that her love for him is doomed and cannot last.

We may also notice a second implication of these ideas: that the tree itself – which lifts its beautiful 'foliage' into the sky, depends on the strength of the underlying rocks. There is a relationship between Catherine's two feelings, then, which is expressed by her choice of two similes that are naturally related to each other. The idea that her feeling for Heathcliff has produced, and sustains, that for Linton, is an uneasy part of Catherine's rationalisation in this scene. She has tried to define how her two feelings are related several times before this moment, and we are encouraged to ask: Does she only love Linton *because* she loves Heathcliff? For example, she said 'I've no more business to marry Edgar Linton than I have to be in heaven; and if the wicked man in there [Hindley] had not brought Heathcliff so low, I shouldn't have thought of it' (p. 80). The imagery we are studying expresses this uneasy relationship between her two 'loves' again.

Finally, we know, from Chapter 2 above, that Catherine invested a great deal of mental effort in suppressing her desire for unity with Heathcliff, pushing her need for him, and particularly the pain of separation from him, down into her unconscious where it was forgotten until her delirious awakening years later. It is therefore appropriate that her image for loving Heathcliff at this time, is of something dark, hidden, with 'little visible' and buried beneath the earth. In the confusion of her mind which is shown by the change from 'foliage' to 'trees' we noticed earlier, it appears that Catherine herself stands in the place of the trees. This idea is again highly suggestive of the state of her character. She depends on the strength of buried feelings about Heathcliff. Yet she temporarily hides herself (as the trunk and boughs of a tree are hidden in summer) inside the dazzling, colourful 'foliage' of courting Linton. If this is a reasonable suggestion, then 'winter' will leave *her* bare and exposed, no longer able to hide behind pretty leaves.

We can also look at the concealment of the tree within its foliage in a different way. Edgar, like the Lintons and Thrushcross Grange generally, shows a decorative, pretty and cultured surface to society. However, *Wuthering Heights* makes it plain that the Lintons exploit and rule the neighbourhood: they have the social and physical power of owners, landlords and magistrates – of the upper class. The violence of this power is revealed in the bulldog Skulker who bit Catherine on her first foray to the Grange, when he was set on her to protect Mr Linton's rents (see pp. 49–50). So, the image relating to Edgar Linton may imply that his appearance is something colourful and dazzling which hides an uglier bare truth. Certainly, the two images suggest that the essence of Edgar is peripheral (foliage) while the essence of Heathcliff is in his core (rocks).

Additionally, we notice that rocks are earlier, or older: trees grow out of rocks, and foliage grows out of trees. This may suggest that Catherine's bond with Heathcliff is primordial or primitive. In the history of society, it is an early, original kind of bond, while her feeling for Linton is like a late flowering of culture upon a social structure that has grown out of original, primitive nature.

We have indulged in an extended discussion of our example in relation to Catherine's character and other themes of the novel, in order to show how rich in suggestion these image-ideas are, and how subtly they portray the volatile, confusing state of her emotions. Some of our discussion is based on the slightest of hints; notice, however, that we have been able to support our suggestions by referring to other parts of the text, to confirm our interpretations.

The third stage in analysing an image is to look for similar images elsewhere in the text. To do this, choose one of the 'attributes' from your notes in stage two, and look for other images which share this 'attribute'. We can begin by picking the ideas of 'foliage' being high up, in the air, and colourful (with the contrasting ideas of rocks as 'beneath', in the ground, and monochrome). On page 101, Catherine warns Isabella against Heathcliff, saying:

> 'Heathcliff is . . . an arid wilderness of furze and whinstone. I'd as soon put that little canary into the park on a winter's day as recommend you to bestow your heart on him!'

In this metaphor, Heathcliff is again associated with the earth 'beneath', which is drained of colour, being 'arid'. Isabella Linton is a colourful but fragile bird – a figurative idea which connects with the light, fragile attributes of foliage we noticed in our example. A further striking connection between these two image-ideas for the Lintons, is that they are both unable to survive the winter: foliage dies in winter, and the 'little canary' also succumbs to the fatal attack of winter.

There is a connection between these two images, then: we have found that there is a recurring idea of height, lightness and fragility, associated with both of the Lintons. This image, however, adds a further dimension as well. The 'little canary' is a tame bird which lives in a protected environment controlled by civilisation (i.e., in a cage in a house). Heathcliff contrasts with this – he is described as a 'wilderness', 'unreclaimed', 'without refinement – without cultivation'. So, a contrast between wildness and tameness is added to our lists of attributes. In this case, then, Emily Brontë has echoed elements from the first image-idea, and enlarged on them. We could say that there is a 'thread' of images running through the novel, which evoke the Lintons, and Heathcliff, in contrasting terms. These images share various attributes, but Emily Brontë uses the succession of images to build further details and qualities into our growing sense of the contrast between Heathcliff and the Lintons.

Example: Devil daddy

> 'Tell us where you got your lessons, and you shall have it,' said I.
> 'Who's your master?'
> 'Devil daddy,' was his answer.
> 'And what do you learn from Daddy?' I continued.
> He jumped at the fruit; I raised it higher. 'What does he teach
> you?' I asked.
> 'Naught,' said he, 'but to keep out of his gait – Daddy cannot bide
> me, because I swear at him.'
> 'Ah! and the devil teaches you to swear at Daddy?' I observed.
> 'Aye – nay,' he drawled.
> 'Who then?'
> 'Heathcliff.'
>
> (pp. 108–9)

This extract is from dialogue between Nelly and the small boy
Hareton, soon after Heathcliff's return. The image compares either
Hindley or Heathcliff, or both of them, to the devil. **The first stage**
of analysis is completed by this statement, so we move on to **stage
two.**

The figurative idea is of the devil. Hareton initially thinks of his
father, Hindley, as the devil, but his devilish attributes are confused.
He taught Hareton to swear, but in Hareton's mind his father seems
'devil' like because he rails at him and prevents him from doing as he
likes. Yet the boy's moral sense is ambiguous: his first reaction when
asked if the devil encouraged him to swear at Hindley, is 'Aye', and
this would identify Heathcliff's promotion of conflict in the house
as 'devil' like. Nelly clearly identifies Heathcliff as like the 'devil'
with her suggestion that 'the devil teaches you to swear at Daddy?'
This is confirmed later on the same page, when she runs from
Heathcliff 'feeling as scared as if I had raised a Goblin'.

What, then, are the attributes of a 'devil'? We associate devils with
Hell, a place of fire and torment commonly thought of as under the
ground. They bring to mind fear of evil and power, and they lie in
wait for the weak, tempting them to their own destruction. Devils
are also proverbially cunning and deceitful.

We can now move to **stage three** of our analysis. Images of devils and Hell are plentiful in *Wuthering Heights*, and the image of Heathcliff as a creature of evil is a commonplace of the book, so we can quickly find further examples. As early as Chapter 2, Lockwood describes Heathcliff wearing 'an almost diabolical sneer' (p. 13); and at his death, Nelly mentions his 'sharp, white teeth,' while Joseph comments that 'Th'divil's harried off his soul' (p. 332); Nelly sees 'not Mr Heathcliff, but a goblin' (p. 326); Isabella declares that 'He's not a human being' because of his 'devilish nature' (p. 172), describes his 'diabolical' forehead and 'basilisk eyes' (p. 178), and tells Hindley that Heathcliff's 'mouth watered to tear you with his teeth' because 'he's only half a man – not so much' (p. 179); Catherine calls him 'a fierce, pitiless, wolfish man' (p. 102) and young Cathy calls him 'lonely, like the devil, and envious like him' (p. 285), while Heathcliff himself says to Nelly 'I believe you think me a fiend!' and to Cathy 'to you, I've made myself worse than the devil' (p. 331). These are only a few examples of comparisons between Heathcliff and a creature of evil. The image clearly applies to him tormenting others – particularly Isabella and young Cathy – during his revenge, yet some of the imagery seems to go further. Young Cathy penetrates the inner experience of a 'devil' who is 'lonely' and 'envious'; and the attributes of a werewolf are the focus of Nelly's description of his teeth, which connects with another strand of images where Heathcliff is seen as a savage beast, such as Catherine's 'fierce, pitiless, wolfish man!' (p. 102) and Nelly's 'like a savage beast getting goaded to death with knives and spears' (p. 167).

Our first quick collection of similar images, then, confirms a strong identity between Heathcliff and devils or demons throughout the novel, but also suggests that broader ideas about a life of 'evil' or existing in 'evil' would be worth pursuing. Looking for wider examples, we quickly find the devil image to be, as we suspected, more complicated than simply an epithet for Heathcliff. He ascribes a devilish nature to Catherine, for example: 'Are you possessed with a devil . . . ?' he asks, and surviving her will leave him 'writhing in the torments of hell' (p. 159), while she has treated him 'infernally' (p. 111).

The figurative idea of a 'devil' is broader than merely that of a villainous man, then. As we find further instances of this kind of imagery, we find further, broader applications of the idea. For example, Hindley thinks of Heathcliff as a devil, saying that Hell will be made 'ten times blacker' by Heathcliff's soul (p. 139); on the other hand, he says that 'it is some devil that urges me to thwart my own schemes by killing him – you fight against that devil, for love, as long as you may' (p. 138), comparing his own vengeful fury to a devil. We know that Heathcliff is seen as a devil by others, and young Cathy penetrates the source of his apparent 'evil' when she descibes him as 'lonely' and 'envious' as the devil: 'however miserable you make us, we shall still have the revenge of thinking that your cruelty rises from your greater misery!' (p. 285). Heathcliff uses the term 'hell' repeatedly to describe the torment of being separated from Catherine (for example, on page 159, and the description 'this abyss, where I cannot find you!' on page 167). Heathcliff, then, sees 'hell' as an experience of pain in which he lives; but it is not his natural habitat as it would be for the 'goblin' or 'devil' that others see him as. It is a state he longs to escape. Just before his death, for example, he says that 'Last night, I was on the threshold of hell. To-day, I am within sight of my heaven' (p. 325). Our knowledge of the novel tells us clearly that Heathcliff, Isabella (after her marriage), and Hindley all inflict on others the 'hell' they have suffered themselves. The recurrent image-ideas of 'hell' and 'devil', then, stand for a cycle of tortures that are self-perpetuating, and the vengeful, vindictive emotions that drive these hurts.

We began this analysis with a straightforward image, comparing two characters with the devil. The only complication was the ambivalence of Hareton's perceptions, and Nelly's different view, which hinted at a more complex idea behind the word 'devil'. Notice that, as we pursue these images by analysing attributes and searching for analogous instances elsewhere in the text, the ideas have become connected to other strands of imagery. So Heathcliff's 'devil' persona is connected to ideas likening him to a werewolf, a goblin, or a savage beast. The specific image-ideas 'devil' and 'hell' have also become broadened and are defined more fully in relation to the story, with each new example we find. 'Hell' now evokes an experience of extreme emotional pain, together with the unending cycle of characters inflicting misery on each other, which is driven by that agony.

This is a characteristic process in analysing imagery. In **stage two** of our analytical method, we broaden the scope of study by looking at the wider qualities associated with the image-idea. So, when we studied Hareton's remark 'Devil daddy', we used the idea of torment; this led us to consider torture and pain, and this in turn led us to further complexities and details in the text, which are connected to each other by the fact that their imagery shares attributes.

Of course, most imagery has more than one 'attribute', so **stage three** can often be investigated several times, each enquiry following up one particular attribute of the image-idea. For example, our analysis of 'foliage' and 'rocks' (example 1, above) focused on the attributes of height and colour, depth and lack of colour. We could also focus on the contrast between small and large in 'foliage' and 'rocks'. This would in turn lead us to Heathcliff's image for the difference between Cathy's and Edgar's emotional capacities:

> And Catherine has a heart as deep as I have; the sea could be as readily contained in that horse-trough, as her whole affection be monopolised by him.
>
> (p. 147)

Studying this image, we might concentrate on the concept of a limited container ('horse-trough') and natural power ('sea'), which would lead us to Heathcliff's contempt for Edgar's Christian virtues:

> And that insipid, paltry creature attending her from *duty* and *humanity*! From *pity* and *charity*! He might as well plant an oak in a flower-pot, and expect it to thrive, as imagine he can restore her to vigour in the soil of his shallow cares!
>
> (p. 151)

Once we have arrived at this point, we notice that Heathcliff's image for Catherine is of a tree – and this connects back to her idea of her love for Linton as 'foliage', with the implication that she depends on the massive, solid support of the 'rocks' which represent her feeling for Heathcliff. These two images, then, seem to *add to each other*, so the absurdity of a large tree in a flowerpot, contrasted with roots in massive and secure earth and rocks, becomes a new expression of the characters' relationships. However, this 'whole' image-idea comes to us gradually, at different times. Our minds naturally add image-ideas together, and recall previous ones, as we read: so it is natural for us to conflate these two different images, expressed by different characters in different circumstances.

In other words, whatever particular focus we follow when studying imagery, will lead us to make connections between different parts of the text: we find ourselves working in an interconnected network of image-ideas which has its own way of conveying the author's essential concerns. The two examples we have studied belong to two extensive 'networks' of imagery in *Wuthering Heights*. 'Foliage' and 'rocks', our first example, belongs in the wide network of nature-imagery in the novel. 'Devil' and 'hell', our second example, belongs in another extensively-used network of images drawn from religion and superstition. A moment's thought about the whole novel tells us that each of these large networks contains numerous criss-crossing strands. Think, for example, about birds (Isabella is a 'canary', Linton has 'dove's eyes', Catherine protects her 'lapwings') in the nature-imagery of *Wuthering Heights*. We touched this 'strand' of the 'network' when we came across Catherine's idea of Isabella as a 'canary' exposed to winter, but we were following a different 'strand' at the time, and we cannot explore the whole network in this short chapter. Similarly, think about the many images of witches and spells (Nelly is a 'hag' gathering 'elf-bolts'; Heathcliff calls young Cathy a 'witch' when she perceives his devilish misery). We would come across this 'strand' of superstitious images next to Cathy's comparison of Heathcliff to a 'lonely' devil. Again, we were following a different 'strand' at the time, and passed over the connection.

Symbolism

It is important to be clear about the distinction between images and symbols. Definitions in dictionaries and literary 'companions' can be extremely confusing. However, if we use our common sense, we can cut away much of the complication and use a clear method to tell one from the other.

When do we need to know which is which? It happens when we are in the middle of studying a text. We have come across something in the text which suggests further meaning, or resonates in our minds, as if it carries extra significance and cries out to be interpreted. We do not need to go back to dictionary definitions, then: we are already involved in studying literature. Simply, we have found something in the text that provokes us to think in an exciting, referential way, as if something in the text *stands for* an idea, or is attached to a feeling. All we want to know is what to call it: image or symbol?

At this point, simply ask yourself a question: Is the thing you have found a real thing that is literally there in the story? If the answer is yes, then you are studying a **symbol**. If the answer is no, then the 'thing' you have come across must be an image-idea, an idea the author brings in as a comparison to something in the story, and you are studying **imagery**. Two examples show how the distinction works in practice.

Think back to our first analysis of imagery. You have noticed the idea of 'eternal rocks beneath' on page 82 of *Wuthering Heights*. This is a noticeable, evocative idea: you sense that it adds feelings of power, permanence and strength to the text at that point. Ask yourself: Are the 'eternal rocks' really there as literal things in the story? No, they are not. Cathy's feelings for Heathcliff are really there – they are an actual part of the story, but the rocks are not. They are imagined, figurative rocks: they are an **image**.

Example: Penistone Craggs

Now look at the following extract from Chapter 4, Volume 2. Nelly and young Cathy are talking:

> 'And what are those golden rocks like, when you stand under them?' she once asked.
> The abrupt descent of Penistone Craggs particularly attracted her

notice, especially when the setting sun shone on it, and the topmost Heights, and the whole extent of landscape besides lay in shadow. I explained that they were bare masses of stone, with hardly enough earth in their clefts to nourish a stunted tree. 'And why are they bright so long after it is evening here?' she pursued.

'Because they are a great deal higher up than we are,' replied I; 'you could not climb them, they are too high and steep. In winter the frost is always there before it comes to us; and, deep into summer, I have found snow under that black hollow on the north-east side!'

'Oh, you have been on them!' she cried, gleefully. 'Then I can go, too, when I am a woman. Has papa been, Ellen?'

'Papa would tell you, Miss,' I answered, hastily, 'that they are not worth the trouble of visiting. The moors, where you ramble with him, are much nicer; and Thrushcross park is the finest place in the world.'

'But I know the park, and I don't know those,' she murmured to herself.   (p. 188)

Reading this passage, we are struck by the amount of emotion and meaning attached to Penistone Craggs. Cathy longs to go there, they shine 'golden' to her, and her discussion with Nelly gives provocatively conflicting interpretations of their attraction or hostility (Cathy sees them 'golden' and 'bright', but to Nelly they are 'bare masses of stone'). Penistone Craggs also seems to mean something: Cathy's remark 'But I know the park, and I don't know those' places the Craggs with the wonder of a wider world, and connects them to the excitement and adventure of youth. It is not going too far to say that they represent the fascination of the unknown, in this passage. Now ask the question: are Penistone Craggs really there, literally and actually a part of the story of *Wuthering Heights*? The answer is yes: Cathy can really see them through her window; Nelly has really visited them. In this case, then, when you study Penistone Craggs and their significance in the novel, you are studying **symbolism**.

We have had no difficulty distinguishing between two lots of rocks: the 'eternal rocks' on page 82 are an **image**, but Penistone Craggs on page 188 are **symbolic**. The distinction is quite clear, and should help you to classify what you are studying.

When thinking about symbols, we must be careful not to add unwarranted meanings to all the natural things in the story. For example, remember that Heathcliff is in a settle when he overhears Catherine's conversation with Nelly in Chapter 9 of Volume 1. It is a crucial and exciting scene, which leads to Heathcliff's disappearance. It is tempting to see everything about that scene as significant, and we may be tempted to think that the settle means something: it represents the division between Catherine and Heathcliff, perhaps, as a hard, intractable barrier between them? We should resist these temptations and remember our common sense. Does Emily Brontë add emotions, attitudes, controversy or descriptive mood to the settle? No, she does not. It is mentioned in passing, only, and it serves the simple physical purpose of hiding Heathcliff from the other two. So, the settle is a straightforward plot device, not **symbolic** at all. Other items of furniture in the novel do have powerful feelings attached to them, and are described with additional characteristics by the author. The panelled bed which was once Catherine's, in which Lockwood dreams and Heathcliff dies, clearly is a significant piece of furniture, as is the 'black press' Catherine sees in her delirium. If we make judgements in this way, relying on common sense and keeping a sense of proportion, we will avoid the error of seeing symbolism everywhere.

We now turn to some examples from *Wuthering Heights*, to show how studying symbolism enriches our understanding of the novel. The two houses, Wuthering Heights and Thrushcross Grange, and their environments – the high moorland and the park – are dominant, pervasive symbols in *Wuthering Heights*. However, we will discuss the duality of these two places in Chapter 4 as part of the 'structure' of the novel. In the remainder of this chapter, we will look at some more limited examples, where Brontë implies a larger meaning around the objects and events of her story.

Example: Isabella's dog

> In passing the garden to reach the road, at a place where a bridle hook is driven into the wall, I saw something white moved irregularly, evidently by another agent than the wind. Notwithstanding my

hurry, I staid to examine it, lest ever after I should have the conviction impressed on my imagination that it was a creature of the other world.

My surprise and perplexity were great to discover, by touch more than vision, Miss Isabella's springer, Fanny, suspended to a handkerchief, and nearly at its last gasp. I quickly released the animal, and lifted it into the garden. I had seen it follow its mistress upstairs, when she went to bed, and wondered much how it could have got out there, and what mischievous person had treated it so.

While untying the knot round the hook, it seemed to me that I repeatedly caught the beat of horses' feet galloping at some distance, but there were such a number of things to occupy my reflections that I hardly gave the circumstance a thought, though it was a strange sound, in that place, at two o'clock in the morning.

(pp. 127–8)

This is Nelly's account of finding Isabella's dog hanging from the park wall. We later learn that Heathcliff hanged it there when he eloped with Isabella. Is the hanging of the dog **symbolic**? In other words, is this simply a gruesome part of the story, or does the event of the dog embody any further meaning? To answer this question, we need to examine the passage closely, focusing on how Emily Brontë describes the event.

The dog is first mentioned as 'something white'. Its movement attracts Nelly's attention because it seems unnatural: it moves 'irregularly' and the wind does not account for this. Brontë reminds us that Nelly is rushing to fetch the doctor, because Mrs Linton is critically ill. Clearly, the irregular movement of 'something white' arrests Nelly powerfully: she stops to investigate 'Notwithstanding my hurry'. Nelly then explains even more fully why she stopped. She is a sensitive, suggestible person, as we know from other parts of the text (for example, when Heathcliff returns and accosts her in the porch, she is 'uncertain whether to regard him as a worldly visiter' – p. 93), yet she clings to her homespun morality and common sense. On this occasion, Nelly feels a need to bring something apparently supernatural down into the world of reason. She is frightened in case she will be haunted by the mystery for the rest of her life: 'lest ever after I should have the conviction impressed on my imagination that it was a creature of the other world'. Emily Brontë, then, introduces the hanging dog in a carefully built-up aura of unnatural mystery and power. Even then, the strangeness of the dog is not dispelled. Nelly recognises it 'by touch more than vision' and remains in great 'surprise and perplexity,' which makes her wonder 'much' how it came to be there. While she is releasing the dog, another mystery is introduced in the 'strange sound' of galloping hoofbeats 'at some distance'. The hoofbeats resemble Nelly's first glimpse of the dog in being indistinct: she says that 'it seemed' that she 'caught the beat of horses' feet'. Brontë, then, places a heavy emphasis on the difficulty Nelly has in discerning the truth of either the dog or the distant sound of hooves. She emphasises hearing and touch at the expense of indistinct sight.

So, although the dog is real enough, its appearance in the narrative is shrouded in mystery and powerful speculations about the supernatural: it calls to a part of Nelly's mind that disturbs her deeply because it threatens to unsettle her reason. Brontë has clearly endowed the hanging dog with ominous attributes, then. Like Heathcliff's reappearance after three years, or her strange presentiment and the vision of an infant Hindley/Hareton which leads her to Wuthering Heights, the dog seems to be another sign of impending horror and doom, which strongly arouses Nelly's fearful, superstitious nature. So the hanging dog is **symbolic**. It is an ominous sign of cruelties and tragic revelations to come.

Having established that the hanging dog is symbolic, by closely examining its context, we can now move to the second stage of analysing a symbol. This involves thinking about the text in an interpretative way, noting how the symbol we have found relates to other major symbols in the text, or to major themes and characters. This can be done by noting down a series of statements about the symbol and thinking about them to see where they lead. Some of these statements (see the first on my list below) may seem laughably obvious. Remember that they are only starting-points, and that the obvious is a necessary stage in any analysis. Here are some statements about the dog:

1. It is a dog.
2. It belongs to Isabella; it is a dependent, petted creature.
3. Heathcliff hanged it.
4. It is hanging on the wall of Thrushcross Grange park, next to the road, outside the garden.

These are plain, straightforward statements, but clear enough for us to build upon. We will take each one in turn, and think about it in relation to the rest of the novel.

First, it is a dog. Do dogs bear any specific relationship to Isabella? Think back to Isabella's first introduction in the novel:

> 'Isabella . . . lay screaming at the farther end of the room, shrieking as if witches were running red hot needles into her. Edgar stood on the hearth weeping silently, and in the middle of the table sat a little dog, shaking its paw and yelping, which, from their mutual accusations, we understood they had nearly pulled in two between them.'
>
> (p. 48)

Heathcliff contemptuously calls the dog 'a heap of warm hair' and the Linton children 'idiots' for quarrelling over it. So, the first character-note we have about Isabella Linton is her attention-seeking tantrum: she is 'screaming' and 'shrieking', and her love is selfish: the desire to possess a comforting object. She also appears capable of insensitive cruelty – she is prepared to hurt the dog ('nearly pulled in two') in order to possess it.

The hanging dog is the successor to that 'heap of warm hair'. Nelly remembers seeing it 'follow its mistress upstairs, when she went to bed'. It is pathetically attached to Isabella, for Nelly finds it 'yelping' when she returns, and it 'coursed up and down snuffing the grass, and would have escaped to the road' to follow Isabella wherever she had gone, had Nelly not seized it (p. 129). When Isabella leaves Heathcliff and runs away to the south, she is 'accompanied by Fanny, who yelped wild with joy at recovering her mistress' (p. 181).

Heathcliff describes Isabella's character in terms of the hanging of the dog, saying that she saw him hang it and pleaded for it, but still eloped with him: 'But no brutality disgusted her – I suppose she has an innate admiration of it, if only her precious person were secure from injury!' (p. 149).

Isabella has one other encounter with a dog. On arriving at Wuthering Heights she approaches Hareton, who threatens her with 'Throttler', a 'half-bred bulldog', and Isabella retreats in fear. Later, however, she recognises Throttler as having spent its 'whelphood' at Thrushcross Grange: old Mr Linton gave it to Hindley as a present. Isabella comments 'I fancy it knew me – it pushed its nose against mine by way of salute, and then hastened to devour the porridge' (p. 142). In the middle of her story of hostility and neglect at Wuthering Heights, Throttler's half-memory of her from the Grange is the only comfort Isabella receives. We notice that Throttler's memory of Isabella does not detain him long from his selfish instincts: he quickly turns to devouring the porridge. In this encounter, Throttler may be said to represent Isabella herself: gently raised at first, but then transplanted to the hostile household of Wuthering Heights. Like Throttler, she is learning to survive, and later we find her eating 'heartily' the morning after Heathcliff's fight with Hindley (p. 178).

In the light of these details about Isabella and dogs, what does the hanging of Fanny tell us? The first and clearest idea that springs to mind is that Fanny represents Isabella's cossetted, self-centred upbringing at Thrushcross Grange, and this takes us on to our second statement, that Fanny is a 'dependent, petted creature'. In particular, the possessive/dependent relationship of owner and pet is all Isabella has known up to now. These thoughts suggest that the dog stands for Isabella's protected background, and also that it stands for Isabella herself, as she has been a dependent, petted creature like Fanny. There is no need for us to tie a symbol down to a single meaning, however: the dog seems to have significance in both of these ways.

Two other ideas about the hanging dog are more shadowy, but nonetheless strongly suggested by the text. When Nelly fears that it is 'a creature of the other world', this brings to mind something hidden and evil. We should remember Isabella's self-centred tantrum over the first dog, when she was first seen in the novel. Here, again, she pursues selfish gratification: she abandons Fanny with the very man who brutally hangs her, pursuing his attention to herself. In this sense, we can argue that the hanging dog represents the underlying cruelty of Isabella's nature, her basic but hidden need to be the centre of attention and her willingness to be vicious and inflict pain, even to suffer violence, in order to satisfy her rage for attention. There are strong signs of a sado-masochistic element in Isabella's character, elsewhere. For example, Catherine calls her a 'tigress' when she scratches her to bleeding (p. 105), and Heathcliff's opinion of her 'admiration' for brutality is quoted above. Isabella conveys these feelings herself when she talks of tasting 'the delight of paying wrong for wrong' and explains 'what misery laid on Heathcliff could content me, unless I have a hand in it?' (p. 179). We also remember that she betrays Hindley and teases Heathcliff, which leads to Hindley being kicked and trampled almost to death while she herself is first 'unnerved by terror for the consequences of my taunting speech' and afterwards 'in a condition of mind to be shocked at nothing . . . as reckless as some malefactors show themselves at the foot of the gallows' (pages 176 and 177). Isabella, then, seems to enjoy a disturbing mixture of terror and cruelty, and this excites her. The next morning she eats heartily and with a sense of 'satisfaction and superiority', while Heathcliff's grief 'gratified' her (pp. 178–9).

This side of Isabella's nature is something covered with hypocrisy: an underlying rage for attention which, at Thrushcross Grange, showed itself as childish behaviour in her tantrums, sulks and jealousy of Catherine. The hanging dog is an external manifestation of her callous cruelty, and perhaps therefore a sign that the world of Thrushcross Grange – despite its more polished appearance – is no less cruel and selfish underneath than that of Wuthering Heights.

The second shadowy suggestion about the dog is more speculative. It can be argued that Catherine's role at Thrushcross Grange, first as the Lintons' guest and friend, and later as Edgar's wife, has been that of a pampered pet. This is a doubtful point, but the evidence presents it as a suggestive element in the incident of the dog.

Remember that Isabella was 'shrieking' in a tantrum about a 'heap of warm hair', when the Lintons first brought Catherine into their house. Here is Heathcliff's description of how Catherine was treated:

> 'Then the woman servant brought a basin of warm water, and washed her feet, and Mr Linton mixed a tumbler of negus, and Isabella emptied a plateful of cakes into her lap, and Edgar stood gaping at a distance. Afterwards, they dried and combed her beautiful hair, and gave her a pair of enormous slippers, and wheeled her to the fire . . .'
>
> (p. 51)

In this passage, it seems clear that Catherine takes the place of the desired pet, and begins her relationship with the Lintons in that context. During her six months' superficial happiness as Mrs Linton, Catherine continues to be petted and deferred to by the brother and sister:

> They were both very attentive to her comfort, certainly. It was not the thorn bending to the honeysuckles, but the honeysuckles embracing the thorn. There were no mutual concessions; one stood erect, and the others yielded; and who *can* be ill-natured, and bad-tempered, when they encounter neither opposition nor indifference?
>
> (p. 91)

During this time, Isabella and her brother clearly indulged Catherine. Edgar had a 'deep-rooted fear of ruffling her humour' and said that 'the stab of a knife could not inflict a worse pang than he suffered at seeing his lady vexed' (both from p. 91).

It is reasonable to suppose that Isabella suppressed selfish feelings during this time, allowing Catherine to monopolise the household's attention. When she does voice a complaint after Heathcliff's return, her words suggest a long-term, hidden resentment of the other girl: 'You are a dog in the manger, Cathy, and desire no one to be loved but yourself.' (p. 101).

It is therefore possible to argue that Isabella acquiesces in the hanging of Fanny partly because Fanny, like Catherine, is a pampered pet of Thrushcross Grange. In a shadowy, unconscious way, disposing of her pet dog takes the place of disposing of Catherine, her hated rival. This suggestion interprets Isabella's psychology beyond any thoughts she would express herself. Brontë's central interest is in the characters of Heathcliff and Catherine, and in comparison to theirs, Isabella's personality is economically sketched in. However, it is a measure of the depth of the author's sensitivity to human nature, that this strand of possible feeling in Isabella is subtly completed by the incident of the dog. The incident happens at the very time when Isabella imagines that she is taking Catherine's place by stealing Heathcliff from her.

Our third statement was the plain fact: 'Heathcliff hanged it.' Does thinking about Heathcliff's action add to the significance of this event? He tells us that, while hanging the dog, 'the first words I uttered were a wish that I had the hanging of every being belonging to her' (p. 149), and this remark provides a clear symbolic meaning for his action: Heathcliff was symbolically hanging the whole Linton household. This interpretation is supported by the language he uses later in the same speech, when he applies diction appropriate to dogs, to Isabella: she is a 'brach', and will endure torture but 'still creep shamefully cringing back' (p. 149). His future cruelty to Isabella and his vicious revenge on the Linton family, then, are all prefigured in the symbolic hanging of Fanny.

Our last statement noted that the dog is hanged on the outer wall of Thrushcross Grange park. We have already remarked that the two houses and their surroundings have a symbolic role in the novel, which will be discussed in more detail in Chapter 4. The incident of the dog is clearly placed within this symbolic setting: Thrushcross Grange is a protected and sheltered environment, and its garden or 'park' is cultivated and civilised. In contrast, the high moors around Wuthering Heights are wild. The fact that Isabella's dog is hanged from the park wall gives the reader a measure of Heathcliff's attack upon the Lintons and their possessions: his power and cruelty has reached as far as the wall of the park, where the dog hangs.

The hanging of Isabella's dog, then, is a symbolic event in several ways. We have looked at its significance in relation to Isabella, Heathcliff and the conflict between the two houses. We have found it to be symbolic on several levels: Heathcliff clearly knows that he is hanging a symbol of the hated Lintons; and Isabella may sense that Fanny represents the cosseted life she has lived up to now. However, Isabella is not aware of her own callous selfishness, and would vehemently deny it; and she would be shocked by the suggestion that she wished to murder her sister-in-law. So Emily Brontë has created a symbolic event which works on many levels, and in different contexts. It is important to remember the various complex interpretations suggested by the hanging dog, as Brontë's symbols often work in this way. They are complex elements in the life of the novel, never reducible to one simple meaning.

Finally, notice that there are several other times in *Wuthering Heights* when dogs seem to play a significant role, so further study of dogs in the novel would be rewarding. For example, the threatening, animal atmosphere of Wuthering Heights is evoked in Lockwood's description 'other dogs haunted other recesses' (p. 5); the bulldog Skulker protects property and attacks Catherine when she and Heathcliff are spying into Thrushcross Grange; when Isabella runs from the Heights, she mentions in passing that 'I knocked over Hareton, who was hanging a litter of puppies from a chair back in the doorway' (p. 181, and a gruesome echo of the hanging of Fanny); and young Cathy's two pointers are mauled by the wilder dogs at the Heights: they are returned to her 'limping, and hanging their heads' after she has rejected Hareton's peace-offering of 'a fine crooked-legged terrier whelp from the kennel' (pages 195 and 194 respectively). Her 'old hound' is wiser about visiting the Heights, and finds its own way home. The conflict between tame and wild people, then, is closely mirrored by a series of incidents involving their dogs, throughout the novel.

Example: Gardening at the Heights

> She got downstairs before me, and out into the garden, where she had seen her cousin performing some easy work; and when I went to bid them come to breakfast, I saw she had persuaded him to clear a large space of ground from currant and gooseberry bushes, and they were busy planning together an importation of plants from the Grange.
> I was terrified at the devastation which had been accomplished in a

brief half hour; the black currant trees were the apple of Joseph's eye, and she had just fixed her choice of a flower bed in the midst of them!

(p. 314)

The gardening that Hareton and Cathy begin at Wuthering Heights, not long before Heathcliff's death, is narrated in this matter-of-fact manner. We quickly realise that it is significant, however, in the context of references to plants and flowers throughout *Wuthering Heights*. In this passage, the 'black' currant-bushes (which are dark, wild and hardy, with thorns) are the type of vegetation that suits the Heights. We remember Lockwood's description of 'a range of gaunt thorns all stretching their limbs one way, as if craving alms of the sun' (p. 4). A flowerbed and flowers, on the other hand, are to be 'imported from the Grange', where the garden is enclosed and cultivated.

Cultivating a garden at Wuthering Heights, then, symbolises Cathy's civilising influence (like her teaching Hareton to read), importing the culture in which she was brought up and softening the wildness of the old house. The suggestion that this activity is like a symbolic spring after the long winter of pain, deaths and Heathcliff's destructive revenge, is reinforced by other slight touches during the final chapters of the novel. For example, when they go inside for breakfast, Catherine teases Hareton by 'sticking primroses in his plate of porridge' (p. 315); and Lockwood is surprised on his final visit to the Heights, to notice 'a fragrance of stocks and wall flowers, wafted on the air, from amongst the homely fruit trees' (p. 304). Cathy's and Hareton's gardening, then, is a straightforward symbol of renewal and growth; an external sign of their youth, love, and re-born hope.

We can also develop our ideas about the garden in the context of the Heights and the Grange, and their long conflict. Joseph's currant-bushes suit the Heights because they provide food: everything at the Heights has a purpose related to the work of the farm (we remember that nobody could be spared to guide Lockwood home through the snow, because they had to tend the livestock – see pp. 12–17). Brontë only mentions two objects with a decorative purpose in connection with the Heights: one is the 'wilderness of shameless little boys' carved above the entrance, a celebration of primitive sexuality, and the other is the fiddle Hindley wanted, which was smashed before it could arrive. The Grange, on the other hand, is full of decoration, culture and beauty for its own sake, from the chandelier and bordered ceiling (p. 48) to Edgar's library of unread books (p. 119). The flowers Cathy intends to 'import' bring the superfluous – beauty for its own sake, because flowers do not provide food – from the Grange to the Heights. To make room for them, part of the food supply is sacrificed. Symbolically, then, the Heights is moving forward in cultural history, shedding some of its primitive practicality and taking on the more refined culture of the Grange. This also means that the Heights is beginning to separate itself from the source of its wealth. The transformation of currant-bushes into flowerbeds is the beginning of a process, then, which ends in a life like Mr Linton's. He receives rents, and does not work: he lives as a leisured gentleman, insulated from the work of his own tenant-farmers.

This simple part of the narrative has self-evident significance, then. However, it also subtly recalls other mentions of flowers in the novel, and is ironically connected to the story of Heathcliff at the end of his life.

We may remember some other flowers when we read about the planned garden at the Heights. For example, when Catherine was convalescent, Edgar brought her some crocuses: ' "These are the earliest flowers at the Heights!" she exclaimed. "They remind me of soft thaw winds, and warm sunshine, and nearly melted snow" ' (p. 132). Catherine's memory is of a hopeful early springtime, and her eyes 'shone delighted'. The gift of crocuses is a symbol of Edgar's hope: he feels that the air blows so 'sweetly' on the hills that 'it would cure you'. To Catherine, on the other hand, the flowers represent the past and her death is inevitable. Emily Brontë constructs the significance of flowers in the novel carefully. We have noticed 'primroses' making part of Cathy's springtime teasing of Hareton (p. 315), and 'crocuses' as a symbol of youth and hope (p. 132). When Mrs Dean describes the weather on the day following Catherine's funeral, we read that 'the primroses and crocuses were hidden under wintry drifts' (p. 169), a passing reference which seems to resonate both backwards and forwards in the novel, as well as reversing the 'thaw winds' and 'nearly melted snow' that crocuses inspired in Catherine's mind.

Thinking about the garden in relation to Heathcliff's progress reminds us that the thaw between Cathy and Hareton, and the clearing of the bushes, happen between Heathcliff's two long monologues (see our analysis of these in Chapter 2). We know that Heathcliff has been unnaturally haunted by his vision of Catherine above the earth, for eighteen years. When Edgar dies, he pays a second visit to her grave, and having seen that she is in her coffin Heathcliff is 'pacified – a little' (p. 288). Shortly after the young couple begin their garden, Heathcliff says to Nelly that 'There is a strange change approaching' (p. 320). In this context, we can think of the garden as part of the reassertion of nature and reality in Heathcliff: a symbol of the end of his revenge, because he cannot remain frozen in a 'winter' of superstition and hate any longer. So, in this sense, the garden is ironically a new spring for Heathcliff as well as for the young people, although his new life is destined to be underground. In this connection, we can understand the significance of Hareton's final act as a gardener, covering Heathcliff's grave:

> Hareton, with a streaming face, dug green sods, and laid them over the brown mould himself: at present it is as smooth and verdant as its companion mounds.
>
> (p. 333)

After eighteen years, Heathcliff finally recognised that Catherine was naturally dead, and buried in her grave, not unnaturally walking the earth to haunt him. That moment, when he looked at her corpse and became 'pacified', was the beginning of a process in which he himself was able to follow his 'nature' again. His negative efforts at revenge, focusing on the past, became less important, and his hope of reunion with Catherine through his own natural death, a focus on the future, and change, became his growing preoccupation. Heathcliff had tried to hold the world still, to freeze it at a moment in the past when Catherine was still above ground; but the world moves on. Cathy's and Hareton's gardening is therefore a part of the final movement for Heathcliff: the world 're-starts' itself around him, and the turf Hareton lays over the grave is a sign that Heathcliff's body has now joined a continuing natural world: it will rot in the earth (as Heathcliff himself has planned), and the grass grows 'verdant' above it.

Conclusions

1. Emily Brontë uses imagery in such a way that single images usually connect with others in the novel, because they have qualities or 'attributes' in common. For example, we found that the image of Heathcliff as 'rocks' connected with Catherine's description of him as 'an arid wilderness of furze and whinstone', both being dark or monochrome, and both being of the earth beneath.

2. The images connect into elaborate networks of imagery, where recurrent characteristics continually reappear in image-ideas. We noticed two particularly widespread 'networks' of imagery: that relating to nature, landscape and the seasons; and that relating to religion and superstition.

3. Many elements in the story of *Wuthering Heights* have extra significance added to them, either by the way in which the author describes them, or through one or more characters' emotions being projected through them. These objects and events are **symbolic**: we can discuss and interpret their significance.

4. The significance of Emily Brontë's **symbols** is never a single, straightforward meaning. She creates symbols with complex co-existing meanings, and with meaning that varies on different levels. **Symbols** are often differently significant to different characters, or even ambiguously significant to one character (for example, we noticed that Fanny might embody both her own past life, and Catherine, for Isabella).

5. Therefore, both **imagery** and **symbolism** in *Wuthering Heights* grow out of the natural surroundings, actual objects and events of the story; and they are intimately related to the emotions and experiences of the characters. In this way, Emily Brontë has

created a seamless continuum from narrative reality to symbolic meaning, where metaphor and themes on the one hand, and physical elements in the story on the other hand, work together. This has the effect of persuading the reader that *Wuthering Heights* is a 'whole' significant world.

Methods of Analysis

[A] When you are studying imagery, use the following three stages:

1. **Stage one:** clearly define the literal and figurative sides of the comparison.
2. **Stage two:** make notes about the qualities or 'attributes' of the image-idea, the figurative side of the comparison. Begin with the attributes Brontë draws to our attention (for example, Catherine called the 'rocks' she compared with love for Heathcliff 'eternal', so their endurance is an attribute the text draws to our attention). Then add notes about other common attributes and associations of the image-idea.
3. **Stage three:** choose an attribute or attributes to study further, and look elsewhere in the text for other examples of image-ideas with the same attributes. This will lead you to recurrences of similar imagery, and into a 'network' of imagery which adds to your insight into story, characters, and the author's concerns.

[B] To distinguish between **imagery** and **symbolism**, when you have found something you sense to be significant and worthy of further study, ask yourself whether what you have found is actually, literally, there in the story. If it is, you are studying a **symbol**; if it is not, but is an idea imagined for the sake of a comparison, you are studying an **image-idea**.

[C] When studying a **symbol**:

1. Begin by making sure that the 'symbol' you have found does provoke a sense of added significance, in the text. Closely study

the way it is described or discussed by the author and characters. For example, we found that the description of the hanging dog raised disturbing questions, and conveyed a strong sense of mystery.

2. Make simple statements about the 'symbol' you have found. These statements may seem naïve, or self-evident, but still provide a useful starting-point for thinking about the symbol and its meaning.

3. Take each of your statements in turn, and think about them in the context of the rest of the novel. This stage of analysis will lead you to look at other passages from other parts of the novel, where related symbols appear. Your aim is to understand a complex of significances, and you should not expect your 'symbol' to have a single clear meaning.

Suggested Work

- Choose a single image and carry out a study by tracing it, and its analogues, in other parts of the text. Any single image would make a suitable starting-point for your study. A suggestion is Edgar's description of Heathcliff's hair as 'a colt's mane' (p. 58). In this case, stage three of your study will lead you into the 'network' of animal comparisons in *Wuthering Heights*.

- Choose a symbolic element in the text to study. A fascinating study in symbolism concerns doors and windows at both Wuthering Heights and Thrushcross Grange. A study could usefully start from page 19, when Lockwood describes his sleeping-closet, the panelled bed.

4

Structure in *Wuthering Heights*

The 'structure' of a text is present in anything the author does to give a 'shape' to our experience as we read. So, we begin to study 'structure' by thinking about the text in a particular way, concentrating on the question of its 'shape', and how it is all fitted together.

Studying structure begins by standing back from the details of the novel and taking an *overall* view. This can be quite difficult to do when you have just read the novel for the first time. *Wuthering Heights* is fast-moving and full of small incidents; and the story is complicated, because different events are occurring to different characters in different places at the same time. When you have finished reading it for the first time, and try to think of the 'whole' novel, you are likely to see nothing but a very large number of scenes all in a long line: the story, event after event after event, from the beginning to the end.

Notice, however, that we have already thought about 'structure' in *Wuthering Heights*. At the beginning of Chapter 1, we discussed the narrative 'frame' of the novel, and the word 'frame' immediately introduces a visual concept. In our mind's eye, we see a distant picture of people in a landscape (the story itself), then we see Nelly as a rectangle of moulded wood, a 'frame', around this picture, and Lockwood as another, larger rectangle of wood (another 'frame') around that. You may have imagined the pane of glass in both frames, so you imagined the story itself, the distant picture, having to pass through these panes of glass before we can see it.

In Chapter 1 we used visual ideas to help us discuss the effect of

Brontë's narrative structure. For example, we said that Lockwood was '*a long way removed* from the actual experiences of the story', and described the contrast between the characters' plain, vigorous diction and Lockwood's precious words as a '*linguistic journey*'. We noted that the story itself sometimes seems to be too alive, and shatters the 'frame' that tries to contain it. We used another image for this: it is 'like a flood trying to get through a hosepipe'. The point is that in Chapter 1 we conceived of the whole book as a kind of visual picture, or diagram, with the story as a distant thing, trying to pass through frames (and 'filters') to get to us.

Thinking about the overall 'shape' of the novel, as we did in Chapter 1, is what we mean by thinking about the 'structure'. Then, we focused on the 'narrative structure' Emily Brontë has given to her novel. In this chapter we look at structure in *Wuthering Heights* with a particular focus on three topics. First, Emily Brontë's use of time in the plot of *Wuthering Heights*; secondly, the structure of families, social groups and relationships in the novel; and thirdly, the structure of the setting, which is dominated by the two houses Wuthering Heights and Thrushcross Grange.

Time

Emily Brontë has plotted *Wuthering Heights* carefully. We are given the relative ages of the various characters, and the amount of time that passes between events, so we are able to reconstruct the story with dates. In the 1995 Penguin Classics edition we find a 'Genealogical Table' on page xxv, which tells us, for example, that old Mr Earnshaw died in October 1777, that Hareton is six years older than young Cathy, and that they marry in January 1803. There are also frequent precise references to time passing, in the text. For example, Lockwood says that he was ill for 'four weeks' (p. 90); Heathcliff's return was 'on a mellow evening in September'; Cathy unlocked her door 'on the third day' (p. 119), was ill for 'two months' until 'the commencement of the following March' (p. 132) when she was moved from her bedchamber into the parlour and then into another room on the lower floor. The day of Catherine's funeral 'made the last of our fine days, for a month' (p. 169). Sometimes the reference to time is very precise indeed, as when Nelly finds the hanging dog 'at two o'clock in the morning' (p. 128). There is, then, an elaborate and carefully-planned sequence of events in this novel.[1] However, the narrative does not march evenly through time. Long periods of time are discussed in a few paragraphs; other short episodes are treated in great detail. A brief study of one of these more detailed episodes will show how carefully Emily Brontë constructs simultaneous events. Between pages 132 and 182, the narrative explains every day: during the month of March, Catherine moves downstairs, Isabella writes about her return as Mrs Heathcliff, Nelly visits the Heights, Heathcliff visits Catherine for the last time, Catherine dies and is buried, young Cathy is born, and Isabella escapes to 'somewhere in the south'.

This intense, short period of time is introduced on page 132. The first paragraph gives a summary of two months. The second paragraph introduces a particular morning when Edgar brought crocuses to Catherine, and that day fixes Catherine downstairs. However, Nelly then backtracks to 'some six weeks from her [Isabella's] departure', with a half-apology for telling things in the wrong order: 'I should mention that . . .' (p. 133). She then moves past 'a fortnight more', back to the time of Catherine's move downstairs, when she receives Isabella's letter. Isabella begins with a statement that she arrived 'last night' followed by a reference to two months ago ('my heart returned to Thrushcross Grange in twenty-four hours after I left it' – p. 134) and a general account of the two months from her viewpoint, before she enters into a detailed account of her first evening at the Heights.

It is clear from this analysis, that Emily Brontë approaches the detailed, crisis episode of Catherine's death with care. She pays elaborate attention to altering the time-focus of the story, from a general survey in which time passes quickly, and the characters' behaviour is

---

[1] There is a detailed chronology of *Wuthering Heights* in C. P. Sanger, *The Structure of Wuthering Heights* (London: Hogarth Press, 1926). This is reprinted in *Critical Essays on Emily Brontë*, ed. Thomas John Winnifrith (New York, 1997), pp. 140–3.

described in general terms ('No mother could have nursed an only child more devotedly than Edgar tended her' – p. 132), to a close account of actions and conversations, specific to particular times ('The sun set behind the Grange, as we turned on to the moors' – p. 135). The change from time passing rapidly, to moment-by-moment narrative, is far from simple: first, it happens twice, in both Nelly's and Isabella's narratives. Secondly, in both of these parallel narratives it contains movements backwards and forwards in time, before it settles into a detailed, precise account.

The same elaborate flexibility of time appears in the text again, at the end of the episode we are studying. Nelly tells of Isabella's departure, late at night on the evening after Catherine's funeral. She then narrates two brief conversations with Heathcliff, the first quite soon after Isabella's flight, and the other some time later – but both unspecified in time. Suddenly, in passing, she mentions that Isabella died about thirteen years later, before returning very precisely to 'the day succeeding Isabella's visit' (p. 182). Time-focus then alters again, mentioning 'a few days' (p. 182) when Edgar's mourning was so intense that he did not notice his daughter, before passing another considerable period of time, 'scarcely six months' to the announcement of Hindley's death, which begins another close account of what we can call 'actual' time: '"Well, Nelly," said he [Doctor Kenneth], riding into the yard, one morning' (p. 183).

Again, in these three pages, the narrative seems to extend and compress its focus on time repeatedly, moving from actual time to jump over thirteen years, then to a single day, several days, six months, and back into 'actual' time. Clearly, Brontë pays close attention to the link between a period of intense activity, which we live through in what we have called 'actual' time narratives (such as Isabella's account of her first evening at the Heights, or Nelly's account of the final meeting between Catherine and Heathcliff), and periods when the characters live on and the narrative passes over months or years, giving only a generalised description of how life proceeds. Emily Brontë does not link these different time-frames by passing gradually from one to the other: our analysis has found that she passes in and out of 'actual time' rapidly, several times, extending and compressing time so that the narrative seems to 'flex', at these linking points in the story. It is as if the story itself pulls backwards and forwards, or zooms into and out of focus, before settling into either a close or a distant focus on time.

One further point about the structure of time in this episode deserves mention. The few days between Isabella's return (and Catherine's move downstairs) and Catherine's funeral, are narrated twice, and partly narrated a third time, much later in the novel. Nelly gives a more-or-less continuous account of these days on pages 144–68. We then live through the same period of time again, from Isabella's viewpoint, on pages 169–81. The same period of time is further narrated by Heathcliff, on pages 285–8. We realise from this that Brontë's 'time' is not a single strand: it is three narratives which move through time alongside each other, with a complex ironic relationship to each other. The effect of this doubling and trebling of accounts of a single time, is to give extraordinary richness of comparison between them, and a strong sense of the complexity of experience. We have already remarked on the contrast between Heathcliff's account of the fight with Earnshaw (ten words) and Isabella's account which details Heathcliff forcing her to tell Joseph that Hindley was the aggressor, and watches her scrub Hindley's blood off the floor. Which of these two versions is 'the truth'? We are left with the impression that there are very different realities, each hardly recognisable to another character, and each seen from a self-absorbed perspective. By constructing several simultaneous strands of narrative, then, Emily Brontë succeeds in emphasising the power of subjective emotion in determining what characters perceive, and the separate worlds of self in which they live.

We will look at one further feature of Brontë's use of time in the novel, before moving on to consider families and social structures. We have noticed that time is carefully and elaborately plotted in *Wuthering Heights*, and our analysis above is of a time for which the novel contains three parallel accounts. During our analysis we have found that Brontë employs different focuses in her narrative, using a general descriptive summary to survey long periods of time when the plot is uneventful. For example, the beginning of Chapter 4 in Volume 2 (pp. 187–9) surveys the first twelve years of young Cathy's life. Nelly mentions her 'trifling illnesses' and gives a general account of her character without referring to specific incidents: 'her anger was never furious; her love never fierce; it was deep and tender' (p. 187). However, on one occasion in the novel, Brontë does not sew the narrative together in this way. There is a gap, and no character or narrator fills it. The gap occurs when Nelly is 'sent out of the house' (p. 37) on the morning following Heathcliff's arrival at the Heights. Nelly resumes the narrative 'on coming back a few days afterwards' (p. 38).

This gap of several days draws our attention because it is the only gap in the novel. It is also intriguing because of the importance of what happens while Nelly is away. Catherine's response to Heathcliff on his first arrival, before the gap, is hostile: she 'showed her humour by grinning and spitting at the stupid little thing' (p. 37), and she joins Hindley in refusing to have it in bed with them. On Nelly's return, however, 'Miss Cathy and he were now very thick' (p. 38). The bond between Catherine and Heathcliff that endures throughout the remainder of the novel and their lives, and drives Heathcliff to his death, is formed during the few days when Nelly is absent from the Heights, and is a complete reversal of feeling on Catherine's part. What is the purpose and effect of withholding any narrative of these crucial few days?

In *Wuthering Heights* we are encouraged to think about the characters' childhood experiences, and understand how these early emotions and events formed their later personalities. We are also encouraged to interpret the story, looking for explanations of later character in childhood symbolism. For example, the two presents Hindley and Catherine requested from their father, are obvious emblems of their characters. The imperious Catherine, caught in the powerless family position of younger daughter, wanted a whip; while Hindley reveals his desire for a softer and more civilised life by asking for a fiddle. These details are all significant, yet Brontë refuses to give us a narrative of the crucial moment when Heathcliff and Catherine became friends. We can only conclude that the *lack* of connected meaning, or explanation, during the forming of the lovers' childhood bond, is also significant.

What does this 'gap in time' tell us? First, and most obviously, it enhances the idea that the bond between the two children was inevitable, and natural. Other characters and events are ascribed causes, and we understand their origin. Hindley's destructive resentment of his family, for example, comes from the broken fiddle and jealousy of his father's affection for Heathcliff. The feeling between Catherine and Heathcliff, on the other hand, has no origin or cause: the reader is left with a mystery. Their love just 'is', but it did not grow out of events or come from anywhere. In this way, the gap in Nelly's narrative enhances our admiration of their feelings. Secondly, Catherine's attitudes on either side of the 'gap' contradict each other. We leave her spitting at the little Heathcliff, and return to find them inseparable. So, Brontë's abrupt jump over 'a few days' also emphasises the overwhelming power of the couple's bond. Not only do we find it unexplainable, it is more than that: it is irrational, and overthrows Catherine's strong pre-existing hostility.

Later in the story, we find that the love between Catherine and Heathcliff keeps this unquestionable quality: it is a 'given fact', like the Earth and the sky – and there is no point in questioning it or seeking to explain it. For example, when Nelly mentions that marriage to Edgar will divide her from Heathcliff, Catherine replies with indignation and astonishment, as if any separation between them is quite unthinkable: how could it cross Nelly's mind? 'He quite deserted! we separated! . . . Who is to separate us, pray? They'll meet the fate of Milo!' (p. 81). The gap in the narrative, when this extraordinary love is born, stands out in the time-structure of *Wuthering Heights* like a rip in the fabric of day-to-day life: like a hole through which, if Brontë let us look, we would see something older and more fundamental behind the close-up texture of details on which the story depends.

Families and Social 'Structure'

We are looking at the structure of *Wuthering Heights*, so we think about the characters we meet in the novel, as a group, looking for a 'shape' among them. Is there anything in their relationships, or in the types of character found in the book, that creates a 'structure' in and among these people? This is the first stage: to find a hypothesis about the structure of the characters, a theory about the 'shape' they may present.

The main characters of *Wuthering Heights* belong with two families, the Earnshaws and the Lintons, and on the surface this would seem an obvious way to group them into two contrasting types. Our first thoughts about these groupings may provide some supporting evidence, such as a difference in looks that is discussed several times, and the combination of traits described in young Cathy; the contrasting environments of the Heights and the Grange (exposed and wild/protected and civilised), and so on. The two family groups, then, give us a theory about structure in the characters. Our next task is to make notes which group the characters in this way, then examine these groupings critically to discover whether they 'work'. By this we mean: Are the family groups consistent, sharing common character-traits? Do these family groups seem to be significant in the overall meaning of the novel? In this way, we can test our theory. Here is a list of the characters, grouped by family:

Earnshaws	Lintons
Mr Earnshaw	Mr Linton
Mrs Earnshaw	Mrs Linton
Hindley Earnshaw	Edgar Linton
Catherine Earnshaw	Isabella Linton
Frances Earnshaw	Cathy Linton
Hareton Earnshaw	
Heathcliff	
Linton Heathcliff	

Notes: Nelly Dean and Doctor Kenneth seem to belong equally to both groups. Joseph and Zillah are servants who belong predominantly with the Earnshaws.

It is important to carry out this second stage in developing ideas on structure. We had a theory about family groups which, on the face of it, seemed persuasive and meaningful. However, as I listed the main characters by family group, I was struck by contradictions: several times, allocating the character to one or the other family group went against my sense of that person from the novel. Here are a number of objections to the above list:

Earnshaws

1. Heathcliff is not an Earnshaw.

2. Hindley was an effeminate boy who longed for a violin and 'blubbered aloud' when it was broken (p. 37). His 'paradise on the hearth' (p. 22) and childish love with his wife; and his denial that anything is wrong with her throughout her last illness (see p. 64), have much in common with Edgar Linton, who has a 'deep-rooted fear' of disturbing the artificial harmony of his marriage (p. 91) and hopes for Catherine's cure despite her own certainty that she will die (see pp. 132–3). Does Hindley fit our concept of an 'Earnshaw' at all? His father thinks that he does not: 'Hindley was naught, and would never thrive' (p. 41).

3. Frances Earnshaw is 'rather thin, but young, and fresh complexioned', and her 'delight' in everything at the Heights does not convince Nelly that she belongs: on the contrary, Nelly thinks her 'half silly' and observes that 'we don't in general take to foreigners here' (all from pages 45 and 46).

4. Linton Heathcliff never thrives in the environment of the Heights, and is nothing like our idea of an Earnshaw. The first description of him mentions both his inheritance of Linton characteristics, and his difference from Edgar: 'A pale, delicate, effeminate boy, who might have been taken for my master's younger brother, so strong was the resemblance, but there was a sickly peevishness in his aspect, that Edgar Linton never had' (p. 198).

5. In fact, the facile vision of a hardy, strong and vigorous family of Earnshaws is simply not true. Where, then, did this impression come from? The answer is that it comes from three places. First, old Mr Earnshaw may be seen as a large strong man, since he walked back from Liverpool carrying a struggling, biting seven-year-old under his greatcoat. The other two characters who contribute to this image are Heathcliff, who is not an Earnshaw; and Hareton. Hareton, however, has rather un-Earnshaw-like parentage: he is the son of the consumptive stranger Frances, and Hindley, the atypical member of the original family.

Lintons

The Lintons seem to be a more homogeneous group. Isabella is more wilful and selfish than her brother Edgar, but both of them and their parents share several important characteristics in both looks and personalities. The problem here rests mainly in Cathy Linton/Heathcliff/Earnshaw. Despite their strong affection for each other, and their similarity in looks, young Cathy and her father are not alike in character. Above all, it is not sensible to allocate either her or Linton Heathcliff to a 'family group'.

Our theory, then, does not work. However, trying the idea out in this way has been helpful, because we have reached a number of clear conclusions about the grouping of characters in *Wuthering Heights*, and developed our understanding of how they relate to each other. For example, there are characters whose vigour and hardiness seem to suit the environment of Wuthering Heights: Heathcliff, Catherine before her illness, and Hareton; and the Linton family, before the birth of young Cathy, do seem to have personalities appropriate to the protected, gentle environment of the Grange.

So, this attempt at studying character-groups suggests that we can broadly think about two kinds of people in the novel. On the other hand, we have learned that family and heredity have nothing to do with it.

Is there an alternative way of organising the characters in the novel? The following is another way we may be tempted to group the characters into a 'structure'. We use the same method again, first proposing a theory and then examining the result critically to see whether it fits what we know about the book.

Perhaps early hardship is important? This idea is suggested by the insight that all of the vigorous characters we listed, who are suitable to the environment of the Heights, suffer persecution and deprivation in their childhood. Catherine's diary shows how miserable and downtrodden her existence was under her brother's rule; and Heathcliff is 'brought . . . low' by Hindley's persecution. Heathcliff then subjects Hareton to comparable persecution, denying him education and keeping him to hard labour. In contrast, Isabella and Edgar, and then Linton Heathcliff, are produced from luxurious and protected childhoods. This is an interesting idea, but we quickly find objections which show that it does not apply consistently. For example, young Cathy has a comfortable and protected childhood and is not made to suffer, yet she turns out to be a resilient and generous-hearted person. Conversely, Hindley is persecuted as a child, yet this does not produce the vigour and hardiness in him that is found in Heathcliff and Hareton.

In *Wuthering Heights*, then, a consistent and meaningful shape in the families or social positions of characters seems elusive. Each theory our minds may propose turns out to run up against serious contradictions. Yet, at the same time, the temptation to look at groups and relationships in this way is clearly inspired by Brontë's text. For example, look at Nelly's summary of young Cathy:

> – a real beauty in face – with the Earnshaws' handsome dark eyes, but the Lintons' fair skin, and small features, and yellow curling hair. Her spirit was high, though not rough, and qualified by a heart, sensitive and lively to excess in its affections. That capacity for intense attachments reminded me of her mother; still she did not resemble her; for she could be soft and mild as a dove, and she had a gentle voice, and pensive expression: her anger was never furious; her love never fierce; it was deep and tender.
>
> However, it must be acknowledged, she had faults to foil her gifts. A propensity to be saucy was one; and a perverse will that indulged children invariably acquire, whether they be good tempered or cross.
>
> (p. 187)

In this extract, Brontë explicitly conveys Cathy's looks in terms of Earnshaw and Linton characteristics; and we are strongly tempted to look at her personality in the same way. So, the narrator compares her strong affections to those of the elder Catherine, using the words 'intense' and 'to excess'; but evokes Edgar's character in the terms 'soft', 'mild', 'gentle' and 'pensive'. All of this is in the context of a generalisation about 'the Earnshaws' and 'the Lintons'. If we think about this more carefully, however, we accept that Cathy does combine qualities from her mother and her father; but we remember that Isabella Linton has turned out to be far from 'mild' and 'gentle'; and Hindley Earnshaw's affections are not of the same kind as his sister's. His heart has room for only 'two idols – his wife and himself – he doted on both, and adored one' (p. 64). The words 'doted' and 'adored' are carefully chosen to remind us that Hindley's feelings are predominantly immature and self-centred: different in kind from the 'intense attachments' now ascribed to young Cathy. In short, Nelly is leading us up a false path when she generalises about Earnshaws and Lintons – although some inheritance from both Edgar and Catherine in their daughter seems true enough.

Notice, also, the careful echo of an image from another part of the book. Catherine's character is described as 'soft and mild as a dove', reminding us of Catherine's remark about Edgar's eyes: 'They are dove's eyes – angel's!' (p. 105). The irony is that young Cathy does not have blue Linton eyes. She has the opposite, having inherited 'the Earnshaws' handsome dark eyes', and the dove image is applied to her character, not her appearance.

Finally, Nelly imposes another questionable theory onto her description, mentioning the 'perverse will that indulged children invariably acquire'. This seems to hint that our second theory, about early suffering, may have some validity. However, young Cathy's later suffering and her eventual success as an adult contradict the idea. Young Cathy grows out of the 'perverse will' Nelly describes here. It proves to be superficial, unlike the deeply ingrained need for attention shown by Isabella, and Linton Heathcliff, two other indulged children. In fact, there are ironies surrounding each attempt to classify or categorise characters in this novel. Young Cathy's description of Linton Heathcliff, for example, likens this spoiled and sickly child to his father: 'I know he has a bad nature . . . he's your son' (p. 285); but Nelly emphasises how like the Lintons he is ('who might have been taken for my master's younger brother, so strong was the resemblance' – p. 198), while Young Cathy rejects the idea that she is related to Hareton: '*He* my cousin! . . . Oh, Ellen! don't let them say such things' (p. 193).

So, the theories we have considered are repeatedly canvassed in the text of *Wuthering Heights*; but they do not hold water when more closely examined. In conclusion, then, we can say that Brontë holds out several deceptive suggestions about a meaningful structure in families and social groups, but such ideas lead nowhere and appear to originate in Nelly rather than revealing any truth. This technique of teasing the reader with facile assumptions about characters, which then prove false, has the effect of enhancing our sense that the figures in *Wuthering Heights* have true individuality. Our study of the groups of characters, from a structural point of view, has failed. We have not found an overall 'shape' which contains the people in the novel. On the other hand, we have achieved a greater understanding of how the novel works. The text has provoked us to think about a number of theories of character and social groupings. In other words, Brontë signals several structural possibilities to her reader. This potential for structure is then systematically undermined, leaving us with a strong sense of the individuality and changeable flux of actual life.

Structure in the Setting

The setting of *Wuthering Heights* attracts our attention because, like the plotting of time discussed earlier in this chapter, it is so fully and precisely created for us. As soon as we begin to consider the setting, we realise that every scene of the story takes place within or between the two houses: Wuthering Heights and Thrushcross Grange. Emily Brontë limits the extent of the setting exactly. Penistone Craggs are beyond Wuthering Heights: they are the most distant visible feature. The narrative does not visit them, although several of the characters have been there and report what they are like. In the other direction, Thrushcross Grange itself is as far as the story travels. There is a village, Gimmerton; and a chapel and churchyard at the edge of the cultivated valley, half-exposed on the moors. We never see the other side of the valley (i.e., looking in the other direction from Thrushcross Grange). The characters who leave this limited area go out of the knowledge of the narrative (Mr Earnshaw, Hindley, Heathcliff, Isabella). The characters who arrive from outside, arrive without any history or information (Heathcliff, Frances Earnshaw. When Linton Heathcliff arrives we know his parentage, and Isabella's letters have called him 'an ailing, peevish creature', but we discover nothing else about his life up to the age of twelve).

The effect of such a clear demarcation of the setting is to provide a strong topographical structure to the novel. As we remarked in Chapter 1, it is as if the drama is acted out on a single stage, without a change of scenery. Brontë repeatedly reminds us of the exact extent of *Wuthering Heights*'s world, as in this incidental description:

> They sat together in a window whose lattice lay back against the wall, and displayed beyond the garden trees and the wild green park, the valley of Gimmerton, with a long line of mist winding nearly to its top (for very soon after you pass the chapel, as you may have noticed, the sough that runs from the marshes joins a beck which follows the bend of the glen). Wuthering Heights rose above this silvery vapour; but our old house was invisible – it rather dips down on the other side.
>
> (p. 93)

The two houses dominate this stage, and each house takes its character from its immediate surroundings. A brief discussion of each house's character will amplify this statement. First, the houses' names are significant. 'Wuthering' is a local word for stormy weather, as Lockwood explains on page 4. A 'thrush' is a valley bird, a woodland or garden bird with an attractive song. 'Cross', in a place-name, may signify a crossroads, a place where journeys and people meet; but it also suggests the idea of Christianity and its conventional church emblem, a cross. 'Grange' means a barn, a storehouse for agricultural produce. The word suggests cultivation, harvest and plenty.

Wuthering Heights is often in darkness, and dark corners are emphasised when Lockwood hears sounds from 'deep within' and imagines other dogs which 'haunted other recesses' (p. 5). Isabella, sitting on the stairs, 'remained in the dark' when Joseph took the candle away, and to clear up the mess she 'groped from step to step' (p. 142). Thrushcross Grange, in contrast, is full of light. In the first description of the Grange, Heathcliff emphasises light: 'a pure white ceiling bordered by gold, a shower of glass-drops hanging in silver chains from the centre, and shimmering with little soft tapers' (p. 48). This motif continues, and on Heathcliff's return, he stands in the Lintons' drawing-room 'now fully revealed by the fire and candlelight' (p. 95).

The vegetation around Wuthering Heights is sparse, and the house exposed. Lockwood describes 'a few, stunted firs' which have an 'excessive slant' due to 'the power of the north wind, blowing over the edge'. The strong prevailing wind has also shaped 'a range of gaunt thorns' (p. 4). Thrushcross Grange, in contrast, is surrounded by 'garden trees' and 'the high wall of the court', then outside the garden is the wooded 'wild green park' and the park wall, alongside which runs the road to Gimmerton and 'the south'. Many passing details throughout the novel contribute to these impressions of exposed, bare Wuthering Heights, and enclosed, protected Thrushcross Grange. For example, on Lockwood's second visit to the Heights he calls it a 'bleak hill-top' and runs to the door past 'gooseberry-bushes', but is still exposed to the snow, which 'began to drive thickly', when standing at the house door (pages 9 and 10); while Heathcliff describes reaching Thrushcross Grange by crawling through a hedge, following a path, and standing on 'a flower-pot' (p. 48). Lockwood comments on the air of the Heights: 'pure, bracing ventilation they must have up there, at all times' (p. 4); while Nelly stops in the kitchen doorway at the Grange to 'draw in a few more breaths of the soft, sweet air' (p. 92).

We could pursue this research through the novel, and pick out numerous further details of the physical contrast between Wuthering Heights and Thrushcross Grange, and their attendant landscapes. However, we should now move on to the next stage of analysing this contrast as a part of the novel's structure. Clearly, the two houses dominate the landscape, and have contrasting characteristics and atmospheres. Does this physical contrast extend to other aspects of the novel's world?

To begin answering this question, we want to think outwards from the houses themselves, to other aspects of life associated with them. Here are some wider topics, beginning with a reminder of points we have already discussed. First, we have looked at the two families, and found that they do not show a consistent attachment to their house of origin in the sense of sharing its character. However, the Lintons do seem to be a homogeneous group, rather spoiled, pampering and conventional (remember Mr Linton's xeno-phobic prejudice against the 'vulgar young ruffian' Heathcliff); but the main contrast to their character is borne by Heathcliff alone. He is not a native of the Heights, although many parts of the text associate him closely with that wilder landscape (remember Catherine's description of him as 'an arid wilderness of furze and whinstone' – p. 101). Secondly, we discussed dogs in the previous chapter, and concluded that those of Thrushcross Grange are tamer, more friendly and weaker than the aggressive dogs found at the Heights. On the other hand, we noticed that this distinction is not absolute. Skulker, the bulldog that injures Catherine, attacks savagely when his master orders him to; and Throttler remembers a gentler puppyhood, and remembers Isabella, from before he became a Heights dog.

Food in the two houses also contrasts. At the Heights there is an emphasis on meat: 'clusters of legs of beef, mutton and ham' (p. 5); while the Grange is repeatedly described in connection with flowers, plants and fruits. For example, Nelly is carrying 'a heavy basket of apples' (p. 92) on the day of Heathcliff's return. The emphasis on meat at the Heights is expanded by occasional details of farm work, which are to do with livestock. Hareton famously hangs 'a litter of puppies' from a chairback (p. 181), Lockwood steals the lantern from Joseph when he is 'milking the cows', and Heathcliff cannot spare a guide because 'who is to look after the horses, eh?', after he has ordered Hareton to 'drive those dozen sheep into the barn porch. They'll be covered if left in the fold all night' (see pages 14–17). In contrast to this, both the Mr Lintons are magistrates, and Edgar spends time in studying ('he is continually among his books' – p. 120). Young Cathy plays make-believe games in the park of Thrushcross Grange, 'now on foot, and now on a pony'. For example, one day she 'said she was that day an Arabian merchant, going to cross the Desert with his caravan' (p. 190). In short, the Lintons and Thrushcross Grange represent the governing, educated class, upholding the law and conventional morality in the community. Their activities are intellectual or imaginative, in contrast to those at Wuthering Heights, where work is a primitive labour, a practical necessity for survival.

We have found, then, that the physical contrast between the two houses, reflected in the contrasting landscapes with which they are surrounded, is extended into the nature of foods, social class and economic roles associated with them. The religions and ethics of the two houses are also in contrast. Joseph is the mouthpiece for religion at Wuthering Heights. It is a punishing form of puritanism which emphasises sin, damnation and hellfire. The following sample of his preaching is typical:

> 'It's a blazing shaime, ut Aw cannut oppen t'Blessed Book, bud yah set up them glories tuh sattan, un' all t'flaysome wickednesses ut iver wer born intuh t' warld! . . . O, Lord, judge 'em, fur they's norther law nur justice amang wer rullers!'
>
> (p. 305)

Joseph's vindictive form of religion, with its vivid picture of hell and damnation, is liberally laced with superstition. So, when Cathy teases him by pretending to be a witch, he is 'trembling with sincere horror' (p. 15), and he imagines Nelly and Cathy to have cast a wicked spell over Hareton (p. 305).

The form of Christian belief that prevails in Thrushcross Grange is altogether different. Here, the emphasis is on tolerance and for-giveness, and hope of heaven is emphasised rather than torments in hell. For example, Edgar receives consolation from his faith, fol-lowing Catherine's death:

> *He* didn't pray for Catherine's soul to haunt him: Time brought res-ignation, and a melancholy sweeter than common joy. He recalled her memory with ardent, tender love, and hopeful aspiring to the better world, where, he doubted not, she was gone.
>
> (p. 182)

According to Nelly, Edgar 'displayed the true courage of a loyal and faithful soul: he trusted God; and God comforted him' (p. 183). Edgar Linton's hopeful faith is carried through to his last words: 'I am going to her, and you darling child shall come to us' (p. 280), while his final weeks are spent agonising over the character of his nephew Linton, hoping that he will turn out well: 'is he changed for the better, or is there a prospect of improvement, as he grows a man?' (p. 253).

There is a weakness at the heart of the Thrushcross Grange faith, however. Edgar's hopeful last words are uttered in the context of false belief. Nelly has told Cathy to say that she will be happy with Linton, and the worst of Heathcliff's brutalities are hidden from him because of Nelly's intention 'to add no bitterness, if I could help it, to his already overflowing cup' (p. 279). His consoling belief that Catherine has gone to heaven is also questioned, by Nelly herself. We remember her doubts, which Lockwood called 'something heterodox': 'Retracing the course of Catherine Linton, I fear we have no right to think she is [happy in the other world]' (p. 165). This view is supported by Catherine's dream, when she finds herself miserable in Heaven and cries to be returned to the open moors (p. 80).

Edgar's faith does not see the truth clearly, then; and his hopes for salvation seem rosily over-optimistic in the case of Catherine. Additionally, he himself does not live up to the standards of charity and forgiveness such a faith enjoins. Two examples underline this point. First, Edgar's reaction to Isabella's elopement is angry and judgemental, and his resentment is equally unforgiving two months later: 'It is out of the question my going to see her, however; we are eternally divided' (p. 144). Here, Edgar's use of the word 'eternally' smacks of passing a judgement he has no right to utter. Secondly, Edgar submits to Nelly's persuasion, and believes Catherine to be shamming her fit. In self-righteousness, he waits for his wife to 'ask pardon'. This failure of charity finally dissolves her affection for him. She is outraged at his insensitivity ('What in the name of all that feels, has he to do with *books*, when I am dying?' – p. 121). When Edgar eventually arrives in the room, she dismisses him from her life: 'I don't want you, Edgar; I'm past wanting you' (pp. 126–7).

What have we discovered from this discussion of the two houses and their ambience? It appears that the houses have distinctive characters, which are strong and opposed to each other; and these two characters dominate the setting. In addition, we can say that the 'character of Wuthering Heights' or the 'character of Thrushcross Grange' extends into many other aspects of the novel. The result is that the story is played out within a dualism, embodied in the topography of two houses and two landscapes, which reaches into every aspect of the text. So Wuthering Heights, with its associated emphasis on meat and livestock, is a concept which also informs some animal behaviour of the characters: when Heathcliff 'howled, not like a man, but like a savage beast getting goaded to death' (p. 167), for example, the animal associations of Wuthering Heights are called to mind. The influence of the two houses seems to pervade the text, and the effect is to enlarge our understanding of Heathcliff's emotion by connecting it with the many-faceted, broad concept that is embodied in Wuthering Heights. At the same time, Heathcliff's emotion extends our concept of the house and its significance.

The dualism of the two houses, then, provides a conceptual structure to the novel. We can suggest abstract ideas which are associated with the two sides of this dualism. For example, we could say that Wuthering Heights stands for the primitive, and depth; Thrushcross Grange for civilisation, and shallowness; conflict is embodied in Wuthering Heights, while Thrushcross Grange represents compromise.

Conclusions

1. Emily Brontë uses time very effectively in *Wuthering Heights*. The narrative includes close accounts in 'actual time', summary accounts of the passage of time, and Brontë carefully manages the transitions between these different narrative modes. The narrative, within its framework of different narrators, is often structured to provide alternative accounts of the same period of time. In this way time becomes complex, being made up of different strands representing different perceptions. The gap in the narrative following Heathcliff's arrival at the Heights, when the bond between him and Catherine is formed, stands out as a mystery and hints that the love between these two poses unanswerable questions. Brontë has drawn attention to this gap by setting it within the detailed time-plotting of the rest of the novel.

2. In this chapter we have experienced some difficulty in defining the 'structural' elements of *Wuthering Heights*. In particular, the text seems to signal assumptions about structure which are

undermined when we examine more thoroughly. For example, the text frequently refers to family-based characteristics and personalities, belonging to 'Earnshaws' and 'Lintons', but these turn out to be deceptive.

3. The major dualism in *Wuthering Heights* is not contained in characters or groups of characters, but is broader and more conceptual than this. Two pervasive and dominant concepts of life, in the book, are apparent in the experiences and actions of various characters, and in many elements of the text. These two dominant concepts are most prominently embodied in the two houses, Wuthering Heights and Thrushcross Grange, and their surrounding landscapes. They are comprehensively contrasted to each other throughout the novel.

4. The prominence of the two houses is enhanced by Brontë's rigid demarcation of the novel's setting. The limited, single 'stage' on which all events take place is an important structuring 'shape' in *Wuthering Heights*.

Methods of Analysis

- When studying the structure of a text, begin by 'standing back' from the details, and thinking of the work as a whole. This will enable you to formulate a theory about a 'structural' aspect of the text.

- Test your theory by making notes on how the 'structure' you have found works in relation to characters and events. Is the relationship between your idea, and the details of the text, consistent or contradictory? Even if your more detailed thinking forces you to abandon or modify your theory, this stage is vital and is likely to be illuminating.

- Find examples, in the text, of places where the 'structure' you have found is apparent. In this way, you will study how the author weaves larger ideas into the page-by-page texture of the writing.

Suggested Work

Make a study of two elements of the structure of *Wuthering Heights*, using the methods we have employed in this chapter:

[a] Study the Thrushcross Grange park wall, analysing how it figures as a border or boundary, as part of the physical setting of the novel. You will be interested in occasions when scenes occur at the wall itself, and occasions when the wall is crossed (e.g., when Heathcliff enters the garden on the night of Catherine's death; when young Cathy jumps the wall on her first excursion towards Penistone Craggs).

[b] Study seasons and generations in the novel. This will involve thinking of a theory about such 'large' elements in the plot, and then testing your theory by referring closely to particular elements of the text, as we did in this chapter when considering families.

5

Themes

Themes are simply subjects the author is concerned with. When we think of the elements of a novel, we tend to think rather glibly of 'characters, plot, themes, style' and so on; but we should recognise that 'themes' are different from these other elements, because the author does not identify and name them, we do. So, we might quite reasonably discuss a 'theme of revenge' in *Wuthering Heights*, and in our discussion we could look at Heathcliff's long pursuit of revenge against both the Earnshaws and the Lintons, Hindley's attempt to revenge himself upon Heathcliff, and Edgar Linton's refusal to be reconciled to Isabella. This discussion might be enlightening and useful, but we should never forget that we chose the subject 'revenge'. What is 'revenge'? It follows 'injury', in the sense that Heathcliff was injured by Hindley's tyranny and Catherine's marriage; Edgar was injured by Heathcliff's destruction of his marriage; Hindley was injured by Heathcliff stripping him of his authority and property. It stands to reason that there is no 'revenge' without prior 'injury'. So, perhaps we should discuss a 'theme of injury and revenge' instead of just 'revenge'? A theme, then, is a subject *we think* is important in the text, and it is *selected and defined by us*. A theme is also not a literal thing, created by the author, like a character or an event.

It follows that we can find any number of 'themes' in a text, and also that different critics can call the same 'theme' by different names. A quick read through past examination questions on *Wuthering Heights*, for example, would show that some of them mention a 'theme of emotion' and others mention the 'theme of love'. Love, of course, is an emotion. We know from reading *Wuthering Heights* that deep and shallow 'love', or deep and shallow 'emotion', is a major element in the conflict between Catherine and Heathcliff on the one hand, and Edgar on the other. The two ideas are not the same, of course, but they overlap. Themes, then, present two difficulties: the terms used to describe them are often arbitrary, and you can always think of more of them to study.

These difficulties are much more troublesome in the case of *Wuthering Heights*, than in the study of some other texts. For example, there is a theme of racial prejudice in Mark Twain's *Huckleberry Finn*. It is quite clear that this subject is a major element in the book, and the way racial issues are woven into the story is distinct and identifiable. Equally, there is a theme of marriage in Jane Austen's *Emma*. So much of the novel revolves around matchmaking, courtship, proposals, expectations of and actual weddings, that it feels entirely natural to discuss the 'theme of marriage': the subject is easily identified in the text. *Wuthering Heights* is not like these other texts, however. It is a book which defies the critic's attempt to take it to pieces. Our example of a 'theme of revenge' underlines this quality in the novel. We can discuss 'revenge'; but we become increasingly aware that 'revenge' is not really a separate and separable subject in the novel. A brief discussion will make this clear.

Revenge, in *Wuthering Heights*, is closely linked to cruelty and suffering. In the case of Heathcliff, we have discussed his revenge as a psychological diversion from Catherine's challenge that he should die to join her (see Chapter 2, above). Hindley's revenge is an attempt to compensate for his own weakness. Revenge is also part of the contrast between the more primitive world-view and punitive religion of the Heights, and the gentler Christianity of resignation, forgiveness and consolation practised at Thrushcross Grange. Can we call Edgar's refusal to write to Isabella 'revenge' at all?

This brief attempt to discuss revenge in the novel shows how bafflingly an apparent 'theme' is integrated into the text, with other 'themes', characters and events. It seems that, whatever subject we try to isolate and discuss, we inevitably end up thinking of the novel as a single whole. Two other texts where themes are notoriously difficult to isolate from one another, are Shakespeare's *Hamlet*, and Coleridge's *The Ancient Mariner*. These texts seem to share a special quality with *Wuthering Heights*: their authors have succeeded in integrating all the elements of the text into a single, many-sided whole, to an extraordinary degree.

Despite these difficulties, it would be helpful for us to find a way to think about *Wuthering Heights*: a way to discuss the novel's meaning and its major concerns. We can do this by trying to find something underlying. What we are looking for is a concept, an idea rather than just a subject like 'revenge' or 'love' which might be part of the characters' lives. The remainder of this chapter is an attempt to find and explore such a concept. We begin with a close examination of Lockwood's two dreams, because they stand at the start of the narrative, like an introduction to the story. We hope, therefore, that the fundamental concepts of the novel may be visible in these dreams in a clearer form than they show once the momentum of story and complexity of characters takes over.

Lockwood's Dreams

Here is the whole of the passage describing Lockwood's two dreams:

> I began to nod drowsily over the dim page; my eye wandered from manuscript to print. I saw a red ornamented title . . . 'Seventy Times Seven, and the First of the Seventy First. A Pious Discourse delivered by the Reverend Jabes Branderham, in the Chapel of Gimmerton Sough.' And while I was, half consciously, worrying my brain to guess what Jabes Branderham would make of his subject, I sank back in bed, and fell asleep.
>
> Alas, for the effects of bad tea and bad temper! what else could it be that made me pass such a terrible night? I don't remember another that I can at all compare with it since I was capable of suffering.
>
> I began to dream, almost before I ceased to be sensible of my locality. I thought it was morning; and I had set out on my way home, with Joseph for a guide. The snow lay yards deep on our road; and, as we floundered on, my companion wearied me with constant reproaches that I had not brought a pilgrim's staff: telling me I could

never get into the house without one, and boastfully flourishing a heavy-headed cudgel, which I understood to be so denominated. For a moment I considered it absurd that I should need such a weapon to gain admittance into my own residence. Then, a new idea flashed across me. I was not going there; we were journeying to hear the famous Jabes Branderham preach from the text – 'Seventy Times Seven'; and either Joseph, the preacher, or I had committed the 'First of the Seventy First,' and were to be publicly exposed and excommunicated.

We came to the chapel – I have passed it really in my walks, twice or thrice: it lies in a hollow, between two hills – an elevated hollow – near a swamp, whose peaty moisture is said to answer all the purposes of embalming on the few corpses deposited there. The rood has been kept whole hitherto, but, as the clergyman's stipend is only twenty pounds per annum, and a house with two rooms, threatening speedily to determine into one, no clergyman will undertake the duties of pastor, especially as it is currently reported that his flock would rather let him starve than increase the living by one penny from their own pockets. However, in my dream, Jabes had a full and attentive congregation: and he preached – Good God – what a sermon! divided into *four hundred and ninety* parts – each fully equal to an ordinary address from the pulpit – and each discussing a separate sin! Where he searched for them, I cannot tell; he had his private manner of interpreting the phrase, and it seemed necessary the brother should sin different sins on every occasion.

They were of the most curious character – odd transgressions that I never imagined previously.

Oh, how weary I grew. How I writhed, and yawned, and nodded, and revived! How I pinched and pricked myself, and rubbed my eyes, and stood up, and sat down again, and nudged Joseph to inform me if he would *ever* have done!

I was condemned to hear all out – finally, he reached the *'First of the Seventy First.'* At that crisis, a sudden inspiration descended on me; I was moved to rise and denounce Jabes Branderham as the sinner of the sin that no Christian need pardon.

'Sir,' I exclaimed, 'sitting here, within these four walls, at one stretch, I have endured and forgiven the four hundred and ninety heads of your discourse. Seventy times seven times have I plucked up my hat, and been about to depart – Seventy times seven times have you preposterously forced me to resume my seat. The four hundred and ninety first is too much. Fellow martyrs, have at him! Drag him down, and crush him to atoms, that the place which knows him may know him no more!'

'*Thou art the man!*' cried Jabes, after a solemn pause, leaning over his cushion. 'Seventy times seven times didst thou gapingly contort thy visage – seventy times seven times did I take counsel with my soul – Lo, this is human weakness; this also may be absolved! The First of the Seventy First is come. Brethren, execute upon him the judgment written! Such honour have all His saints!'

With that concluding word, the whole assembly, exalting their pilgrim's staves, rushed round me in a body, and I, having no weapon to raise in self-defence, commenced grappling with Joseph, my nearest and most ferocious assailant, for his. In the confluence of the multitude, several clubs crossed; blows, aimed at me, fell on other sconces. Presently the whole chapel resounded with rappings and counter-rappings. Every man's hand was against his neighbour, and Branderham, unwilling to remain idle, poured forth his zeal in a shower of loud taps on the boards of the pulpit, which responded so smartly that, at last, to my unspeakable relief, they woke me.

And what was it that had suggested the tremendous tumult, what had played Jabes' part in the row? Merely, the branch of a fir-tree that touched my lattice, as the blast wailed by, and rattled its dry cones against the panes!

I listened doubtingly an instant; detected the disturber, then turned and dozed, and dreamt again; if possible, still more disagreeably than before.

This time, I remembered I was lying in the oak closet, and I heard distinctly the gusty wind, and the driving of the snow; I heard, also, the fir-bough repeat its teasing sound, and ascribed it to the right cause: but, it annoyed me so much, that I resolved to silence it, if possible; and, I thought, I rose and endeavoured to unhasp the casement. The hook was soldered to the staple, a circumstance observed by me, when awake, but forgotten.

'I must stop it, nevertheless!' I muttered, knocking my knuckles through the glass, and stretching an arm out to seize the importunate branch: instead of which, my fingers closed on the fingers of a little, ice-cold hand!

The intense horror of nightmare came over me; I tried to draw back my arm, but, the hand clung to it, and a most melancholy voice sobbed,

'Let me in – let me in!'

'Who are you?' I asked, struggling, meanwhile, to disengage myself.

'Catherine Linton,' it replied, shiveringly (why did I think of *Linton*? I had read *Earnshaw* twenty times for Linton). 'I'm come home, I'd lost my way on the moor!'

As it spoke, I discerned, obscurely, a child's face looking through the window – Terror made me cruel; and, finding it useless to attempt shaking the creature off, I pulled its wrist on to the broken pane, and rubbed it to and fro till the blood ran down and soaked the bedclothes: still it wailed, 'Let me in!' and maintained its tenacious gripe, almost maddening me with fear.

'How can I?' I said at length. 'Let *me* go, if you want me to let you in!'

The fingers relaxed, I snatched mine through the hole, hurriedly piled the books up in a pyramid against it, and stopped my ears to exclude the lamentable prayer.

I seemed to keep them closed above a quarter of an hour, yet, the instant I listened again, there was the doleful cry moaning on!

'Begone!' I shouted, 'I'll never let you in, not if you beg for twenty years!'

'It's twenty years,' mourned the voice, 'twenty years, I've been a waif for twenty years!'

Threat began a feeble scratching outside, and the pile of books moved as if thrust forward.

I tried to jump up; but, could not stir a limb; and so yelled aloud, in a frenzy of fright.

(pp. 22–6)

We can begin by assessing the status of this passage. How much authority and what kind of authority should we accord to these dreams?

To answer this question, we can look immediately around the extract. We are struck by the amount of trouble Emily Brontë has taken to prepare the elements which appear in Lockwood's dreams. For example, on page 15 he witnessed the argument between Cathy and Joseph, where the old servant's dour, rigid religion was emphasised, and the woman was accused of being a witch. The title-page of the book he is reading as he falls asleep blends into his first dream as he is 'half consciously, worrying my brain to guess what Jabes Branderham would make of his subject'. The suggestive surnames for Catherine: Earnshaw, Heathcliff or Linton, appeared all over the margins of the book, and the extract from her diary provided yet more evidence of Joseph's persecutions in the name of religion. The author's careful realism continues into and through the narrative of the dreams themselves. Elements of dream and physical worlds are related to each other in close detail. So the chapel Lockwood dreams of is real ('I have passed it really in my walks, twice or thrice'); the noise of Jabes Branderham hammering the floor with his staff is a dream-representation of 'the branch of a fir-tree that touched my lattice . . . and rattled its dry cones against the glass'; and in his dream he piles up the real books, a detail remembered from his actual surroundings, to keep out Catherine's ghost. The narrative returns to this detail when 'the pile of books moved as if thrust forward'.

Emily Brontë has been equally thorough in providing psychological justifications for these dreams. Lockwood's admission that 'terror made me cruel' before he tried to cut the ghost's wrist on the glass, echoes the cold rejection of emotional appeals we already know to be characteristic of him. He has told us that he cruelly rebuffed the advances of 'a fascinating creature, a real goddess' when at a sea-coast resort (see page 6). After waking, Lockwood provides Heathcliff with an explanation. He had never heard the name 'Catherine Linton' before, but 'reading it often over produced an impression which personified itself when I had no longer my imagination under control' (p. 28).

Brontë ensures that we have a clear understanding of the relationship between the real world and Lockwood's dream visions, then. The dreams have no physical effect, either. The glass was not broken when Heathcliff 'wrenched open the lattice' after the dream, and Lockwood's voice is deliberately ironic in observing that 'The spectre showed a spectre's ordinary caprice; it gave no sign of being' (pp. 28–9). We can therefore conclude that the dreams are two vivid, dramatised stories made out of elements from the real waking world: objects and observations that have recently surrounded Lockwood; and pre-existing traits of his character, which we can trace clearly between waking and dream worlds.

We asked what sort of authority we should accord these dreams. We have already found the first part of an answer: the raw material of the dreams is in the narrative already – they are a vivid presentation of what Lockwood has met since coming to the area, and of what he is. Should we, then, think of the dreams as nothing more than an insight into Lockwood's own tense and exhausted mind? If we think about our answer, however, it seems to indicate more. What has Lockwood met? He has met a series of people with grotesque and outlandish manners (Heathcliff, Joseph, Cathy, Hareton) in a wild and frightening place where he has experienced rage and terror. He has met confusing mysteries about their relationships and history, made even more insoluble by Catherine's diary. In short, he has been confronted by the riddle of the novel's central story – the riddle of *Wuthering Heights* itself. It is therefore likely that these dreams are, at least, a vivid presentation of the unfamiliar 'world' of the story, distilled through Lockwood's brain. In other words, the dreams are more than mere characterisation of Lockwood: they say something about the whole 'world' of *Wuthering Heights*.

Our next task is to look at the passage closely, asking whether we can see any features that give further clues: does anything in the passage itself indicate a larger or wider meaning in the dreams?

There are two elements in the passage that indicate a stronger meaning for these visions. First, we notice that Lockwood contradicts himself. When recounting his dream, he remarks in brackets: 'why did I think of *Linton*? I had read *Earnshaw* twenty times for Linton'. Afterwards, on the other hand, he gives Heathcliff to understand that he only, and repetitively, read 'Linton'. So Lockwood suppresses the one unlikely 'coincidence' in his dream: the one detail he could not have known or imagined at the time. This does not mean that there was a real ghost, of course; but it does suggest that the dream may have more to tell us than merely about Lockwood's nervous exhaustion.

Secondly, one of the dreams is full of biblical allusions. This vision contains verbal references to four different books of the Bible, including the first book (Genesis), a New Testament gospel (Matthew) and two other books in between. On the surface of the dream-story, the question of sin and punishment seems to be set in irrational terms: there is a sermon lasting hundreds of hours, then the congregation starts cudgelling the dreamer. However, the biblical references imply that there is a wider subtext. As readers, we need to interpret the dream, using our knowledge of the scriptures to help amplify and explain what seems to be irrational in Lockwood's vision.

We have noticed that Brontë goes to considerable trouble to make these dreams realistic, as imaginings synthesised by Lockwood's brain. On the other hand, the coincidence of the name and biblical references imply a wider meaning as well. The evidence so far, then, does not allow us to believe in the dreams literally – so we should not believe in ghosts. On the other hand, it suggests that they have meaning: we are meant to interpret the dreams, and their meaning will illuminate the significance of the novel as a whole. Remember, also, that Emily Brontë was very familiar with the Bible, and could expect her readers to be familiar with biblical references.

We begin by interpreting the first dream. This means that we put ourselves in the position of nineteenth-century readers by making sure that we know the biblical references as well as they would have done. We then turn our knowledge into as many questions as we can think of, and return to the passage itself looking for answers. The first biblical reference is the words 'Seventy Times Seven' in the title of Branderham's sermon. This, as the note to most editions will tell you, is a reference to Matthew, Chapter 18:

> Then came Peter to him, and said, Lord, how oft shall my brother sin against me, and I forgive him? till seven times? Jesus saith unto him, I say not unto thee, Until seven times: but, Until seventy times seven.[1]

The sense of this seems to be clear: Peter asks whether there is a limit to forgiveness, and if so, what is that limit. Jesus, by multiplying 'seven' to 'seventy times seven', suggests an unending, infinite forgiveness. It is clear that Jesus does not mean 'four-hundred-and-

---

[1] The Holy Bible (King James Version), Standard Text Edition (Cambridge University Press). This quotation is Matthew, 18: 21–2 (p. 968). Further quotations from the Bible will give the book, chapter and verse, and page references to this edition.

ninety times, and no more!' Instead, he means, 'go on forgiving until you have lost count of the times'. On the other hand, Branderham's sermon also mentions the words 'First of the Seventy First'. Logically, this means one more than the forgivable sins: one sin that need not be forgiven. This interpretation is confirmed by Lockwood, who denounces Branderham for sinning 'the sin that no Christian need pardon'.

The notes in a modern edition of *Wuthering Heights* have helped us thus far; and it is important to read the notes, since otherwise a modern reader not versed in the Bible may miss the allusion altogether. We are wiser about the reference, and the idea of repeated, endless forgiveness even 'Until seventy times seven'. However, we are still uninformed about the 'First of the Seventy First', and at this point it is important to recognise that the editor's note is limited. Nineteenth-century readers would know their Gospels well: they would do more than merely recognise one phrase; they would remember the whole conversation between Jesus and Peter. Here is the parable which ends Matthew, Chapter 18:

> Therefore is the kingdom of heaven likened unto a certain king, which would take account of his servants. And when he had begun to reckon, one was brought unto him, which owed him ten thousand talents. But forasmuch as he had not to pay, his lord commanded him to be sold, and his wife, and children, and all that he had, and payment to be made. The servant therefore fell down, and worshipped him, saying, 'Lord, have patience with me, and I will pay thee all'. Then the lord of that servant was moved with compassion, and loosed him, and forgave him the debt. But the same servant went out, and found one of his fellowservants, which owed him an hundred pence: and he laid hands on him, and took him by the throat, saying, 'Pay me that thou owest'. And his fellowservant fell down at his feet, and besought him, saying, 'Have patience with me, and I will pay thee all'. And he would not: but went and cast him into prison, till he should pay the debt. So when his fellowservants saw what was done, they were very sorry, and came and told unto their lord all that was done. Then his lord, after that he had called him, said unto him, 'O thou wicked servant, I forgave thee all that debt, because thou desiredst me: shouldest not thou also have had compassion on thy fellowservant, even as I had pity on thee?' And his

lord was wroth, and delivered him to the tormentors, till he should pay all that was due unto him. So likewise shall my heavenly Father do also unto you, if ye from your hearts forgive not every one his brother their trespasses.

(Matthew, 18: 23–35)

The import of this parable is not complicated, but it adds a great deal to our understanding of Jesus's message. We were right to conclude that there is no limit to the number of times a sin can be forgiven. On the other hand, there is one kind of sin that will be punished, and cannot be forgiven: it is intolerance, the failure to forgive. The context of the parable shows that the servant had a legal 'right' to punish his fellowservant, but he must not stick to the letter of the law, or any concept of 'justice', by judging or punishing his fellow. Intolerance, lack of patience, failure to give another the benefit of the doubt, failure to forgive another, passing judgement, punishing others or taking revenge on them. These are all descriptions of the sin that will not be forgiven by God, according to the parable at the end of Matthew, Chapter 18. These, then, are descriptions of the 'First of the Seventy First'.

This is crucial understanding of the author's allusion to the Bible. Notice that we have had to go beyond the modern editor's cursory note, looking up the biblical reference for ourselves and reading around it. This makes sure that we know the whole of what Emily Brontë and her readers would have thought relevant.

The next question is: how is this relevant to *Wuthering Heights*? To answer this, we return to the passage with our new understanding of what Jesus meant by the unforgivable sin, the 'First of the Seventy First'. In Lockwood's dream, two people are accused of this sin. First, he accuses Branderham because he preached an unendurably long sermon. Then, Branderham identifies Lockwood himself as the sinner, in the words '*Thou art the man!*' The dream fits Jesus's words, telling us clearly that Lockwood is wrong and Branderham is right. Lockwood endured the four-hundred-and-ninety separate parts of the sermon, but there came a time when his oppression by Branderham was 'too much'. At this point he became intolerant. He judged and condemned the preacher, in cruel terms: 'Drag him down, and crush him to atoms.' Lockwood clearly commits the sin of intolerance. The biblical reference explains to us that the unforgivable sin is not a matter of numbers of sins – the spirit of Jesus's remark 'Until seventy times seven' is that any *number* of sins can be forgiven. It is the specific *kind* of sin that brings down punishment: the sin of intolerance, of judging and punishing one's fellow human. This is the offence Lockwood commits by saying that one more section of sermon is 'too much'.

The passage, however, tells us more about Emily Brontë's concept of intolerance. How does she describe the sins against Lockwood? First, the peculiar and private content of Branderham's sermon is emphasised. Branderham had 'his private manner of interpreting' so each sin is an 'odd' transgression 'that I never imagined previously'. This highlights the gulf between Lockwood's thoughts and those of Branderham: they see the world from different perspectives, and Lockwood finds it impossible to understand the preacher's viewpoint. Remember that Lockwood's opening narrative has insistently raised this question for the reader, also. In Chapter 1, we analysed his way of writing, showing that it is full of guesswork about the other characters, and he even catches himself projecting his own feelings onto Heathcliff whom he does not know. On that occasion, Lockwood admits his ignorance about other human beings and their inner feelings: 'Mr Heathcliff may have entirely dissimilar reasons . . . to those which actuate me' (p. 6). We could adapt this quotation to the circumstances of the dream, thus: *Branderham may have entirely dissimilar ideas about sin, to those which I recognise.* Emily Brontë, then, has given this dream to a character whose failure in understanding others is already prominent in the novel. His response to the sermon, including his easy assumption that his own ideas are common, while those of Branderham are 'odd' and 'curious', is self-centred and judgemental.

Secondly, Brontë leaves us in no doubt that Branderham's sermon is far too long: 'good God – what a sermon! divided into *four hundred and ninety* parts – each fully equal to an ordinary address from the pulpit'. If we think of an hour's sermon and multiply that, Branderham's went on for more than twenty days and nights without stopping. Lockwood's discomfort is also given in detail:

'How I writhed, and yawned, and nodded, and revived! How I pinched and pricked myself', and so on. We agree, then, that Branderham is utterly unreasonable – the length of the sermon is grotesque. Nobody should be asked to sit through such an address. In fact, Branderham makes a disproportionate, unreasonable, unjust demand on Lockwood. Just like the servant in the parable, who had the 'right' to demand his money and punish his fellowservant, Lockwood has the 'right' to complain.

These two points – Lockwood's lack of understanding of another, and Branderham's unjust demands – are strongly emphasised in the passage. In this way, Emily Brontë elaborates the Gospel. The unendurable, unending sins of another, are seen in terms of an outrageously exaggerated demand for forbearance. Lockwood uses the phrase 'preposterously forced' for the way he has been treated, and we understand how he comes to regard himself as a 'martyr'. Intolerance and judgement come easily, because other people seem so difficult to understand, so 'odd'.

So far, we have developed our ideas in relation to the main biblical reference – that to Matthew, Chapter 18. However, both Lockwood and then Branderham denounce each other in biblical terms. Lockwood says 'that the place which knows him may know him no more'. This is a quotation from the Book of Job of the Old Testament. Here is an extract from Job, Chapter 7, including the quotation Lockwood uses:

> The eye of him that hath seen me shall see me no more:
> Thine eyes are upon me, and I am not.
> As the cloud is consumed and vanisheth away:
> So he that goeth down to the grave shall come up no more.
> He shall return no more to his house,
> Neither shall his place know him any more.
> Therefore I will not refrain my mouth;
> I will speak in the anguish of my spirit;
> I will complain in the bitterness of my soul.
>   (Job, 7: 8–11)

The context of this quotation is surprising. The Book of Job is not about sin or punishment, but focuses on a man whom God has destroyed 'without cause'. Job is silent for seven days and nights in his affliction; then, when he begins to speak, he curses life: 'Let the day perish wherein I was born' (Job, 3: 3). The passage from Chapter 7 in which Lockwood's quotation occurs is about death, and the loss of contact with God – it is more concerned with loss of faith, and absolute extinction of life, than with sin and punishment. Why does Lockwood go to the disturbing, tragic nihilism of the Book of Job for his condemnation of Branderham, rather than quoting from a more appropriate source? There is no specific answer to this question, but in the wider context of *Wuthering Heights*, where life is suffering for so many of the characters, a reference to the tortures suffered by Job seems apt. Job is a man who lives on in pain after his chief happiness has been destroyed. This situation is shared by Hindley, Edgar and Heathcliff, who all painfully survive for many years following the deaths of Frances and Catherine.

Branderham quotes Psalm 149: 'execute upon him the judgment written! Such honour have all His saints.' Here is more of the relevant Psalm:

> For the Lord taketh pleasure in his people:
> He will beautify the meek with salvation.
> Let the saints be joyful in glory:
> Let them sing aloud upon their beds.
> Let the high praises of God be in their mouth,
> And a two-edged sword in their hand;
> To execute vengeance upon the heathen,
> And punishments upon the people;
> To bind their kings with chains,
> And their nobles with fetters of iron;
> To execute upon them the judgment written:
> This honour have all his saints.
> Praise ye the Lord.
>   (Psalms, 149: 4–9)

The context of Branderham's quotation makes clearer sense in relation to the dream than does Lockwood's. The Psalm mentions 'He will beautify the meek with salvation', and suggests that those to be punished will be of an arrogant, autocratic kind, by identifying 'their kings' and 'their nobles'. The general sense seems to be to bring down the arrogant, and exalt the lowly. This action is described in terms of 'glory' and 'honour'. Branderham, then, refers to a text with a more positive view of sin and punishment. In the Psalm, the work of a God who exalts the weak and brings down the arrogant and strong is associated with 'honour' and 'glory'. The Psalm says that the Lord 'taketh pleasure' in his people.

There is, perhaps, an amusing irony in this, since it is followed by a violent attack with cudgels. However, in the broader context of the whole novel, we should not forget this gloss, and the final line 'Praise ye the Lord'.

The final biblical quotation of this dream comes in Lockwood's description of the fight: 'Every man's hand was against his neighbour.' This is from Genesis, Chapter 16, and the relevant passage is:

> 'Behold, thou art with child, and shalt bear a son, and shalt call his name Ishmael; because the Lord hath heard thy affliction. And he will be a wild man; his hand will be against every man, and every man's hand against him; and he shall dwell in the presence of all his brethren.'
>
> (Genesis, 16: 11–12)

These words are spoken to Hagar by an angel. The story is that Abraham and Sarah could not have children, so Sarah arranged for Abraham to sleep with her maid, Hagar. When Hagar conceived, she and Sarah quarrelled, and Hagar ran away into the wilderness. Here, the angel appeared to her and induced her to return to Abraham's house, as well as speaking the prophecy about her child, which would be called Ishmael. Following Hagar's return and the birth of Ishmael, God miraculously makes the aged Sarah conceive to produce Isaac, Abraham's heir. When Ishmael is thirteen, he and his mother are cast out from Abraham's house, and go wandering away; but Ishmael is protected by God:

> And God was with the lad; and he grew, and dwelt in the wilderness,

and became an archer. And he dwelt in the wilderness of Paran: and his mother took him a wife out of the land of Egypt.

(Genesis, 21: 20–1)

Hagar and Ishmael are sent away at the insistence of Sarah, who refuses to allow the illegitimate boy to stay once she has her own son and heir, Isaac. Abraham sends them away against his will: 'the thing was very grievous in Abraham's sight because of his son' (Genesis, 21: 11).

The reference to Genesis raises a number of parallels with the story of *Wuthering Heights*. In particular, Ishmael's story is reminiscent of Heathcliff's. They are both interlopers, who compete with a legitimate heir and have the affection of the father but the hatred and jealousy of others. The prophecy is quite apt to Heathcliff, also. He does become cast out, and the description 'he will be a wild man; his hand will be against every man' suits the later events of the book.

Emily Brontë has used the four quotations from the Bible, then, to provide wider connections between Lockwood's dream and the main narrative of *Wuthering Heights*. The reference to the Gospel of Matthew, the 'Seventy times Seven' and 'First of the Seventy First', elaborates ideas of sin and punishment which help us to understand Brontë's unconventional concepts of suffering and forgiveness and so interpret the remainder of the novel, as we shall see. The quotations from the Book of Job, the Psalms and Genesis all provide highly suggestive contexts which provoke us to think about the nature of the story we are about to read. The stories of Job and Ishmael, in particular, provoke wider thought about life as suffering, and Heathcliff's position in relation to the Earnshaw family.

What have we found in this dream? Our first conclusion must be that we can accord authority to the dream: it can be interpreted, and it does carry a significant meaning in relation to the main story of *Wuthering Heights*. The biblical references to Job and Genesis relate to the main experiences of the novel in a broad and suggestive way. The ideas – about death and suffering, and a wild outcast – go far beyond the range of Lockwood the character. The moral framework of the dream also has authority. Brontë has clearly elaborated the concepts from Matthew, Chapter 18. She has emphasised a 'preposterous', unending demand on the individual, and at the same time she underlines the need to forgive, and the sin that is committed when an individual sets a limit on forgiveness, takes justice into his own hands, passes judgement and metes out punishment.

The problem Brontë presents in this dream, then, is one of intolerable demands: demands that go far beyond any ordinary human capacity to endure. In the dream, Lockwood is faced with the prospect of a sermon that will never end: it reaches its allotted limit at the end of 'Seventy times Seven', yet it then continues, for Branderham begins the 'First of the Seventy First'. The demand, then, passes even beyond the 'preposterous', unendurable length of four hundred and ninety sermons. We can say that the sermon will *never* end. Lockwood must endure *infinitely*, and forgive *all*. These words, 'never', 'infinitely' and 'all' are absolutes, so we can conclude that the dream is about **absolute demands** on the individual, or absolute forbearance and forgiveness.

Disaster follows Lockwood's failure to meet this absolute demand: his understandable, human decision to set a limit, to judge that Branderham is unreasonable in asking so much. In his objection to the sermon, Lockwood urges fairness and justice. He has listened to *so much*, and it is unfair for him to listen to *more*. There must be a *limit* to the sermon, otherwise it will be out of *proportion* or 'preposterous'. These ideas, 'so much', 'more', 'limit' and 'proportion', all have to do with measurement and balance. If we see life in these terms, we expect to reach a reasonable **limitation**, a reasonable boundary around and between conflicting needs.

These two principles, the **absolute** and **limitation**, are in conflict. Emily Brontë presents them to us in the form of a problem that she does not resolve, so that the two principles remain a living quandary in our minds. We cannot take a moral stance using a simple idea of 'right' and 'wrong'. After all, Lockwood is 'right' to say that the sermon is far too long, but he commits a sin – he is 'wrong' – when he tries to act upon this 'right'.

The irrelevance of 'right' and 'wrong' to the conflict between these two principles takes us back to the Book of Job, where we were less sure of our interpretation. The cause of Job's suffering (a wager between God and Satan) is insufficient, trivial: it appears that he suffers pointlessly, for no reason. Yet the power of God is infinite, as represented in the Book of Job. We can say, then, that Job suffers under an amoral absolute power. God is neither 'right' nor 'wrong', simply **absolute**. The emphasis on unreasoning, infinite demands and pain in Lockwood's dream therefore seems to connect with the incomprehensible but absolute tyranny of God in the Book of Job.

We have found that Lockwood's first dream is full of significance, so our next task is to take our conclusions, and test them upon other parts of the text. This will tell us whether the dream acts as a 'key', helping us to interpret other dilemmas and events in the novel. We begin by looking at the second dream, examining it in terms of the principles of the **absolute** and **limitation** we have arrived at from the first dream.

The second dream also makes a demand on Lockwood, and he again tries to set a limit on it. This time, he reacts to the unending knocking at the window, feeling that he 'must stop it'. This makes him break the glass, and the horrific events of the dream unfold from there. However, the focus in this dream is on terror and violence. Lockwood goes through the same sequence of events as in the first dream: he suffers from an unending irritation, tries to control it and bring it to an end, and becomes cruel in doing so. This time, however, the accent in the writing is upon the wildness of Lockwood's emotions and actions: it is a less theoretical, more personal experience.

Lockwood feels 'The intense horror of nightmare' and the voice speaks to him 'shiveringly'. Then 'Terror made me cruel' and the small hand's grip was 'almost maddening me with fear'. Even when he has freed his hand, Lockwood finds the voice unbearable and 'stopped my ears to exclude the lamentable prayer'. Eventually, the unending voice provokes a crisis in Lockwood and he 'yelled aloud, in a frenzy of fright'. These emotions develop our sense of human reactions to infinite demand. The author leaves us in no doubt about the ruling emotion in Lockwood, using 'horror', 'shiveringly', 'terror', 'fear' and 'fright' in quick succession.

Explicitly, fear produces cruelty. The dreamer shows vicious and cunning cruelty under the pressure of 'Terror'. Brontë describes this graphically: 'I pulled its wrist onto the broken pane, and rubbed it to and fro till the blood ran down and soaked the bedclothes.' The gory horror of this picture has a powerful effect, and convinces us that the dreamer's terror will make him stop at nothing – he will violently murder – in order to shut out the unacceptable demand.

Finally, there is an exchange that reminds us of the numbers in 'Seventy times Seven' and the 'First of the Seventy First'. Lockwood uses an absolute term, saying he will 'never' let her in; then he defines 'never' with a number, as 'twenty years'. The waif's answer is that 'twenty years' have already passed. In this exchange, Brontë again raises the issue of numbers and limits. Ironically, Lockwood's idea of infinity is limited: 'never', to him, is a long time – twenty years. Just as in the earlier dream, demand passes beyond its limit: Lockwood's 'never' has already passed, and still the waif's voice pleads. This echoes Branderham, who reached the end of 'Seventy times Seven', but then continued. In this dream also, then, the demand is clearly presented as an infinite, or **absolute** demand; and in conflict with this, Lockwood's human capacity is limited: he tries to set a limit, to introduce his concepts of quantity and numbers, because he cannot face the challenge of the absolute.

The meaning of the second dream is similar to that of the first, then. However, it takes us further into human experience, and emphasises the trappings of nightmare – blood, cruelty and ghosts. In a sense, we could say that the second dream shows us what Jesus's parable means, in terms of actual human experience. At the same time, the author emphasises fear, as the governing emotion which produces cruelty and deception. Specifically, this fear is the result of being unable to face infinity. We see a limited human capacity facing something much larger, more demanding, than it can cope with.

Remember that we are developing our understanding of underlying 'concepts' in *Wuthering Heights*. We have identified the conflict between two principles, because it lies at the heart of interpreting Lockwood's two dreams. These two principles are, first, the **absolute** (infinity, going beyond all limits, unlimited personal demands and unlimited commitment); and second, the principle of **limitation** (balance, fairness, justice: setting limits and reaching agreement within reasonable bounds). Now we want to find whether these principles, and the conflict between them, can be said to be 'underlying' throughout the novel. To do this, we will look at extracts from other parts of the text, trying to interpret them in terms of a conflict between the **absolute** and **limitation**.

* * *

Here is a part of the final conversation between Heathcliff and Catherine, taken from the first chapter of Volume 2 (Chapter 15):

> 'I wish I could hold you,' she continued, bitterly, 'till we were both dead! I shouldn't care what you suffered. I care nothing for your sufferings. Why shouldn't you suffer? I do! Will you forget me – will you be happy when I am in the earth? Will you say twenty years hence, "That's the grave of Catherine Earnshaw. I loved her long ago, and was wretched to lose her; but it is past. I've loved many others since – my children are dearer to me than she was, and, at death, I shall not rejoice that I am going to her, I shall be sorry that I must leave them!" Will you say so, Heathcliff?'
>
> 'Don't torture me till I'm as mad as yourself,' cried he, wrenching his head free, and grinding his teeth.
>
> The two, to a cool spectator, made a strange and fearful picture. Well might Catherine deem that Heaven would be a land of exile to her, unless, with her mortal body, she cast away her mortal character also. Her present countenance had a wild vindictiveness in its white cheek, and a bloodless lip, and scintillating eye; and she retained, in her closed fingers, a portion of the locks she had been grasping. As to her companion, while raising himself with one hand, he had taken her arm with the other; and so inadequate was his stock of gentleness to the requirements of her condition, that on his letting go, I saw four distinct impressions left blue in the colourless skin.
>
> 'Are you possessed with a devil,' he pursued, savagely, 'to talk in that manner to me, when you are dying? Do you reflect that all those words will be branded in my memory, and eating deeper eternally, after you have left me? You know you lie to say I have killed you; and, Catherine, you know that I could as soon forget you, as my existence! Is it not sufficient for your infernal selfishness, that while you are at peace I shall writhe in the torments of hell?'
>
> 'I shall not be at peace,' moaned Catherine, recalled to a sense of

physical weakness by the violent, unequal throbbing of her heart, which beat visibly and audibly under this excess of agitation.

She said nothing further until the paroxysm was over; then she continued, more kindly –

'I'm not wishing you greater torment than I have, Heathcliff! I only wish us never to be parted – and should a word of mine distress you hereafter, think I feel the same distress underground, and for my own sake, forgive me! Come here and kneel down again! You never harmed me in your life. Nay, if you nurse anger, that will be worse to remember than my harsh words! Won't you come here again? Do!'

Heathcliff went to the back of her chair, and leant over, but not so far as to let her see his face, which was livid with emotion. She bent round to look at him; he would not permit it; turning abruptly, he walked to the fire-place, where he stood, silent, with his back towards us.

Mrs Linton's glance followed him suspiciously: every movement woke a new sentiment in her. After a pause, and a prolonged gaze, she resumed, addressing me in accents of indignant disappointment.

'Oh, you see, Nelly! he would not relent a moment, to keep me out of the grave! *That* is how I'm loved! Well, never mind! That is not *my* Heathcliff. I shall love mine yet; and take him with me – he's in my soul. And,' added she, musingly, 'the thing that irks me most is this shattered prison, after all. I'm tired, tired of being enclosed here. I'm wearying to escape into that glorious world, and to be always there; not seeing it dimly through tears, and yearning for it through the walls of an aching heart; but really with it, and in it.'

(pp. 158–60)

Catherine and Heathcliff complain about each others' shortcomings in love. Catherine's initial speech plays on the conflict between a reality that is all too common – that the passing of time will lessen grief, and the surviving lover will find new consolations – and the eternal, unchanging devotion she feels and wishes him to feel. She tortures him by supposing he will say 'I loved her once . . . but it is past'; and asks him 'Will you say so, Heathcliff?' In response, he declares that change and time will not affect his love: 'Catherine, you know that I could as soon forget you, as my existence!' Instead, he complains that her teasing words are hurtful, and their hurt will grow after she is dead. He is particularly goaded because she talks of compromises – of change and time – in the face of the absolute, death: 'Are you possessed with a devil . . . to talk in that manner to me, when you are dying?'

Both Heathcliff and Catherine, then, have a standard of **absolute love**, and their quarrel is about probing, goading and teasing each other to live up to this standard. They both fear that the other is not absolute in love. Catherine is frightened that Heathcliff will forget her after she dies; and Heathcliff rejects her demeaning talk, angrily dismissing all ideas of limitation in the face of his absolute love. He emphasises the absolute, death, which she faces.

Catherine's two speeches later in the extract develop the ideas with which she began the passage: 'I wish I could hold you . . . till we were both dead! I shouldn't care what you suffered . . . why shouldn't you suffer? I do!' This begins two themes: first, the idea that their love is so absolute it cannot be fulfilled except through the deaths of both of them (and at the same time, the demand that they sacrifice life for each other); and secondly, the need for each to imagine what the other feels. Catherine says that they suffer equally, and returns to this idea later: 'I'm not wishing you greater torment than I have, Heathcliff!' Since she understands that he suffers as painfully as she does, she asks for the same understanding from him: 'should a word of mine distress you hereafter, think I feel the same distress underground, and for my own sake, forgive me!' Later in their dialogue, Heathcliff accuses her of being solely responsible for parting them, and her response, again, is a plea for both of them to continue forgiving each other: 'If I've done wrong, I'm dying for it. It is enough! You left me too; but I won't upbraid you! I forgive you. Forgive me!' (p. 161). Clearly, the theme of absolute love includes an insistent need for each to forgive the other, and to continue forgiving the other no matter what their sin. This emphasis reminds us of Branderham's 'Seventy times Seven' and the 'First of the Seventy First'.

The idea that their love is so absolute, they must pass through death to reach union, is present in Catherine's wish to hold him until they are both dead. This is not a new idea, but one Catherine has talked of twice before. We remember that she dared Heathcliff to follow her through death, in her delirium: 'If you do, I'll keep you.

I'll not lie there by myself; they may bury me twelve feet deep, and throw the church down over me; but I won't rest till you are with me' (p. 125). The second time she mentioned this idea was to Edgar, when she excluded him from her life-after-death: 'my soul will be on that hill-top before you lay hands on me again. I don't want you, Edgar' (p. 126). The distinction Catherine makes is clear: her love with Heathcliff is absolute: she may demand the ultimate sacrifice from him. The love between her and Edgar, on the other hand, is of a different, lower, more limited order, and will disappear when she dies.

In the present extract, Catherine takes this idea a stage further. She seems to have two concepts of Heathcliff. One is the living man, who continually fails her, and cannot forgive her for what she has done to him. By withholding his forgiveness, he prolongs the painful breach between them. Catherine then thinks of '*my* Heathcliff' who is not in the real world but 'in my soul'. It is this perfect Heathcliff, who meets her absolute demands, who will pass through death and be with her: 'I shall love mine yet; and take him with me.' The agonies the real Heathcliff endures in this scene, and those he passes through after Catherine's death, are put into context by this remark. His struggles to set himself free from the tyranny of his physical existence, the long conflict between his desire to be one with Catherine and his stubborn instinct for survival, has been fully discussed in Chapter 2. Here, Catherine expresses her own final weariness of life: she is eager to discard her body, 'the thing that irks me most is this shattered prison, after all. I'm tired, tired of being enclosed here.' These words should be set beside Heathcliff's near his death: 'I have a single wish, and my whole being, and faculties are yearning to attain it' (p. 321). We remember the weary effort he finds it to make his heart beat, when he is near to death (see p. 321 and Chapter 2 above).

What Catherine expresses here is set in language which contrasts life – a limiting, unsatisfactory compromise – with death, a desired absolute. Life is a 'shattered prison' and she feels her soul to be 'enclosed'. The image of life as a barrier she must pass through or escape to attain what she desires, is continued in the image of 'that glorious world' which, in life, can only be seen 'dimly through tears' and 'through the walls of an aching heart'. The implication of this speech, with its perfected Heathcliff and its desire to leave the 'prison' of physical life, is that Catherine has an overwhelming yearning for infinity, for the **absolute**. Unity with Heathcliff, the absolute aim of her love, is here closely associated with the absolute of death. We could say that love and death are so closely interwoven in *Wuthering Heights*, because they are both absolute principles – they are both irked by the limitations and compromises of physical existence.

In this extract, then, we have found that Brontë's text continues to play upon the conflicts between **absolutes** and **limitation**. Issues clearly rehearsed in Lockwood's dreams, which are further developed here, include the question of forgiveness beyond the call of justice, and the 'preposterous' demand of the ultimate sacrifice – life itself. The absolutes present in this extract are love and death, and the narrative focuses insistently on the sufferings and struggles of Heathcliff and Catherine, in their efforts to meet the superhuman demand of their emotions.

Lockwood's dream helps us with this scene, because the parable of the 'Seventy times Seven' provides an interpretative framework. Catherine has undoubtedly 'sinned' against Heathcliff and their love by marrying Edgar. Heathcliff urges this point powerfully on the next page: 'Because misery, and degradation, and death, and nothing that God or satan could inflict would have parted us, *you*, of your own will, did it' (pp. 160–1). However, remember that Jesus's 'servant' had the 'right' to punish his 'fellowservant'; and Lockwood was 'right' to complain of the length of Branderham's sermon. It is not a question of 'right' and 'wrong', then, and Heathcliff should not urge any concept of justice. Catherine asks him to pass beyond such limitations: if his love is absolute, his forgiveness should also be infinite: 'I forgive you. Forgive me!' (p. 161). We can say, in Branderham's terms, that Heathcliff still commits the sin of the 'First of the Seventy First', until he forgives Catherine her sins against him. In our extract, he also fails to imagine her experiences and focuses on his own agony – as Lockwood did while enduring Branderham's sermon (Heathcliff says that she will be 'at peace' while he will 'writhe in the torments of hell'). Catherine, on the other hand, seems to imagine his feelings as equalling her own.

Examining this extract, then, has confirmed that the principles of the absolute and limitation are in conflict here as well. Lockwood's dream, and the concepts of sin, punishment, justice, forgiveness and so on that are elaborated by Emily Brontë in that vision, becomes a useful tool to help us interpret the violent passions and wild demands of Heathcliff's and Catherine's final meeting. Emily Brontë presents an idea of romantic love that matches the framework of the dream. The lover's commitment is no less than that proposed by Jesus in his parable: the sins of the loved one are to be forgiven 'Until seventy times seven'; and any judgement or intolerance, any attempt to punish a wrong, is the unforgivable sin, the 'First of the Seventy First'. In this scene Heathcliff struggles violently to overcome his sense of injustice and the suffering she has caused him, to meet Catherine's extreme demands, and succeed in forgiving her.

*　　*　　*

The next extract we will examine is from a less melodramatic part of the novel. Young Cathy is determined to be reconciled to Hareton. The two have hurt each other grievously in the past, and the present scene deals with overcoming fear and resentment in order to be friends:

'. . . when she hates me, and does not think me fit to wipe her shoon! Nay, if it made me a king, I'd not be scorned for seeking her good will any more.'

'It is not I who hate you, it is you who hate me!' wept Cathy, no longer disguising her trouble. 'You hate me as much as Mr Heathcliff does, and more.'

'You're a damned liar,' began Earnshaw; 'why have I made him angry, by taking your part then, a hundred times? and that, when you sneered at, and despised me, and – Go on plaguing me, and I'll step in yonder, and say you worried me out of the kitchen!'

'I didn't know you took my part,' she answered, drying her eyes; 'and I was miserable and bitter at every body; but, now I thank you, and beg you to forgive me, what can I do besides?'

She returned to the hearth, and frankly extended her hand.

He blackened, and scowled like a thunder cloud, and kept his fists resolutely clenched, and his gaze fixed on the ground.

Catherine, by instinct, must have divined it was obdurate perversity, and not dislike, that prompted this dogged conduct; for, after remaining an instant, undecided, she stooped, and impressed on his cheek a gentle kiss.

The little rogue thought I had not seen her, and, drawing back, she took her former station by the window, quite demurely.

I shook my head reprovingly; and then she blushed, and whispered – 'Well! what should I have done, Ellen? he wouldn't shake hands, and he wouldn't look – I must show him some way that I like him, that I want to be friends.'

(pp. 310–11)

This extract is clear. We know that the kiss succeeds, and Cathy and Hareton are reconciled. Our interest focuses on the stages Cathy passes through in her effort to overcome Hareton's resistance.

Before the start of our extract, Cathy has asked Hareton to be friends, but she concealed her feelings: 'chewing her lip, and endeavouring, by humming an eccentric tune, to conceal a growing tendency to sob'. When she asked him to be friends, her diction was still in an imperious form: 'Come, you shall take notice of me, Hareton – you are my cousin, and you shall own me' (both p. 310). In the extract, the barriers in Cathy's words and behaviour come down in stages. First, she gives up the attempt to conceal her feelings, and this shows her as a vulnerable person, suffering: 'wept Cathy, no longer disguising her trouble'. Next, she acknowledges suffering in her words ('and I was miserable and bitter at every body') and acknowledges that she has wronged him ('and beg you to forgive me'). The outcome of this movement is that she behaves as his equal, and accepts that he is equal with her. This is shown by her gesture when she goes to him 'and frankly extended her hand'.

At this point, Cathy has expended all the resources of normal behaviour and normal intercourse. She has apologised, revealed her vulnerable feelings, and asked for forgiveness as an equal. Hareton's behaviour has been hostile, however. He expresses his anger at how she has hurt him, and he cannot allow himself to be hurt in the same way again: 'Nay, if it made me a king, I'd not be scorned for seeking her good will any more.' In the face of her climb-down, Hareton maintains his hostile stance. At this point, then, the scene is at an impasse. Hareton 'scowled like a thunder cloud', and Cathy seems to have exhausted all her ideas of how to break through to him. She even expresses the fact that there is nothing more she can do: 'what can I do besides?'

The measures of normal and reasonable behaviour provide no guide here, yet normal and reasonable behaviour is clearly not enough. Brontë is careful in describing what happens next. Cathy cannot think of what to do, because reason cannot help her in this impasse; but 'by instinct' she 'divined' his feelings, and after a moment's hesitation, she breaks the normal bounds of behaviour and kisses him. Two further details complete our picture. First, it is clear that Cathy has passed beyond conventional limitations: she was aware of this herself, when she 'blushed', and Nelly underlines the fact by shaking her head 'reprovingly'. Second, Cathy justifies her action by referring to an absolute need that will not be denied. She says that she 'must' show him her liking 'some way'.

This is altogether a gentler and happier scene than our last extract. However, we can recognise the same underlying concepts at work here as well. Cathy is confronted by boundaries and limitations: she is only allowed a certain range of behaviour, which does not include kissing an angry man. On the other hand, her feelings go beyond this: her love for Hareton is an imperative emotion, much stronger than the limits of social manners. In this scene, then, Cathy clearly goes beyond **limitations** and pursues the **absolute** ('I *must* show him some way'). Her ability to overcome her own defensive shyness, and his hostility, displays the strength of her feeling for him. It is also associated with intuitive understanding of his feelings. Emily Brontë makes it clear that her intuition also goes beyond the normal – it is beyond the limits of reason and thinking. It is only 'by instinct' that Cathy 'divined' his feelings and knew what to do.

In the terms of Lockwood's dream, this scene shows Cathy breaking through the boundaries we can call the 'First of the Seventy First'. She does so because her emotion is strong enough to compel her beyond the conventions that would otherwise restrain her, so she 'must' find a way when all normal means have been exhausted; and because she intuitively understands Hareton's inner feelings, despite the deceptive anger he displays on the outside.

Absolutes and Limitations

In this section we will enlarge on the principles of the 'absolute' in conflict with 'limitations', that we have found in Lockwood's dreams, and confirmed as underlying concepts by examining two scenes from other parts of the text. Our discussion will look back at some parts of the novel met in earlier chapters, and briefly consider Edgar Linton in the context of Lockwood's dream.

In Chapter 3 we discussed imagery in *Wuthering Heights*, and noticed a contrast between Catherine's image for Heathcliff, and that she applies to Edgar Linton. Much of the imagery in the novel can now be classified into two groups: images conveying the **absolute**, and images of **limitations**. For example, the 'foliage' which is Catherine's love for Edgar is temporary, an image of something limited, in contrast to the permanence, or absolute, of her love for Heathcliff as 'the eternal rocks beneath'. In the same way, Edgar's emotional capacity is compared to a limited 'horse-trough' which cannot contain Catherine's love, a love which Heathcliff likens to the infinite depth of 'the sea'. Catherine tries to explain the difference between Edgar's soul and those of herself and Heathcliff, in terms of absolute brightness and heat ('lightning' and 'fire') in contrast to the limited image-ideas 'moonbeam' and 'frost' (p. 80). Heathcliff specifically relates these images of shallowness and infinite depth, to love in contrast to shallower emotions: 'And that insipid, paltry creature attending her from *duty* and *humanity*! From *pity* and *charity*! He might as well plant an oak in a flower-pot, and expect it to thrive, as imagine he can restore her to vigour in the soil of his shallow cares!' (p. 151). The images of **limitation** we have noticed include small containers like the 'horse-trough' and 'flower-pot'; and this motif links with images which bring to mind imprisonment and enclosure, like Catherine's ideas of seeing a 'glorious world' dimly 'through tears' or 'through the walls of an aching heart', which we met in our extract from Volume 2, Chapter 1.

Both Catherine and Heathcliff suggest that they will not be confined by death unless they are finally together: the infinity of their desire will escape the physical confines of coffin, earth, and whatever else may be placed about them. Catherine says they may 'throw the church down over me; but I won't rest till you are with me . . . I never will' (p. 125); and Heathcliff warns Nelly that she will have 'a better chance of keeping me underground, when I get there' now he has seen that Catherine is in her grave (p. 286). Heathcliff proposes to remove the physical barriers between their corpses, also, by removing the coffin-sides. The image-idea of enclosures and walls further links to the setting of *Wuthering Heights*. Edgar's fear of his daughter passing beyond the enclosed 'park' of Thrushcross Grange is clearly a sign of his **limitation**: he only wishes her to experience a part of life (Nelly comments that she grew up like a 'perfect recluse' – p. 188), and is frightened of the unlimited, unbounded experience she might meet if she ventured farther afield. Edgar's servants maintain his seclusion:

> There was a labourer working at a fence round a plantation, on the borders of the grounds. I enquired of him if he had seen our young lady?
> 'I saw her at morn,' he replied; 'she would have me to cut her a hazel switch, and then she leapt her galloway over the hedge yonder, where it is lowest, and galloped out of sight.'
>
> (p. 190)

Young Cathy's boundless desire to see 'what lies on the other side' of Penistone Craggs (p. 188), and her determination in jumping her father's flimsy hedge, can be seen as another example of the infinite character passing beyond its prescribed **limitations**. The low part of the hedge, and the 'gap which the man was repairing', through which Nelly issues in pursuit, ironically underline that all attempts to imprison an **absolute** human spirit are full of holes, and futile. The position of Catherine's grave is a further example of limited civilisation's failure to contain her:

> The place of Catherine's interment, to the surprise of the villagers, was neither in the chapel, under the carved monument of the

Lintons, nor yet by the tombs of her own relations, outside. It was dug on a green slope, in a corner of the kirkyard, where the wall is so low that heath and bilberry plants have climbed over it from the moor; and peat mould almost buries it.

(p. 168)

Notice that we have traced image-ideas of shallowness, containment, **limitation**, in contrast to more **absolute** principles of infinity, eternity and freedom, beginning with the incidental similes and metaphors of the text; we have then linked these to similar ideas in the deliberate actions of the characters (notably Heathcliff's plans for the graves, and Cathy's escape from the Park); finally, we have found the same ideas expressed on a larger, more passive scale, in the topographical setting throughout the novel. Along our way, we have found these ideas associated with emotions and attitudes of **limitation** (Edgar's fears, which lead him to limit his daughter's experiences; the emotions of duty, humanity, pity and charity on which Heathcliff pours scorn), and more **absolute** values (Cathy's desire to see Penistone Craggs, her determination to go beyond all confines, Heathcliff's love, Catherine's escape from the 'shattered prison' of her body). So, as we continue to pursue these two underlying concepts in the novel, our understanding of their complexity, and their many ramifications, becomes more and more enriched.

We can now turn to a comparison between Edgar Linton's behaviour during the crucial period following Heathcliff's return, and Lockwood's role in his first dream. We remember that Lockwood endured the interminable sermon for a long time. By his own account, 'I have endured and forgiven the four hundred and ninety heads of your discourse' (p. 24). Edgar Linton is in a similar situation in relation to his wife, after their marriage:

> It was not the thorn bending to the honeysuckles, but the honeysuckles embracing the thorn. There were no mutual concessions; one stood erect, and the others yielded; and who *can* be ill-natured, and bad-tempered, when they encounter neither opposition nor indifference?
>
> I observed that Mr Edgar had a deep-rooted fear of ruffling her humour. He concealed it from her; but if ever he heard me answer

sharply, or saw any other servant grow cloudy at some imperious order of hers, he would show his trouble by a frown of displeasure . . .

(p. 91)

We discussed this situation in relation to Isabella and the hanging of her dog, in Chapter 3. Here, it is clear that Edgar endures Catherine's faults or 'sins' of moodiness and imperious behaviour, not because he believes her to be right, but out of fear. We remember the importance of fear as the ruling emotion of Lockwood's dreams.

In the dream, Branderham reaches the expected period of his sermon, and then begins to go further. Something similar to this happens in Edgar's life with Catherine. Following Heathcliff's return, her 'sins' against him continue, and go beyond anything she had attempted before. We know that Edgar is against Heathcliff being admitted as a visitor to Thrushcross Grange in the first place (at their first meeting 'he grew pale with pure annoyance' and was 'striving to preserve his ordinary tone, and a due measure of politeness' – p. 96). Just as Branderham began the 'First of the Seventy First', so Catherine now ignores Edgar and focuses all her attention on Heathcliff.

Matters come to a head during the quarrel in Chapter 11. We remember that, at the crucial moment when Branderham looked set to go on for ever, Lockwood found that 'an inspiration descended' upon him, and he was 'moved to rise and denounce' the preacher, thus committing the unforgivable sin of reaching the limit of his tolerance: judging his fellow man, and calling for punishment. In the main story, Edgar is finally moved to take a stand. Here is the language he uses:

> 'You *must* answer it; and that violence does not alarm me. I have found that you can be as stoical as any one, when you please. Will you give up Heathcliff hereafter, or will you give up me? It is impossible for you to be *my* friend, and *his* at the same time; and I absolutely *require* to know which you choose.'

(p. 116)

This speech reveals Edgar in several ways. First, notice that the italicised words, 'must', 'my', 'his' and 'require' are all about compulsion and possession. Secondly, Edgar is rigid in imposing his judgement, seeking to erect an impassable barrier around Catherine. His use of 'impossible' and 'absolutely' show this.

Finally, he rejects her appeal to his fear and sympathy: 'that violence does not alarm me'; and he uses evidence to support this judgement, as if he has been observing her and judging her: 'I have found that you can be as stoical as any one, when you please.' Edgar is a magistrate, and his diction here reminds us of his attempted dignity towards Heathcliff on page 113, which also sounded like a pronouncement from the bench. Ironically, Edgar then used the same verb to Heathcliff as he now uses on his wife, saying 'I *require* your instant departure.'

In Lockwood's dream, we understood his sufferings and sympathised with them: the sermon was outrageously long. In the same way, we sympathise with Edgar and we agree that Catherine's behaviour has been – in conventional terms – dreadful. On the other hand, we should recognise that Edgar here commits the sin 'no Christian need pardon', the sin of intolerance and self-righteous judgement, the 'First of the Seventy First'; just as in the dream, Edgar's is not a sin against 'right' and 'wrong'; but it is a sin against love and faith. Edgar continues in an obdurate and self-righteous frame of mind through the succeeding days. He 'did not inquire concerning his wife's occupations' (p. 117), and Brontë's language is filled with the concepts of right and wrong and justice when he is described expecting that Catherine, 'repenting', would 'ask pardon' and seek a 'reconciliation' (p. 119).

The effect of Edgar revealing the limitation of his patience cannot be exaggerated. Like Branderham, Catherine judges him in her turn. Notice, however, that she does not judge him to be 'wrong'. Instead, she concludes that he does not love her, telling Nelly 'I thought . . . they could not avoid loving me – and they have all turned to enemies in a few hours', and pictures an insincere Edgar 'standing solemnly by to see it over; then offering prayers of thanks to God for restoring peace to his house' (pp. 120–21). In consequence, she has no further use for him: 'I don't want you, Edgar; I'm past wanting you. . . . Return to your books. . . . I'm glad you possess a consolation, for all you had in me is gone' (pp. 126–7). Catherine is outraged, and her rejection of Edgar is powerful and final, but it is always because he has sinned against feeling, not because she 'judges' him in a conventional sense: 'What in the name of all that feels, has he to do with *books*, when I am dying?' (p. 121).

The breach between them, caused by Edgar's recourse to righteous judgement, is not healed before her death. Even in her gentler mood during her rally, she does no more than tell Edgar that he is about to lose her. It is clear, then, that Lockwood's dream can be closely applied to the situation during these chapters. Edgar endures and forgives the 'Seventy Times Seven', but then – under extreme provocation – he becomes self-righteous and intolerant, and commits the unforgivable sin, the 'First of the Seventy First'.

Finally, we should look at the issue that has accompanied the idea of 'Seventy times Seven' in every context we have discussed: understanding of other people. Lockwood could not accept Branderham's ideas, finding them 'odd' and 'curious'; Catherine, on the other hand, realises Heathcliff's suffering, and urges him to make a similar effort to imagine her feelings. The present discussion began with imagery which suggests that Edgar and Catherine are from different, incompatible species: he is a 'honeysuckle' while she is a 'thorn'. When he denounces his wife, Edgar rejects understanding, and judges her to be acting her illnesses: 'you can be as stoical as any one, when you please'. However, he becomes uncertain when Catherine has a fit, and it is Nelly who shores up his resolve, saying 'There is nothing in the world the matter' and telling him 'Never mind!' Clearly, Edgar lacks understanding of his wife, and does not trust her; but during the crucial three days, the influence of Nelly's irritated, unsympathetic judgements is powerful. The narrative tone is brusque and dismissive as she tells us that she 'wasted no condolences . . . expostulations . . . nor did I pay any attention'; Nelly is convinced that she is right because she is the 'one sensible soul' in the Grange, and 'I determined that they should come about as they pleased for me' (all from p. 119). We must conclude, therefore, that Mrs Dean contributes to the 'First of the Seventy First', with her limited sympathy and narrow self-righteousness.

This point is underlined by Mrs Dean's analysis of how the marriage broke down, which she gives on page 92:

It ended. Well, we *must* be for ourselves in the long run; the mild and generous are only more justly selfish than the domineering – and it ended when circumstances caused each to feel that the one's interest was not the chief consideration in the other's thoughts.

In this passage, Nelly voices a cynical philosophy entirely at variance with that of Jesus in Matthew, Chapter 18. Her analysis that Catherine and Edgar divided in selfishness, and that both were goaded to this by feeling that they were ignored by the other, seems to fit the events. On the other hand, there are two revealing ironies. First, Nelly acknowledges that her admired Edgar was – and would necessarily be – as selfish as his naughty wife, for whom she has little patience. Secondly, the truth of Nelly's dictum 'we *must* be for ourselves in the long run' comes to apply to herself particularly, in her fit of self-righteous annoyance following the quarrel.

We can further comment that the idea of being 'more justly selfish' is a nonsense. When we think about this idea in relation to our 'underlying concepts', it simply expresses an attempt to measure different kinds of selfishness within a limited morality. Finally, we should notice that Nelly's cynical statement that 'We *must* be for ourselves in the long run' is a measure of her own limitation throughout the novel. Brontë has chosen a narrator who is incapable of understanding her main characters. This further underlines the observations we made in Chapter 1, that the novel works to a great extent through the tension between the content (and particularly the **absolute** in the form of Catherine's and Heathcliff's relationship) and the **limitation** of Nelly's and Lockwood's narrative viewpoints.

Concluding Discussion

1. We have discussed Edgar's crisis in terms of the 'First of the Seventy First'; however, it should be remembered that the underlying ideas of **limitation** and the demands of the **absolute**, that we deduced from Lockwood's dreams, are relevant throughout *Wuthering Heights*. All of the characters, including Heathcliff and

Catherine, commit the unforgivable sin at one time or another, or pass through phases of self-righteousness, lack of imaginative understanding, and intolerance. So, we should not think of these concepts as sorting out a morality in the novel, which will help *us* to judge the characters. We should not allow this appreciation of themes to lead us into being *anti*-Linton, or *pro*-Catherine and Heathcliff. For example, in Chapter 2 we suggested that Heathcliff's long prosecution of revenge derives from the principle of **limitation** as he struggles over eighteen years to avoid the **absolute** challenge Catherine has set by dying.

2. The underlying conflict between these two principles, then, is not a moral rubric for the novel at all. Rather, it is a framework which helps us to interpret the life-experiences narrated in *Wuthering Heights*, as they occur. The novel is always about the struggle to overcome **limitations**, the failure to do so and the violent conflicts of doing so, and the overwhelming – almost unfaceable – challenge of **absolute** principles such as love, death and freedom.

3. Particular themes in *Wuthering Heights* can now be approached by means of these underlying ideas, and Emily Brontë's concerns become clearer in this way. For example, the 'theme of love' in the novel concerns a love that is **absolute**. It is a tyrannical emotion in which two people seem to be one, without any barrier between them; and in which their desire for each other is infinite, passing beyond physical constraints and ultimately demanding the sacrifice of life itself. Other manifestations of love in the novel are subject to **limitations**: we meet an apparently tolerant affection, which is possessive, but reaches its limits when put under stress (Edgar); and a self-centred, possessive desire which confuses pain with attention (Isabella).

Methods of Analysis

1. We began by recognising that the conventional definition of 'themes' in *Wuthering Heights* presents a difficulty. The novel is many-layered, and numerous apparent 'themes' are integrated

into character, dialogue, events, and narrative standpoint throughout the text.

2. In these circumstances, we chose to look for underlying concepts in the novel, expecting that these, once identified, would be useful because they would help us to understand individual 'themes', and the action of Brontë's ideas within the characters and events, in different parts of *Wuthering Heights*.

3. We analysed Lockwood's two dreams, from Chapter 3, in detail. In doing this, we used a variety of techniques for close analysis that have been shown in previous chapters, and in addition we made use of the editor's notes to draw our attention to biblical references. We further investigated these references, in order to reach a full understanding of how the biblical passage is relevant to the text. This analysis provided us with a working understanding of two principles, which we called the **absolute** and **limitation** respectively.

4. In the later part of the chapter, we have examined further extracts from widely-separated parts of the text. In each case, we confirmed the relevance of a conflict between the **absolute** and **limitation** to the passage studied. These further studies also added depth and complexity to our understanding of underlying principles. For example, our analysis of Cathy's reconciliation with Hareton (pp. 310–11) added detail to our ideas about imagining the feelings of others. Cathy does not understand Hareton's feelings rationally: instead, this understanding comes 'by instinct' or intuitively.

5. A broader discussion of the underlying ideas we have identified in *Wuthering Heights*, suggests various openings for further investigation, and further confirms that this way of approaching the 'themes' of the novel will be rewarding.

Suggested Work

It would be enlightening to take almost any episode from *Wuthering Heights*, and analyse it closely in relation to the underlying principles of the **absolute** and **limitation**.

You could begin by examining the discussion between Nelly Dean and Catherine Earnshaw, which Heathcliff overhears and which induces him to leave Wuthering Heights. Begin your analysis on page 76 when Catherine whispers '"Are you alone, Nelly?"', and study as far as page 82, '"No, I'll not promise," I repeated.'

6

Conclusions to Part 1

This chapter is in two parts. First, we try to draw together the various conclusions about *Wuthering Heights* we have arrived at from all of our detailed study, in a descriptive discussion of the novel as a whole. Secondly, we bring together the various techniques and approaches that have been found useful in the preceding chapters, when analysing *Wuthering Heights*.

Wuthering Heights: What Sort of a Novel is it?

A discussion of the place occupied by *Wuthering Heights* in the history of English novels and their genres, will be found in Chapter 8. The present discussion is not concerned with placing Emily Brontë's masterpiece in the history of literature. Rather, we want to focus our attention on questions that relate to our function as interpretative critics: how is this novel intended to be read? On what level, and in what way, should we take it? What kind of a creation are we studying, and therefore, what are we justified in saying about it?

Each chapter so far has looked at *Wuthering Heights* from a particular standpoint; and in each case, we have been able to reach enlightening conclusions. These are all like staging-posts in developing thought about the novel, and we now want to draw them together.

We began by looking at the narrative framework, and noticed that the relationship between the story itself, and the frame, is fraught with conflict. Our final observation on Mrs Dean, at the end of Chapter 5, returns to this point in the context of the **absolute** and **limitations**: Mrs Dean opines that 'we *must* be for ourselves in the long run', and with this comment defines her limitations. The **absolute** demands and desires of the story and characters must break through her limiting viewpoint to reach the reader. The conclusions of our first and fifth chapters, then, can be considered together: the narrative framework is a further conflict involving the **absolute** and **limitations**, because the narrators represent a principle of 'limitation' in conflict with the 'absolutes' struggling for expression in the story.

In our first chapter we also suggested Aristotle's concept of 'unity', when comparing Brontë's novel to a play. 'Unity' seems a curious concept, in relation to a novel which chronicles the childhood and life of one generation, then brings the second generation to adulthood and marriage, and where there are so many characters. We suggested this idea in the original Aristotelian sense, however, that the novel is 'a complete unit, and the events of which it is made up must be so plotted that if any of these elements is moved or removed the whole is altered and upset'. This comment applies to any successful work of art in an unspecific sense, of course. In the case of *Wuthering Heights*, our Chapters 4 and 5 have added to our understanding of how Brontë achieves an effect of 'unity' in her apparently rambling and disparate work. The dominating dualism of the setting, between its poles of Wuthering Heights and Thrushcross Grange; and the detail with which other parts of the setting are delineated in relation to the two houses, is one unifying force in the novel. Another is the continuous life of two underlying principles – the 'absolute' and 'limitation' – in conflict with each other, and visible wherever we look in the text. These two elements in *Wuthering Heights* pervade the text so that almost every word plays upon one or the other of them, or upon both. The impression of 'unity' is thus appropriate: moving or removing any part of the novel would alter the 'whole' that Brontë has created.

In Chapter 2 we concluded that Emily Brontë builds her characters with the psychological insight we would normally expect from a post-Freudian writer. Catherine and Heathcliff, and to a lesser extent

Isabella and Edgar, are detailed to us in a manner that reminds us of an analyst's case-history. They display repressions, denials, drives and expressions of mental anguish – as well as significant mental events they do not understand themselves. We also noticed the importance of a unitary state, in childhood, as a focus for feelings of traumatic loss and impossible adult desire. Catherine, in particular, longs to re-enter this state. Childhood is remembered as a time of harmony, while growing up brings division from one's self. Catherine and Heathcliff struggle to escape from the pain of self-division; and a single, 'absolute' state of self-unity is their most powerful desire. This conclusion returns us to the idea of an 'absolute' and a struggle against complexities or 'limitations'. However, we can now enlarge our understanding of the 'absolute'. We know that the lovers' desire for final union is closely associated with a desire for death; but it is also fuelled by the pain of a divided self, and desire to re-create the innocent, unitary state of childhood. This insight suggests that the lovers' tragic passion is, at the same time, a rejection of adult life. Their story is thus a version of one of the basic fables of Western culture: it is the story of their 'fall'.

When considering *Wuthering Heights* it is important to change our perspective regularly. The world of Nelly Dean is made up of practical nostrums, respectable opinions, and concepts of behaviour and duty that all embody what we have called 'limitations'. For Edgar, as time passes grief becomes less acute and he finds consolation: 'he was too good to be thoroughly unhappy long. . . . Time brought resignation, and a melancholy sweeter than common joy' (p. 182). If we join the majority, as both Mrs Dean and Edgar do, then we will accept 'limitations', because it is 'normal' to do so, and 'reality' consists of complexities, changes and reasonable compromises.

From this point of view, Catherine and Heathcliff are 'abnormal' people. We did not pursue the question of madness when we studied the characters in Chapter 2; but there is one. For example, Heathcliff is conscious of 'seeming insane' (p. 320); and Nelly states that 'his wits were as sound as mine' apart from his 'monomania' about Catherine (p. 321). Emily Brontë carries on this discussion of sanity and madness intermittently throughout the novel, as if to remind us that the 'absolute' is not the real world, and those who serve it are, from society's practical point of view, 'mad'.

Returning to the narrative framework, it may be helpful to consider this from two points of view also. We have commented that the story itself, the actual experience of the characters, has to 'burst' or 'break' through the framework in order to reach us. However, we have focused on this device because of its effect in conveying a wilder range of emotion to the reader. We can also consider the framework of *Wuthering Heights* as a comment on vision and art – that the infinite imagination of the artist must, after all, pass through a finite channel (the page, the canvas, the range of a musician's instrument) to communicate itself to an audience. The author has shaped her narrative as a great book passing through insipid channels to the public. It pretends to be a novel which cannot be contained within its own covers. This is a conjuring trick of enormous effectiveness, and suggests the immensity of inner life that is contained within contemptible physical constraints, in creative art as in the lives of Brontë's protagonists.

In Chapter 5, we found that the concepts of suffering, terror and intolerance elaborated in Branderham's 'Seventy times Seven' and 'First of the Seventy First' are specifically recalled and applied throughout the text. On the other hand, we warned against using this interpretation as a criterion for judging the characters: they all, at one time or another, pass through intolerant or self-obsessed states, and commit the sin 'no Christian need pardon'. Likewise, in Chapter 4, we found that the characters do not 'belong' in groups – even when they have a family likeness, as do Catherine and Hareton, or Edgar and Isabella. Our various analyses have led us to the perception that we cannot rely on such ideas or turn them into a simple 'guide', when reading *Wuthering Heights*. Rather, we have to look at each particular event without pre-conceptions. The relationships between characters and their 'groups', and between characters and the moral framework of Lockwood's dream, change constantly. Events and people in *Wuthering Heights* all follow their own laws according to the demands of the moment: they do not follow any set 'framework', yet such a 'framework' is powerfully present in each scene.

Looking at the various conclusions we have reached, it is tempting to conflate the two major conflicts that pervade the book: that between Wuthering Heights and Thrushcross Grange, and all they represent; and that between the principles of the **absolute** and **limitation**. Both of these dualisms are like grand templates that can be laid over the whole novel, so that the many details of the story find their places within the template's scope. Both of them therefore make a major contribution to our understanding of the novel. However, just as we found with families, and with Lockwood's dreams, these two grand templates do not match. It is false to say that Thrushcross Grange 'embodies' a principle of **limitation**; and even more false to identify Wuthering Heights and the **absolute**. A brief example will underline this truth.

As the younger Catherine is fetched from Thrushcross Grange to live at Wuthering Heights, she speaks to Heathcliff with extraordinary perception:

> 'I know he has a bad nature,' said Catherine; 'he's your son. But I'm glad I've a better, to forgive it; and I know he loves me and for that reason I love him. Mr Heathcliff, *you* have *nobody* to love you; and, however miserable you make us, we shall still have the revenge of thinking that your cruelty rises from your greater misery! You *are* miserable, are you not? Lonely, like the devil, and envious like him? *Nobody* loves you – *nobody* will cry for you, when you die! I wouldn't be you!'
> Catherine spoke with a kind of dreary triumph: she seemed to have made up her mind to enter into the spirit of her future family, and draw pleasure from the griefs of her enemies.
>
> (p. 285)

Parts of Cathy's speech relate to the 'First of the Seventy First'. For example, she recognises her ability to forgive Linton his faults, even though we know that he is endlessly demanding and irritating, like Branderham's sermon in the dream. It is 'love' that confers power to transcend the littleness of her husband's character. In all of this we hear echoes of an absolute forgiveness – a forgiveness that will not reach its limit, like that of the 'Seventy times Seven'. The remainder of the speech concerns Heathcliff, and Cathy's perception of his misery is extraordinary, as we have remarked before. It is an isolated example of imaginative understanding in a part of the novel dominated by selfish retribution.

On the other hand, Nelly says that Cathy speaks to 'draw pleasure from the griefs of her enemies' – and this idea is supported by the word 'revenge' and Cathy's final jibe: 'I wouldn't be you!' This, according to Nelly, is the 'spirit of her future family' as she moves from Thrushcross Grange to Wuthering Heights. Clearly, in this instance Wuthering Heights represents a destructive **limitation**. Cathy carries something like an **absolute**, in the form of her commitment to Linton in spite of his faults, from the one house to the other. Earlier in the same chapter, Heathcliff's victory over the protective enclosures of the Grange is completed. He 'made no ceremony of knocking . . . [he] availed himself of the master's privilege to walk straight in'. Nelly muses on the changes time has brought: 'It was the same room into which he had been ushered, as a guest, eighteen years before: the same moon shone through the window; and the same autumn landscape lay outside' (both from p. 283). The author continues to sow into the narrative significant details relating to the two houses. For example, Heathcliff remarks of Catherine's portrait that 'I shall have that at home. Not because I need it, but –' (p. 285).

In this instance, then, the scene contains prominent reminders that the two houses are the two poles of *Wuthering Heights'* world; and that the underlying moral concepts which help us to interpret character and action are those of Lockwood's dreams. These two major elements of *Wuthering Heights* continue to live and develop throughout the scene. However, they each develop on their own account, and are not tied together. We could express this simultaneous but independent development of two central dualisms, by saying that the narrative is built out of 'living levels' rather than conforming to any single aesthetic structure. These 'levels' exist and respond continuously throughout the narrative, acting *as themselves*, and not 'shaped' to conform to each other at all. This is similar to the relationship between characters and the groups they superficially belong to. They live their own lives – irrespective of their origin as Earnshaw, or Linton, although that origin is never irrelevant.

This discussion has been an attempt to describe what kind of a novel *Wuthering Heights* is, as a 'whole': an exploration of its nature as a work of literature, and the reasons for its abiding effect. Much of our conclusion merely warns us that we will not find clear and single answers about *Wuthering Heights*: the implications of the fable and the way Emily Brontë has handled its narration are often paradoxical, and are open-ended. We should also beware of being judgemental or sentimental when analysing this text. It presents a series of issues in an ambivalent context. A reminder of Lockwood's dream is apposite: remember that Branderham's sermon is unjust, outrageous and oppressive, so Lockwood's judgement is correct. On the other hand, to endure and forgive so much, and then set a cruel limit, is irrational; and is a sin against understanding, imagination and generosity.

If we want higher authority for not finding definitive answers in the text, we need only look at Brontë's central fable. The novel *Wuthering Heights* concerns the arrival of Heathcliff at the Heights, and the consequences of that event. The central and most powerful relationship in the novel is that between Catherine and Heathcliff. We should remember that Brontë has left Heathcliff's origin as an absolute mystery – we have no information about it at all. Equally, the detailed time-plotting of the story gives prominence to the only gap – the few days of Nelly's absence when Mr Earnshaw sends her out of the house. The origin of the indissoluble bond between Heathcliff and Catherine is thus also left blank – surely a deliberate, carefully-defined omission on the part of the author.

How to Study *Wuthering Heights*

We have approached the text making use of a variety of analytical techniques, in Part 1 of this book. A summary of specific techniques in analysing prose appears at the end of Chapter 1, and these approaches are more or less repeated, as appropriate, in all the analyses we have carried out. The general point of this kind of study is all we need to recall now: observe **the way in which the passage is written** very closely, which involves an open-minded, detailed scrutiny. Whatever you *notice* about the writing is of interest, because it must be *noticeable*, i.e. a feature of the writing. Describe the feature and its effect as accurately as you can. Particular approaches to analysing imagery and symbols, in clear stages, are given at the end of Chapter 3.

In later chapters, we have omitted some of the more detailed stages because we were busy discussing the content of a passage. For example, in Chapter 5 we examined the final conversation between Heathcliff and Catherine. It is noticeable that Catherine's phrases at the start of that extract, when she imagines Heathcliff forgetting her, have a dying cadence. She says 'I loved her long ago' and 'but it is past'. This speech-rhythm conveys the passing of time, and the passing away of all things. It is in strong contrast to Heathcliff's answer. His first three phrases lead up to powerful final words: 'yourself', 'devil' and 'dying'. This example serves as a reminder that detailed analysis remains rewarding: even when we are in pursuit of abstract ideas, we should not forget that they are created in the texture of the writing.

Two other techniques that have been widely used in Part 1 deserve a mention.

Formulating your ideas as questions to ask of the text

Each of the chapters in Part 1 has taken a particular aspect of *Wuthering Heights* as its focus, so we have approached our extracts for analysis with a particular subject in mind. In this connection, it is helpful to turn a subject into question form. So, an interest in imagery becomes, simply, the question: *What images are there in this passage?* Follow up your questions with supplementary questions. In the case of imagery, you might ask: *Do the images I have found have anything in common?* As you study, you will find that formulating leading questions about the text becomes a natural habit, you will do it almost without thinking. The clearer and more practical your questions, the easier and more purposeful your studying will be.

Using summaries

The text is filled with details, including descriptions of people and settings, dialogue, and the narrative of exciting events. It is often helpful to make a concise summary, describing a complex part of the text as briefly as possible. This can bring out the underlying truths about what is happening; or help us to highlight and define important questions to ask. For example, when we are reading Heathcliff's speech from pages 285–8, we are likely to be caught up in the action. Heathcliff conveys his desperate, suicidal frenzy as he digs down towards Catherine's grave. His sensations veer wildly between extremes and soon he is running back to Wuthering Heights. When studying this extract, we summarised the story in simple terms: 'as he is breaking open the coffin, he clearly wishes to die then and there: "I wish they may shovel in the earth over us both!" But he turns, re-fills the grave and goes home.' This short summary highlights the obvious question: *Why* does Heathcliff change his mind at this point? The summary, then, sends us back to the passage with a clear investigative purpose: to find an answer to our question.

Studying the 'Structure' and 'Themes' of *Wuthering Heights*

In Chapters 4 and 5, we found that isolating a 'theme', or looking for a component in the 'structure' of *Wuthering Heights*, is a peculiarly difficult task. Emily Brontë's novel is one of a small number of works where the effect of the 'whole' is powerful, and dazzling; but the work itself resists analysis to an unusual degree. Shakespeare's *Hamlet* and Coleridge's *The Ancient Mariner* are similar to *Wuthering Heights* in this respect.

When studying these texts, there is a danger of gross distortion if we take a single 'theme' or structural component out from the whole work, and examine it in isolation. To put this another way, the more we try to break the work down into parts, the more we are conscious of falsifying its meaning: the more we are led to make statements about it that, when viewed in the perspective of the novel as a whole, are ridiculous. With *Wuthering Heights*, then, it is important to reach an understanding of underlying concepts. These are very broad. Notice, for example, our principle of the **absolute**. This means anything – an idea, action, desire, ideal, word, or any other element of the text – that implies totality and is beyond measurement or change. So the 'absolute' is a very broad abstract concept that can be widely and variously applied.

When you have identified a broad concept like this, it will help you to remain on a reasonable track when you look at more concrete 'themes' in the text. However, *Wuthering Heights* must still be treated with respect. Even the underlying concepts of this novel are handled ambivalently by the author, and we should guard against using them in a simplistic way, as clubs to batter the characters with, or masks for our approval and disapproval of what happens in the story.

Another way of expressing the resistance to piecemeal analysis that is so strong in *Wuthering Heights*, refers back to our observation about 'unity'. In this novel there is a very strong coherence between all the parts, and everything contributes to the one absorbing fable: Heathcliff's arrival at the Heights and its consequences. Aristotle wrote that 'unity' exists in a work where 'the events of which it is made up must be so plotted that if any of these elements is moved or removed the whole is altered and upset'. The 'unity' of *Wuthering Heights* is so strong, that our attempt to remove any part gives us the uncomfortable impression of 'altering' or 'upsetting' the whole.

PART 2

THE CONTEXT
AND THE CRITICS

7

Emily Brontë's Life and Works

Emily Brontë's Life

We will begin with a plain account of Emily Brontë's life. We will then look at the controversies which have raged between her biographers, who interpret the bare facts in such different ways. Different biographies sometimes read as if they are the lives of different people, not one woman, but we will be careful to make limited, objective statements about Emily in our initial account.

Emily Brontë was born in July, 1818. Her father, the Reverend Patrick Brontë, was the clergyman of Thornton, near Bradford. He was the son of an Irish peasant who was lucky enough to be sponsored to go to Cambridge University, take a degree, and enter holy orders. On the way, he changed his name from Brunty to the new spelling 'Brontë', and married a Miss Maria Branwell of Penzance. Emily Brontë was their fifth child. Three daughters were born first: Maria and Elizabeth in 1813 and 1815 respectively, and Charlotte in 1816. The only boy, Branwell, came next in 1817, a year before Emily's birth. The fifth daughter and last child, Anne, was born in 1820. When Anne was about three months old Patrick Brontë was appointed to Haworth, a small town near Keighley in Yorkshire, and the family moved into the Parsonage there. Soon after their arrival, Mrs Brontë became ill, and in September 1821 she died.

Mrs Brontë's sister, Elizabeth Branwell, had been nursing Mrs Brontë before her death and agreed to stay on, helping to run the household and care for the children. She remained with the family until her death twenty-one years later. 'Aunt Branwell' ran the house and instructed her nieces in domestic duties as well as giving them some basic education. In 1824 there was a change of servants, and a widow called Tabitha (Tabby) Aykroyd became the main family servant. She is reported to have been a warm, down-to-earth person who provided the children with friendship and affection. She remained with them and served them until after Emily's death, except for a short time when she broke her leg, when the Brontë daughters insisted on taking on her work and nursing her themselves rather than send her away.

Three of Patrick Brontë's children died before Emily. Maria died in May 1825 while at school at Cowan Bridge; Elizabeth became ill while at Cowan Bridge School, and died soon after being returned home, a month later. They were eleven and ten years old respectively, and Emily – who had been at the school with her three older sisters – was still only six. Emily's brother Branwell died in September 1848, only two months before her own death. Aunt Branwell had died six years earlier, in 1842.

All of the children spent periods of time away from Haworth, either attending schools or attempting to earn their livings; and all of them except Maria, who died while still away at school on her first absence from home, returned between spells of education or work, and lived for periods of time at home in the Parsonage. Emily spent less time away than any of her three surviving siblings. She spent about seven months at Cowan Bridge School with Charlotte, Elizabeth and Maria, when she was six. In 1835, on the day before her seventeenth birthday, Emily went with Charlotte to Miss Wooler's school at Roe Head. She was unhappy and became ill, and returned to Haworth less than three months later. In September 1838, when she was twenty years old, Emily went as a teacher to Miss Patchett's school at Law Hill. The exact dates of her time there are not known, but after about six months she again became ill, and by March 1839 she was back at Haworth Parsonage. Finally, Emily went to Mme Heger's school in Brussels, with Charlotte, and studied there between February and November 1842. She and Charlotte returned from Brussels on hearing the news of Aunt Branwell's illness and death. Emily did not leave Haworth after returning from Brussels.

All of Emily's times away from home were meant to last, then; yet none of them did. Death in her family called her home twice, her own illness sent her home on the other two occasions, and none of her absences lasted longer than a few months. Charlotte, Branwell and Anne all left home for much longer periods than Emily. The longest continuous employment any of them enjoyed was Anne's job as governess with a family called Robinson at Thorp Green, near York. Anne remained in this post for five years, between 1840 and 1845. Branwell was tutor to the son of the same family for three years, from 1842 until 1845, when he was dismissed in some form of scandal. Charlotte had gone to Miss Wooler's school twice – first as a pupil and then as a teacher – and she also returned to Brussels for a second year, in 1842, as a pupil, but with some teaching duties.

These are the facts bounding Emily Brontë's life. There are a number of other 'facts' which seem to tempt her biographers into exciting explanations, but which can still be recounted in more-or-less objective terms. The Brontë children created imaginary worlds together, and wrote copious histories, 'books', magazines, newspapers and poetry adding imagined details to their imagined worlds. These worlds began as 'Glasstown' and 'Angria', a fantasy world shared between all four siblings. At some point Emily and Anne ceased contributing to the world of 'Angria', and created their own different fantasy, calling their land 'Gondal'; while Branwell and Charlotte continued to elaborate 'Angria'. A great deal of material from the 'Glasstown' and 'Angria' writing survives, but hardly anything survives of the world of 'Gondal' except for some hearsay names and other details, Emily's poems and Anne's poems. It is clear that a great deal of prose was also written about 'Gondal', but this has been lost.

Emily kept pets and loved them. In biographies of her we hear about two pet geese, Victoria and Adelaide, a hawk named Hero whom Emily found wounded, brought home and nursed back to health, a cat called Black Tom, and Emily's dogs, Grasper, and later, Keeper. We also hear that Emily was angry with Charlotte on some important occasions. Most notably, Emily was furious with her sister for reading her poems without her permission (1845), and for revealing her existence to the publishers of *Jane Eyre* (1848). Of the three writing sisters, Emily was the most insistent on keeping her identity secret. When Emily became ill following Branwell's death, in the late autumn of 1848, she refused any medicine and refused to see a doctor until the last day of her life. She also increasingly failed to eat, becoming extremely thin and 'emaciated' before she died.

Emily's brother Branwell suffered a series of disappointments and disgraces. He tried several different ways to make a name for himself, as poet, painter and novelist, but failed in all of them. His attempts to earn a living also ended in failure: he was dismissed from his job as a railway clerk, accused of embezzlement; and his stint as tutor for the Robinsons of Thorp Green ended in scandal. He was dismissed in disgrace, and he claimed that his love affair with his employer's wife was the reason for this. Branwell spent the final three years of his life at the Parsonage in Haworth. He was repeatedly summonsed for debt, and he drank and used opium with increasing regularity and in increasing volumes.

Emily's father, the Reverend Patrick, became almost completely blind until he had a cataract operation in 1846, which restored his sight. Emily's sister Charlotte was the prime mover in trying to have the sisters' writings published. This effort began in earnest when she read Emily's poems, which, as we know, roused Emily to fury. Charlotte organised for *Poems* by Currer, Ellis and Acton Bell (pseudonyms for Charlotte, Emily and Anne Brontë) to be published at their own expense, in 1846; and was the driving and organising force behind sending their three novels to publishers. *Wuthering Heights* was published in December 1847.

Emily's appearance struck many observers as odd. She was tall and angular in figure, and she paid no attention to fashion, wearing simple dresses in the styles that had been prevalent when she was a child. Emily said that she liked to wear clothes giving her physical freedom. She was physically brave: on one occasion, she separated fighting dogs in the middle of the village. In this incident she was bitten by a rabid dog. Emily immediately walked into the Parsonage kitchen where Tabby was pressing clothes, and picking up the hot iron, cauterised her own wounded arm. Several accounts of Emily also tell us that she did not make conversation: she said little, and some of those who have described her thought her sulky or rude.

At this point we face a number of issues which cannot be treated objectively, because there is not enough evidence to decide between conflicting interpretations. Was Aunt Branwell stern but fair, and respected by her nieces; or was she cold, withdrawn and bad-tempered? Was Patrick Brontë a cold, distant father who took no interest in his children and brooded alone in his study, isolated from the people of Haworth; or was he a man of liberal beliefs, who was with his children when his duties allowed, and busily involved with local affairs and the surrounding community? Was Branwell a talentless wastrel, a self-pitying wreck who was a parasite in his family's home; or was he a man of great talent, tragically ignored? Was Charlotte selfish and bossy, or sensitive and devoted to her siblings? Was Anne a characterless, submissive girl, or a strong intellect with firm and original beliefs of her own? Was Emily closer and more tolerant with Branwell than any other member of the family, or did she simply ignore him more easily than others did? Was she considerate, kind and affectionate, or daydreaming in her own fantasies most of the time, with little thought to spare for others? Finally, was Emily wild, misanthropic, anorexic, sensitive, self-obsessed, affectionate, hostile, demanding, considerate, self-sacrificing, atheist, superstitious, deluded, suicidal?

All of these 'characters' for Emily and her family, and the questions they pose, are drawn from reading some of the many Brontë biographies you can find in libraries and bookshops. We cannot decide these questions, as the evidence about the Brontës that survives is either external (for example, records of community meetings and church functions Patrick Brontë attended), anecdotal (for example, the recollections of Ellen Nussey, Charlotte's friend from 1831 until the end of her life, who has left her impressions of the Brontës, having stayed at Haworth Parsonage with them several times), or written evidence in the form of diaries and letters, very few of which were written by Emily. So, it is easy to know what Emily did, but difficult to know what she thought and felt. The external evidence records Patrick Brontë's opinions on the social and religious issues of his day, but there is almost none relating to Emily. It is easy to know what other people thought about Emily, even down to descriptions of her appearance and dress, but we have no reliable evidence about what Emily thought of the people around her. Finally, it is easy to read the story of the family, its crises, personalities and vicissitudes, as told by Charlotte in her many letters; it is easy to gather Charlotte's opinions on all sorts of matters, including literary subjects, from her assiduous correspondence with her publishers; and it is easy to savour Branwell's views about the world, Haworth, art and literature, from the many notes, letters and writings he left behind. However, these are Charlotte's and Branwell's views, not Emily's.

We will look at one controversy a little more closely, to show how differently the different biographers deal with Emily. The argument we take up concerns Emily's religious views.

Katherine Frank[1] tells us that Emily's 'peculiar faith was highly unorthodox'. She does not specify what this 'peculiar' faith was, but does bring forward further evidence that Emily was not a Christian in any conventional sense:

> Emily was the only Brontë daughter who was exempted from teaching Sunday school and who did not attend church regularly. And then we have Emily's own verdict on conventional religions in a poem written some years later:

> Vain are the thousand creeds
> That move men's hearts, unutterably vain,
> Worthless as withered weeds
> Or idlest froth amid the boundless main.

Ms Frank then reminds us that in *Wuthering Heights* Joseph's Calvinism 'reduces him to a grotesque caricature', Branderham is 'mocked' for his 'interminable hellfire sermonizing', and the village church falls into disuse and ruin in the course of the novel. She concludes: 'Growing up in the isolated parsonage of an evangelical clergyman, Emily nevertheless remained immune to conventional religious doctrine along with so much else in her environment' (all

---

[1] *Emily Brontë: A Chainless Soul* (London, 1990; page references are to the Penguin edition, 1992).

quotations are from Frank, *op. cit.*, p. 109). Katherine Frank, then, suggests that Emily rejected Christianity.

Juliet Barker[2] disagrees. She writes that Emily's 'misanthropy – and her lack of conventional religious faith – have been vastly overstated by her biographers', and quotes one of the essays Emily wrote in French for her teacher in Brussels, M. Heger. At the end of a composition on the subject of a caterpillar, Emily wrote:

> The created should not judge his Creator, here is a symbol of the world to come. Just as the ugly caterpillar is the origin of the splendid butterfly, so this world is the embryo of a new heaven and a new earth whose poorest beauty will infinitely exceed mortal imagination; and when you see the magnificent outcome of what seems so humble to you now, you will despise your blind presumption in accusing Omniscience for not destroying nature in its infancy.[3]

Juliet Barker's comment is that 'This could hardly be a more eloquent statement of Christian belief' (quotations from *The Brontës* are from pp. 388–9).

A third view is expounded by Thomas John Winnifrith,[4] who offers another quotation from a Brussels essay Emily wrote for Heger:

> God is the God of justice and mercy; then, assuredly, each pain that he inflicts on his creatures, be they human or animal, rational or irrational, each suffering of our unhappy nature is only a seed for that divine harvest which will be gathered . . .[5]

Winnifrith suggests that Emily held a doctrine of 'redemption' through suffering, and identifies three axioms in her belief: '(1) Hell

---

[2] *The Brontës* (London, 1994; page references are to the Phoenix edition, 1995).

[3] Emily Brontë, '*Le Papillon*', 11 August 1842, translated in the transactions of the Brontë Society.

[4] 'Brontë's Religion', from *Critical Essays on Emily Brontë*, ed. Thomas John Winnifrith (New York, 1997).

[5] Quoted by Winnifrith from Emily Brontë, *Five Essays Written in French*, trans. L. W. Nagel (Austin: University of Texas Press, 1955).

exists only on earth, and no souls suffer torment after death. (2) A soul that has suffered sufficiently on earth attains its heaven. (3) A soul that has not suffered is in limbo for a time, but is redeemed by others' sufferings if not by its own, after enduring the *poena damni*, deprivation of the desired heaven' (Winnifrith, *op. cit.*, pp. 8–9). Winnifrith further suggests that Catherine and Heathcliff are united after death, having suffered enough in life to have earned both their own and each others' 'redemption'; but that their 'heaven' is not a conventional one ('For Catherine and Heathcliff to be united would be heaven, even if it were not a tranquil heaven', ibid., p. 15), and may exist on earth (he refers to the boy's story of seeing the couple on the moors, at the end of the novel).

A brief discussion calls all three of these theories into question. First, Katherine Frank is right to say that Emily's religion was not conventional; but she fails to allow the possibility of an individual faith. She argues that, since conventional religion is criticised in *Wuthering Heights*, and 'creeds' are dismissed in the poem, Emily had no faith. However, Katherine Frank seems to be superficial in dismissing Joseph (he is 'grotesque', but his judgements often express ironic truths); and she has completely missed the point of Jabes Branderham's sermon, which is 'mocked' by the shallow Lockwood, not the author. Her argument is entirely founded on the verse beginning 'Vain are the thousand creeds', from the final poem in a notebook of non-Gondal poems that Emily transcribed in February 1844. In the context, it is ludicrous to interpret this single stanza so literally. Emily writes 'I see Heaven's glories shine / And Faith shines equal' in the first stanza, and in the second she describes 'God within my breast / Almightly ever-present Deity / Life'.[6] It is obvious that the 'creeds' are 'vain' because there are a 'thousand' of them; while the poem asserts a strong faith in a single, infinite deity. The

---

[6] Emily Brontë, *The Complete Poems of Emily Jane Brontë*, ed. C. W. Hatfield (New York, 1941), poem no. A31, p. 243.

poet is unconventional, since God is placed 'within my breast' and associated with 'Life', but there is no rejection of faith in the poem. Remember, however, that Emily has left us a very small amount of evidence. Katherine Frank seems to be wrong about the poem, but that does not mean Emily Brontë was a Christian. This is only one poem, representing one moment in her life, and her beliefs may well have changed and fluctuated at other times, so one poem is not evidence of what she believed when she wrote *Wuthering Heights*.

Another reason for not jumping to conclusions is this: we said there is no *rejection* of faith in the poem, but it is also true to say there is no clear *assertion* of faith either. The terms in which Emily Brontë describes God are ambiguous: perhaps she believes in 'Life' and the 'heart', and has no specifically *religious* beliefs? So, Ms Frank's conclusions are not justified, but we cannot come to different conclusions either.

The same kind of objections can be raised against Juliet Barker's views. Her argument relies on the essay about the Caterpillar. Emily's words are ambiguous here as well. She writes of 'the world to come', 'new heaven and new earth', and 'Omniscience'. We can agree that this extract implies some sort of belief, but it is not at all clear what sort of belief. The words 'new heaven and new earth' may, for example, echo *Antony and Cleopatra*, in which case the paradise is one created from romantic passion.[7] Our conclusions must be that Juliet Barker is wrong to read this extract as an 'eloquent statement of Christian belief'; that this essay, in any case, may represent only a temporary state of mind in Emily; that it was written for a devout Catholic teacher at the Pensionnat Heger in Brussels, in a foreign language that Emily did not yet know well – in short, we cannot draw wider conclusions from such evidence.

Finally, we come to Winnifrith. His essay is largely an attempt to point to some consistent doctrine in *Wuthering Heights*, so by and large he is engaged in literary criticism rather than biography. He

---

[7] Shakespeare, *Antony and Cleopatra*, I. i, l.17. Cleopatra imperiously says that she will set a limit on Antony's love, and he replies that this will entail finding a 'new heaven, new earth' (since, by implication, the limit of his love cannot be found in this world or its conventional heaven).

points out that Emily portrays suffering and some form of 'redemption' as inextricably linked, and he mentions in passing that there is potential for 'masochism' in her views, as far as they are revealed in the novel. However, Winnifrith is not clear about Brontë's actual beliefs: at the end of his essay, he shies away from plain statements, saying only that Emily's theology was more radical than that of her sisters. As literary criticism, this is reasonable; but we can object to his extract from a Brussels essay, just as we objected to the use Juliet Barker makes of a similar source. Indeed, the point is rather underlined: here are two extracts from Brussels essays, which lead to different conclusions. Therefore, we should not draw firm conclusions about Emily Brontë's beliefs, on such evidence.

Emily Brontë's life, then, frustrates the biographer. She is one of a small number of enigmatic artists who did not reveal their personal feelings and experiences to posterity. However much historical detail is assembled *around* Emily, and however imaginatively the biographers speculate about her, she herself remains an empty, unknown space in the middle of all the words. She shares this quality with Shakespeare, and it is ironic that such enigmatic figures are the very ones which have generated an excess of biographical writing, as well as alternative theories about the authorship of their works. In Emily's case, for example, one theory is that *Wuthering Heights* is really the work of Branwell.

Brontë's enigmatic life is equally tempting when we consider elements of *Wuthering Heights* in relation to her history – but we must be wary of such suggestiveness. For example, Katherine Frank's theory that Emily was an anorexic, a 'hunger artist', and that this gave her unusual insight into the light-headed moods she portrays in Catherine, and later in Heathcliff, is based on tenuous evidence. Another tempting idea is that Isabella Linton's desperate, dependent – even masochistic – passion for Heathcliff, is drawn from life. Emily's sister Charlotte was hopelessly in love with their Belgian teacher, M. Heger, and her letters to him are as painfully vulnerable as Isabella becomes. However, we must soberly remember the lack of evidence: we do not know whether Charlotte ever told Emily about her passion, or whether it remained her own secret.

For the literary critic, this absence of biographical authority is liberating. Whatever we need to know about Emily Brontë will be found in her works, and there is only one comment worth making with regard to her life: for a vicar's daughter who lived in isolated Haworth at the start of Victorian times, and who only rarely and briefly left home, Emily Brontë was quite extraordinary.

Emily Brontë's Works

There is evidence that Emily was working on a second novel, and may have completed it, before her death. Nobody knows what happened to the manuscript (some biographers guess that the content was even more unconventional than that of *Wuthering Heights*, and that Charlotte destroyed it, for that reason, after her sister's death). At any event, this second novel has been lost. Emily Brontë's works therefore consist of *Wuthering Heights* and her poems. It was Emily's poems that triggered the final, successful enterprise towards publication for the three Brontë sisters.

Charlotte read Emily's poems in October 1845. She was deeply impressed by them, and filled with hope that the world would appreciate Emily's talent. The three sisters agreed to put together a selection of poems by all three of them, and decided on their pseudonyms of Currer, Ellis and Acton Bell. Their joint volume, containing 21 of Emily's poems, was published at their own expense in 1846. The sisters were already at work on their novels by that time, however. Apparently they wrote together around the kitchen table at Haworth Parsonage, in the late evening and into the night, after their father had retired to bed: Charlotte writing *The Professor*, Emily *Wuthering Heights*, and Anne writing *Agnes Grey*. Apparently also, they continually read passages from their novels to each other, and discussed the progress of each others' manuscripts. It is not clear whether *Wuthering Heights* had been begun even before the joint writing venture started, or whether parts of it were adapted from one or more pre-existing Gondal manuscripts, but the bulk of the writing must have been done between 1845 and the middle of 1846, when Charlotte wrote a letter asking for advice on publication of the novels, to Messrs. Aylott and Co., who had printed the *Poems*.

Wuthering Heights and *Agnes Grey* were accepted by Thomas Newby, but he required a returnable advance of fifty pounds from the authors. *The Professor*, Charlotte's first novel, was rejected. Ironically, Charlotte's sudden success with her second novel, *Jane Eyre*, published by Smith, Elder and Co. in October 1847 spurred the dilatory Thomas Newby to finally bring out *Wuthering Heights* and *Agnes Grey*. He clearly hoped to cash in on the sudden notoriety and success of the three 'Bells'.

The poems

The remainder of this chapter gives a very brief account of the poems. A reader will find more detailed accounts of Emily's poetry by following up suggestions in 'Further Reading' at the end of this book.

The bulk of Emily Brontë's poetry was written as part of the evolving saga of 'Gondal', the imagined country she developed with her sister Anne. There are many beautiful poems expressing a variety of moods and situations. However, in these works it is difficult to identify the author's own voice: they are dramatic works, in which the voice, and the feelings expressed, belong to one or another character from the Gondal saga. For example, poem no. 97 in the *Complete Poems* begins with an affecting contrast between grieving people and nature continuing its cycle of rebirth in Spring:

> From our evening fireside now,
> Merry laugh and cheerful tone,
> Smiling eye and cloudless brow,
> Mirth and music, all are flown;
>
> Yet the grass before the door
> Grows as green in April rain;
> And as blithely as of yore
> Larks have poured their day-long strain.
> (*The Complete Poems of Emily Jane Brontë*, p. 102)

However, the 'Gondal' story soon asserts itself, and the speaker,

'R. Gleneden', explains the background to the family's grief and loss. The picture of a silent family who remember joy and laughter, but feel none, is vividly evoked. Nature's fullness outside the house is equally strongly painted in clear, plain phrases. The rhyme is prominent but unforced. We can easily imagine this poem to depict the Brontë family, sitting stunned by grief following one or another family tragedy, or missing Branwell who had left to take up a career in London, or his post as tutor in Cumbria. However, the simple sincerity is deceptive. A quick glance at biographies reveals that the four siblings were all at home in the spring of 1839 when this poem was written, and most of them were relieved to be there. Reading the Gondal poems, then, is partly illuminating but partly puzzling: Emily's poetic voice is emotional and convincing, yet we always seem to be reading at the edges of a story we cannot understand – and we fail to identify the genesis of emotions that are powerfully conveyed.

In February 1844, Emily began to transcribe poems into two notebooks, one marked 'Gondal poems', and the other simply 'E.J.B. Transcribed February, 1844'. The second of these notebooks contains thirty-one poems which appear to be the direct, non-Gondal, output of Emily Brontë. These poems throw some light on themes which reappear in *Wuthering Heights*, and on the author's own beliefs and states of feeling. The poem marked 'A31' beginning 'No coward soul is mine' comes from this notebook, for example. This is the poem we discussed earlier, in which Katherine Frank mistakenly detects a rejection of religious faith.

We were wary of drawing firm conclusions from that poem. However, the poems do highlight themes that were both a part of Emily's own inner life, and that became a part of *Wuthering Heights*. First, several poems show that she was aware of turning away from society, and normal human experiences and concerns. The poem listed as A26,[8] to which we will return later, sets this peculiarity of her character as a question for which she seeks an explanation. She asks 'Reason' to say:

---

[8] *The Complete Poems of Emily Jane Brontë*, pp. 208–9.

> Why I have persevered to shun
> The common paths that others run.
> And on a strange road journeyed on
> Heedless alike of Wealth and Power –

In the poem listed as A7[9] Emily refers to herself as 'Thou lonely dreamer' and acknowledges the lack of human involvement in her heart, writing that 'passion may not fire thee' while the power of 'Nature' can. Nature itself is the speaker of this poem, and holds absolute power over the poet:

> I know my mighty sway,
> I know my magic power
> To drive thy griefs away.

Nature declares that Emily has a rare and different heart, for 'Few hearts to mortals given / On earth so wildly pine', and concludes by urging her to join nature itself and turn away from all human concerns ('Since nought beside can bless thee'). In 'The Night-Wind', the intimate, even seductive relationship between Emily and nature is pitted against her human thoughts and feelings. The wind seems to be speaking to the poet, tempting her to enter its world of 'dream' and 'spirit'. She tries to resist, claiming that the music of the wind has no 'power to reach my mind' and begging it to 'leave my human feelings / In their own course to flow'. However, the conclusion of this poem gives the 'night-wind' the last word. Its temptation does not go away, but instead:

> Its kiss grew warmer still –
> 'O come,' it sighed so sweetly,
> 'I'll win thee 'gainst thy will.'

The final stanza admonishes the poet: she is wasting her time on 'human' feelings, and should join the loving relationship with

---

[9] Ibid., pp. 146–7.

nature. After she is dead there will be plenty of time for nature to 'mourn' her, and for her 'to be alone'. So, nature wins in this conflict: it offers a close, beguiling relationship including 'dreams', while the sum total of Emily's human thoughts and feelings amounts to the three words 'to be alone'.

Many poems express this passionate, even personal, relationship with nature and the earth. The wind, the stars, the moon, the sky are all personified, and the poet addresses them, or they address the poet, in the language of a lover. We have heard the seductive voice of the wind in the poem numbered A6. Emily addressed the stars, in poem A28:[10]

> All through the night, your glorious eyes
> Were gazing down in mine,
> And with a full heart's thankful sighs
> I blessed that watch divine!

Her metaphors for this relationship with natural things, are persistently sensual. Notice that the stars do not gaze down 'on' or 'at' her eyes, but intimately 'in' them. Later, she 'drank your beams', and 'one sweet influence, near and far, / Thrilled through and proved us one', so that after sunrise the poet wishes to revive the night and 'see / Your worlds of solemn light, again / Throb with my heart and me!' There is, then, a strong sensuality, and in many places a self-evident metaphor of sexual passion, in Emily Brontë's response to nature.

Some of the most powerful emotions expressed in the poems, however, are aroused by imagination, 'fancy', or Emily's 'world within'. This seems to be a combination of her strong sensual bond with nature, and the overmastering desire she expresses to enter into 'visions' and 'dreams', and leads her to yearn for her own death. In the poetry, her future death is depicted as simultaneously joining with nature, and being set free from physical constraints into a world of visions. Clearly, there is an escapist element in her desire to live in fantasy. In poem A26 she finds that her visions make her

---

[10] Ibid., pp. 225–6.

numb to the suffering of everyday life ('Deadening me to real cares')
and give her power to escape disappointment:

> And am I wrong to worship where
> Faith cannot doubt nor Hope despair
> Since my own soul can grant my prayer?

A poem written while she was a teacher at Law Hill school in
1838 tells of a brief break between her duties, when she could allow
her mind to enjoy her 'dream'-life. In the end, and too soon, 'truth
has banished fancy's power' when duty calls again, and she concludes
sadly:

> Even as I stood with raptured eye
> Absorbed in bliss so deep and dear
> My hour of rest had fleeted by
> And given me back to weary care.[11]

'Raptured' and 'bliss' convey the intensity with which Emily lived
these fantasies. In A9[12] the poet describes her enraptured state,
noting her 'altered cheek', 'kindled gaze', and 'the words thou scarce
dost speak', to show how 'wildly fancy plays'. The growth of her
belief in the indefinable reality, and endurance, of her visionary
world, can be traced in poem A25, To Imagination.[13] Its escapist
genesis is again frankly stated: 'So hopeless is the world without, /
The world within I doubly prize'; however, as the poem develops,
the despair of objective reality does not matter any more, 'If but
within our bosom's bound / We hold a bright unsullied sky'.
Eventually, the vision-world is credited with a real existence, associated in some way with a victory over death, or a wonderful transformation through death:

> And call a lovelier life from death,

---

[11] Ibid., pp. 93–5.
[12] Ibid., p. 165.
[13] Ibid., pp. 205–6.

And whisper with a voice divine
Of real worlds as bright as thine.

This theme gains its strongest expression in poems which combine a desire for death with the yearning towards a visionary world. One such imagines the liberated soul rising from its 'prison' body. Notice, however, that this is no conventional Christian poem, since Emily Brontë contrasts mortal life, and life, in such a way that we take her final reference to freedom in 'the skies' literally, not as a figure for any 'heaven':

A principle of life, intense,
Lost to mortality.

Thus truly when that breast is cold
Thy prisoned soul shall rise,
The dungeon mingle with the mould –
The captive with the skies.[14]

Another, poem A8,[15] expresses a powerful desire for liberty through both life and death, and the need for the inner self to be free in all circumstances:

Yes, as my swift days near their goal
'Tis all that I implore –
Through life and death, a chainless soul
With courage to endure!

This combination of desires for death, liberty and imagination, seems to be revived in Catherine's and Heathcliff's stories, in *Wuthering Heights*. Perhaps also, the poet who so consciously chose fantasy above reality, is equally able to portray both the untruth, and the convincing realism to her, of Catherine's hallucinations during her delirium.

---

[14] Ibid., poem A9, p. 165.
[15] Ibid., p. 163.

8

The Place of *Wuthering Heights* in English Literature

Wuthering Heights is an extraordinary novel, the individual creation of a writer working in comparative isolation. Emily Brontë read widely, and despite her lack of continuing formal education, she was familiar with classical texts, French and German. However, she was emphatically outside the literary world of early Victorian times: she took no notice of its preferences and opinions, nor did she observe the developing conventions of the novel form. So, although we can trace many influences on *Wuthering Heights*, they are widely spaced in time and drawn together idiosyncratically in this one work.

Many critics have remarked that the names, and even the topography of *Wuthering Heights* show the influence of Sir Walter Scott's novels, which Emily admired and read repeatedly. So, Scott's Thorncliff may have suggested the name for Heathcliff, his Rashleigh Osbaldistone from *Rob Roy* shows similar characteristics, and so on. There are also a number of studies that trace similarities between *Wuthering Heights* and contemporary genres in the novel form. For example, Lyn Pykett suggests that the novel moves between Gothic/romantic form – which predominates in the older generation of Catherine, Heathcliff and Edgar – and the emerging genre of Victorian domestic fiction, so that Brontë's novel moves, say, between Mary Shelley and Dickens and mixes these genres. Pykett suggests that *Wuthering Heights* tells the story of a change in perception of families, and particularly explores the

194

subordinate position of women through these cultural and literary changes.[1]

In this chapter we will look farther afield, focusing on some of the features of *Wuthering Heights* that connect it with other works, more distant than those of Walter Scott. We must remember, however, that Emily Brontë's novel is unique. Whatever similarities we trace between this text and others, and whatever influences we theorise about or detect, are only partial contributions. None of them define this novel. We begin with a discussion of the 'gothic' elements in *Wuthering Heights*.

The 'Gothic' in *Wuthering Heights*

Ghosts, the opening of graves, visions and decaying, overgrown churchyards; peasants and gentry, horror, violence, obsession, and the dramatic backdrop of Penistone Craggs; a dark stranger of mysterious origin, a powerful demon-like character: all of these features are found in *Wuthering Heights*. They can also be found in the 'gothic' novels of Mrs Radcliffe and others, which were so popular in the late eighteenth and early nineteenth centuries, as well as in Mary Shelley's classic of the genre, *Frankenstein*, published in 1818, the year of Emily Brontë's birth.

Many of the elements of Brontë's novel are indeed 'gothic', then. However, her treatment of these elements differs from that of her predecessors. Here is an extract from *The Monk*, by Matthew Lewis, a gothic novel which was published in 1795. In this passage Ambrosio has conjured the devil:

> 'He comes!' exclaimed Matilda in a joyful accent.
> Ambrosio started, and expected the Daemon with terror. What was his surprize, when the Thunder ceasing to roll, a full strain of melodious Music sounded in the air. At the same time the cloud dispersed, and He beheld a Figure more beautiful than Fancy's pencil ever drew. It was a Youth seemingly scarce eighteen, the perfection of

---

[1] Lyn Pykett, *Emily Brontë* (Basingstoke and London, 1989). See particularly pp. 137–8.

whose form and face was unrivalled. He was perfectly naked: A bright
Star sparkled upon his fore-head; Two crimson wings extended themselves from his shoulders; and his silken locks were confined by a
band of many-coloured fires, which played around his head, formed
themselves into a variety of figures, and shone with a brilliance far
surpassing that of precious Stones.

(Matthew Lewis, *The Monk*[2])

This is excitingly written, and has a powerful dramatic effect in
context, since the devil's beauty is so unexpected. Matthew Lewis
uses comparisons with superlatives to help him evoke the supernatural; so, the devil is 'more beautiful, than Fancy's pencil ever drew',
and his fires shine 'with a brilliance far surpassing that of precious
Stones'. However, in Lewis's text, the writer uses all his efforts to
convince us that the supernatural figure really did appear: the devil is
a literal part of the story, and Ambrosio, the human character, really
did meet him – it was no illusion. Looking back to our analysis of
Heathcliff's and Catherine's hallucinations, in Chapter 2, we
remember that Emily Brontë is careful to remain uncommitted in
her attitude to their visions. In *Wuthering Heights*, then, these
'gothic' features are ambiguously entwined with questions of psychology and obsession: they typically occur at moments of violent
anxiety, or when characters are in a heightened state of emotion.
Often (as with Catherine's delirium and Heathcliff's haunting), the
visions are associated with the effects of starvation or illness. We
remember that Heathcliff, not Emily Brontë, was convinced: 'as certainly as you perceive the approach to some substantial body in the
dark, though it cannot be discerned, so certainly I felt that Cathy
was there' (*Wuthering Heights*, p. 287). The phrase 'some substantial
body in the dark' is a fitting description for the shadowy, almost-
physical presence of embodied obsessions, desires and passionate
needs in *Wuthering Heights*.

Brontë's approach to the extraordinary is also different from that of
Mary Shelley. In *Frankenstein*, the protagonist is surrounded by the
paraphernalia of deep studies, and scientific achievement, in order to

---

[2] Matthew Lewis, *The Monk* (Oxford University Press, World's Classics, 1980), pp. 276–7.

convince us that he can succeed in animating the body of his monster, conferring life on a creature made in the laboratory: Shelley's technique is one much used by science-fiction writers today. Her main interest in creating the marvellous, however, is the opportunity it provides to explore moral issues. Any reader of the long debate Frankenstein and his creation engage in on the top of a glacier, will know that the rights and duties of creation, and the creator's obligations to his creature and society, are thoroughly explored. Emily Brontë, as we know, does not develop morality in connection with the 'marvellous' in her novel. The visions are raw, and not subjected to rational analysis. They are, as it were, pure emotion made physical, in the mind of the character who perceives them.

Emily Brontë included suggestions of the supernatural in *Wuthering Heights*, in a most ambiguous and modern manner. I would argue that her interest is different from that of the 'gothic' writers. Like the occasional, disturbing mention of 'ghosts' in E. M. Forster's *A Passage to India*, the visions in *Wuthering Heights* suggest an opposition to the accepted priorities of life – as if Catherine's and Heathcliff's passions are elemental and suppressed, and can only 'live' through the power of subjective perceptions. So Brontë's supernatural is much more closely described as something which exists beyond the range of what conventional society can understand or tolerate. It does not seem to be something which exists outside nature, however: indeed, it could be argued that the 'visions' in *Wuthering Heights* are actually closer to nature than the conventional minds which cannot comprehend them, such as Edgar Linton's or Lockwood's. Brontë's 'gothic', then, harks forward to E. M. Forster, and perhaps even Camus or Kafka, rather than back to the 'gothic' writers of fifty years before.

'Modernist' Novels

Wuthering Heights is so unlike any other production of its own time that it invites comparison with novels of the twentieth century, when several writers set out to challenge or change the conventions of the genre.

In *Wuthering Heights*, the most prominent and lasting impression is made by the passionate emotions of Catherine and Heathcliff: if the story is 'about' anything, it is about this. Yet their love cuts across all the conventional elements of a novel's plot. Catherine does not marry Heathcliff, she marries Edgar Linton. Heathcliff marries Isabella Linton. In terms of the novel's plot, in fact, a 'love affair' between Catherine and Heathcliff never exists. Further, the second half of the novel follows the upbringing and courtship of Hareton and the younger Cathy. On the surface, this would seem to be a conventional courtship structure with the added theme of uniting two families and ending a feud. However, Heathcliff's unresolved passion continues to overshadow the text, and the novel's resolution focuses on Heathcliff's state of mind, and his death, eighteen years after the death of Catherine. We could say that, in *Wuthering Heights*, there is a level of life which does not cause or depend on the 'plot'; and this level is conveyed as of supreme interest and importance.

As a result, events and actions, the traditional stuff of novels, seem secondary. Some modern novelists have constructed their works to achieve a similar effect. In James Joyce's *A Portrait of the Artist as a Young Man*, for example, the hero, Stephen Dedalus, happens to see a young woman wading in the water. This is not an 'event' in the conventional sense: the young woman is a stranger, and never becomes a character. Stephen sees her, but does not approach and meet her. The incident is purely coincidence, something Stephen might have seen on any day of his life. However, Joyce creates this moment as a crucial turning-point in Stephen's development. To readers of the novel, this chance sight means a great deal more than many details of Stephen's literal life, which seem to occupy a vaguely sketched background in contrast to his vivid 'inner' life.

E. M. Forster, in *A Passage to India*, constructs his plot in such a way that the projected visit to the Marabar Caves dominates the first half of the novel, and something which is supposed to have happened there fuels the arrest and trial of Dr Aziz, which dominate the second half. However, Forster's text deliberately and resolutely refuses to clarify anything about the Marabar Caves:

. . . the visitor returns to Chandrapore uncertain whether he has had an interesting experience or a dull one or any experience at all. He finds it difficult to discuss the caves, or to keep them apart in his mind, for the pattern never varies, and no carving, not even a bees' nest or a bat, distinguishes one from another. Nothing, nothing attaches to them, and their reputation – for they have one – does not depend upon human speech.

(E. M. Forster, *A Passage to India*, Penguin, 1981, p. 138)

The event which is supposed to have taken place in one of the caves turns out to be equally indefinable. There is an accusation of rape and a sensational trial, but the final outcome is that even the 'rape' victim cannot say what happened: 'It's as if I ran my finger along that polished wall in the dark, and cannot get further. I am up against something, and so are you' (op. cit., p. 261). Forster, then, makes an elaborate construction of his novel, along conventional lines, but deliberately withholds the central information: the crisis occurs in a place which cannot be described, and consists of an event which is not an event. We can compare this unconventional subversion of a novel's traditional plot, to the persistent reticences of *Wuthering Heights*: the mystery of Heathcliff's origin which is copiously discussed but never explained; and the deliberate gap in Brontë's narrative, when the crucial bond between Catherine and Heathcliff is formed (see Chapter 4).

Another example of a radically revisionary plot is found in Virginia Woolf's *Mrs Dalloway* (1925). In this novel the traditional courtship fable, including a marriage-choice between two suitors, is relegated to the past and narrated in flashbacks, while a chance coincidence between two lives which barely intersect – those of Clarissa Dalloway and Septimus Warren Smith – dominates the actual narrative of the novel's present day. The effect is curiously similar to that of *Wuthering Heights*: Heathcliff's and Catherine's love relegates two courtships and marriages to a pale background, and in the second generation, another conventional courtship fable – that of young Cathy – also fails to dominate the centre of the novel's consciousness.

Our three examples – Joyce, Forster and Woolf – are chosen from among many modern novels which attack the idea that life can be conveyed by a narrative which highlights actions and events, and where motives are a matter of cause and effect. They are not close to *Wuthering Heights* in content or particular themes. However, they do share the quality that they subvert the conventional novel's plot, making it appear irrelevant and insufficient to depict the central concerns of life. In so doing, all of these works subvert the concept of life as a progress with a purpose: they focus our minds on perennial and fundamental questions of existence, rather than on the changeable circumstances of external, material facts.

Relating this to *Wuthering Heights*, we could say that for Catherine and Heathcliff, the underlying states of existence were states of separation from and unity with each other. These underlying states were the same when they were children, as at the end of Heathcliff's nearly forty years of life. The novel highlights these continuing, unchanging parameters of existence, rather than the many external events which occur during the lovers' lives.

Wuthering Heights and Tragedy

There are significant parallels between *Wuthering Heights* and Shakespearian tragedy. In our first chapter, we remarked on the dramatic features of Brontë's narrative, such as the many monologues which resemble stage soliloquies. Remember, for example, Heathcliff's two late monologues, or Catherine's account of her illness, where the listener, Nelly Dean, is treated almost as if she is not there while Catherine and Heathcliff reveal their inner experiences.

However, the resemblance consists of much more than features of dramatic 'form' in *Wuthering Heights*. Here are a few examples of close resemblance between moments in the novel, and similar moments in Shakespeare's tragedies. Heathcliff is a dark figure, 'a tall man dressed in dark clothes, with dark face and hair'. He is set apart from society by his mysterious origin and his outcast position. Many descriptions of Heathcliff's expression are given by Nelly and Isabella, which call to mind Hamlet's statement: 'But I have that within which passeth show; / These, but the trappings and the suits of woe' (*Hamlet*, I.ii. ll. 85–6). Heathcliff carries a cynical and destructive analysis of life within him which reminds us of Hamlet, also. We remember Catherine's belief in 'my' Heathcliff, the absolute and devoted lover she longs for: 'I shall love mine yet; and take him with me – he's in my soul' (p. 159), and this may remind us of Cleopatra's description of Antony, and her question to Dolabella:

> *Cleo.* Think you there was, or might be such a man
>   As this I dreamt of?
> *Dol.*   Gentle madam, no.
> *Cleo.* You lie up to the hearing of the gods.
>   (Shakespeare, *Antony and Cleopatra*, V. ii, ll. 93–5)

There are many other places where the moods and expressions of Catherine or Heathcliff call characters and events from the tragedies to mind.

When we consider the fable of *Wuthering Heights* as a whole, these correspondences become less surprising: there is a likeness between the central experience of the novel, and the tragic condition shown in Shakespeare's plays. It is difficult to pin down this similarity, but two brief discussions will set the comparison in context.

First, a major theme of Shakespearian tragedy is order and disorder. The tragic story shows a time when both social and moral 'order' is exposed as hollow and lacking in truth or justification. In this situation violent, destructive events take place. For example, in *King Lear* the hero abdicates, removing the authority for both social order in the kingdom, and patriarchal authority in his own family. The resulting chaos and civil conflicts reveal subversive truths, such as Lear's insights into justice:

> A man may see how this world goes, with no eyes. Look with thine ears: see how yond justice rails upon yond simple thief. Hark, in thine ear: change places; and, handy-dandy, which is the justice, which is the thief?
> (Shakespeare, *King Lear*, IV. vi, ll. 150–4)

Similarly, in *Macbeth*, the hero's attack on 'order' by assassinating his king and usurping the throne unleashes violent bloodshed throughout Scotland. In *Wuthering Heights*, we can argue that the introduction of Heathcliff the changeling into the 'order' of the Earnshaw family, and the district, brings about a multiple displacing of people from their allotted positions: Hindley is ousted when Heathcliff becomes Mr Earnshaw's favourite, and Heathcliff is subsequently degraded by Hindley. Catherine becomes Heathcliff's wild, outcast companion, but later acquires unnatural authority over Edgar and Isabella at the Grange, while Hareton is deprived of his birthright and brought up to ignorance and labour. Heathcliff then usurps the position of master at the Heights, supplanting Hindley in fact, as he originally supplanted him in his father's affections. During the reign of disorder, there is an accent on the failure of normal social structures, and on the unnatural. For example, the marriage between Catherine and Edgar becomes hollow, and is eclipsed by the subversive relationship between Catherine and Heathcliff; and the marriage between vigorous young Cathy and a dying, sick boy (Linton Heathcliff) is an unnatural mockery. In short, all that is real and powerful takes place outside the social order, which is reduced to impotence in the face of the tragic powers unleashed by Heathcliff's alien presence.

Many critics have remarked that the fruition of the ending, in the courtship and marriage of Cathy and Hareton, is insipid in comparison with the destructive power of Heathcliff's final acts. This is again reminiscent of Shakespearian tragedy, where the final scene shows a fragile restoration of 'order' (such as Edgar's half-reluctant assumption of responsibility at the end of *King Lear*, or Fortinbras's opportunistic takeover of Denmark at the end of *Hamlet*). The feeling a reader is left with when closing *Wuthering Heights* can be closely compared to the delicate cathartic mood at the end of one of these plays: there is a sense of relief, of emotions exhausted by the intensity of destructive passion, or 'purged'; and an awareness that the new start is shallow, overshadowed by the fundamental power and violence of the story that has now ended.

Secondly, in Shakespearian tragedy, the tragic hero is excluded from, or in fundamental opposition to his world. The story is of a battle between an individual and everything around him, and we are fascinated by the extent to which our sympathy with the individual draws us into a negative, 'anti-' world as we take sides with his honesty, and feel his pain, in conflict with injustice and hypocrisy. The tragic process thus reveals uncomfortable truths both about the external world, and in our own emotions; and it touches disturbing truths that we prefer not to think of in our daily lives. For example, Hamlet thinks about death continuously. We, on the other hand, occasionally remember that death is inevitable; but we are likely to dismiss this thought and get on with making the evening meal. We know that if we dwell on thoughts of death we will become morbid and depressed, and unable to pursue our ordinary lives.

In *Wuthering Heights*, Catherine and Heathcliff expose the reader to a comparable experience. We remember that their underlying desires lead to death, and recall the powerful speech in which Catherine conveys the shallow futility of her day-to-day life, in contrast to the power of her suicidal desire for union with Heathcliff beyond the grave:

> . . . the whole last seven years of my life grew a blank! I did not recall that they had been at all. [I was] . . . the wife of a stranger; an exile, and outcast, thenceforth, from what had been my world – You may fancy a glimpse of the abyss where I grovelled!
>
> (p. 124)

Wuthering Heights, then, has this in common with Shakespeare's tragedies: the power of tragic characters carries the audience/reader into an alternative, negative or 'anti-' world, which is made to seem more truthful, enduring and significant than the material details of ordinary life. These, by contrast, seem sham, shallow and worthless.

Wuthering Heights has the qualities of tragic drama. This achievement showed the novel form in a new light, for Brontë was the first novelist to show that it was possible to achieve this intensity of experience, and unity of symbolic theme, by means of a long prose narrative. The attempt to embody a tragic process in novel form was further taken up and developed by Thomas Hardy, towards the end of the nineteenth century.

Wuthering Heights and the Development of Setting

The very structured topography of *Wuthering Heights*, dominated by
two contrasted houses and contrasting landscapes, was discussed in
Chapter 4. Brontë's use of the setting confers significance upon the
landscape and nature, as we pointed out, so that each of the houses
and its ambience suggests a complete way of life, including habits,
atmosphere, weather, and attitudes. Brontë's descriptions of nature
call this symbolic significance to mind, so that she evokes a setting
which reflects the emotions and events of the story. At times, these
descriptions seem to pass beyond naturalism into something symbolic or 'impressionistic', so that the background becomes an active
participant in the novel. We remember, for example, that the furniture at Wuthering Heights includes chairs, 'one or two heavy black
ones lurking in the shade', and the background recedes vaguely into
nightmare with 'other dogs haunted other recesses' (p. 5). Later,
young Cathy describes her own and Linton's contrasting ideals in
terms of landscape:

> He said the pleasantest manner of spending a hot July day was lying
> from morning till evening on a bank of heath in the middle of the
> moors, with the bees humming dreamily about among the bloom,
> and the larks singing high up over head, and the blue sky, and bright
> sun shining steadily and cloudlessly. That was his most perfect idea of
> heaven's happiness – mine was rocking in a rustling green tree, with a
> west wind blowing, and bright, white clouds flitting rapidly above;
> and not only larks, but throstles, and blackbirds, and linnets, and
> cuckoos pouring out music on every side, and the moors seen at a dis-
> tance, broken into cool dusky dells; but close by great swells of long
> grass undulating in waves to the breeze; and woods and sounding
> water, and the whole world awake and wild with joy.
>
> (p. 245)

In this passage, Brontë paints two pictures of the landscape, and
every detail provides us with further insight into the two characters
reflected in these settings. 'Dreamily', 'high up', 'steadily' and 'cloud-
less' convey the stillness of Linton's ideal. The living movement in
Cathy's picture begins with 'rocking', and is further built up by
'rustling', 'blowing', 'flitting', 'pouring', 'swells', 'undulating',

'sounding' and 'wild'. Finally, the landscape's potential for subjective significance seems to provide an open-ended irony at the end of the novel. Lockwood is unwilling to acknowledge the continuing power of Catherine and Heathcliff's story, and this is subtly conveyed by description in the final paragraph of the novel:

> I lingered round them [the graves of Catherine, Edgar and Heathcliff], under that benign sky; watched the moths fluttering among the heath, and hare-bells; listened to the soft wind breathing through the grass; and wondered how anyone could ever imagine unquiet slumbers, for the sleepers in that quiet earth.

However, Lockwood himself has sensed the potential for further havoc and disturbance in his surroundings, only a paragraph earlier:

> . . . decay had made progress, even in seven months – many a window showed black gaps deprived of glass; and slates jutted off, here and there, beyond the right line of the roof, to be gradually worked off in coming autumn storms.
>
> (both quotations are from *Wuthering Heights*, p. 334)

It is clear that the weather and setting of *Wuthering Heights* are much more than an inanimate background. They are an ambiguous, changeable extension of the characters' perceptions and moods, with a significance of their own woven into the text.

This development of the setting into an active element in the story, is echoed in Dickens's later novels: the symbolic use of setting is fully exploited in his famous evocation of the marshes and the hulks around Pip's childhood home, and his use of the London docks and the river, in both *Great Expectations* (1860–1) and *Our Mutual Friend* (1864–5). Dickens's settings are filled with mood and attached to a symbolic significance; and his descriptions extend the sense of place to shadowy speculations about primitive, hidden processes which once took place there, or which continue to happen beneath the surface.[3] However, his evocations are still firmly rooted

---

[3] See, for example, the first two paragraphs of Chapter 46 of *Great Expectations*, which describes the docks with 'ooze and slime and other dregs' and 'rusty anchors blindly biting into the ground'.

in a detailed, representational description founded on convincing observation.

Thomas Hardy, on the other hand, took the technique further. At times the metaphorical elements of his settings overwhelm realism, and nature seems distorted: it behaves in a disturbing, surreal manner that is more metaphor than real. Here, for example, is a description of the barren Flintcomb-Ash, from *Tess of the D'Urbervilles*:

> After this season of congealed dampness came a spell of dry frost, when strange birds from behind the North Pole began to arrive silently on the upland of Flintcomb-Ash; gaunt spectral creatures with tragical eyes – eyes which had witnessed scenes of cataclysmal horror in inaccessible polar regions of a magnitude such as no human being had ever conceived, in curdling temperatures that no man could endure; which had beheld the crash of ice-bergs and the slide of snow-hills by the shooting light of the Aurora; been half blinded by the whirl of colossal storms and terraqueous distortions.
> (Hardy, *Tess of the D'Urbervilles*, Everyman, 1984, vol. 2, p. 129)

In this description, Hardy carries us beyond nature. That 'frost' should follow 'dampness' is believable, and the arrival of 'spectral' and 'gaunt' birds from the north is also natural. However, the hint of a surreal or supernatural metaphor enters with the nonsense-phrase 'from behind the North Pole', and soon we are involved in an alien landscape imagined through the eyes of these strange birds. This is no longer the bleak upland of Flintcomb-Ash, but a cold violent destruction which evokes Tess's futile misery: a place where 'ice-bergs' crash and even the 'shooting light of the Aurora' is weird. Finally, Hardy evokes 'terraqueous distortions', a kind of bulging and squeezing of the earth and oceans themselves, on a planetary scale.

It can be argued that such 'visionary' extension of the novelist's descriptive range is a development from Emily Brontë's characterisation of landscape, and the distortion of reality by emotion that we find in *Wuthering Heights*.

Concluding Discussion

We have not attempted to reach any systematic conclusion about the place of *Wuthering Heights* in the history of the English novel: we accepted from the outset that this is such an original and idiosyncratic text, that it stands outside any continuity in literary development. Rather, we have tried to show that *Wuthering Heights* draws on a variety of inspirations from further afield than its immediate precursors, and brings influences together into an unprecedented 'whole'; and we have suggested that Brontë's achievement had the effect of opening a wide range of new possibilities for the novel, that had not been imagined before it appeared. In short, the influences upon *Wuthering Heights* are unquantifiable, and its own influence is incalculable.

In particular, we have discussed this novel's likeness to works of literature which were predominantly in dramatic form. Emily Brontë's achievement was to treat tragedy in the Shakespearian manner, in a novel. It is difficult to define the effect of this achievement on succeeding authors. *Wuthering Heights* transcends the traditional view of the novel form as suiting a 'chronicle' or 'biography', in which we may expect a long picaresque narrative like Fielding's *Tom Jones*, or a voyage like Defoe's *Robinson Crusoe*. She also shows the novel subverting stories of courtship and romance, such as the 'marriage'-tales of Jane Austen, and stories of sensational horror like the 'gothic' productions of Mrs Radcliffe, or Mary Shelley's *Frankenstein*.

All this is only to say that *Wuthering Heights* does something different with the novel form: something previously only attempted in drama or verse. Its influence on more recent writers has been enormous. Simply, *Wuthering Heights* showed that you can do anything with a novel, from evoking the core of tragedy, to cutting across all literary norms in a subversive anti-text, to exploring the nature of the human condition in a modern manner, by re-ordering perceptions of existence, experience, and purpose.

9

A Sample of Critical Views

Hundreds of books and articles have been written about *Wuthering Heights* by academic critics, and many more are published each year. They are often written in a confusing, over-complicated style: academics are just as fond of showing off as anybody else. It is important to remember that you have read and studied Emily Brontë's novel, so your ideas are just as valid as theirs. Always be sceptical in approaching their ideas: you are not under an obligation to agree with them. Your mind can be stimulated by discussing the text with your teachers and lecturers, or in a class. Treat the critics in the same way: it is stimulating to debate *Wuthering Heights* by reading their books and articles, challenging your ideas and theirs. This is the spirit in which you should read 'the critics'.

In this chapter we look at three different critics' reactions to the novel, but without any pretence that they are 'representative'. Those who are interested in the varieties of critical theory and approach should go on to read from the suggestions in *Further Reading* following this chapter, and make use of further bibliographies in the critical works themselves to pursue their research. Such reading will reveal that there are several very different strands of each of feminist, psychoanalytical, cultural, structuralist and post-structuralist criticisms, as well as a wealth of other critics who have no single theoretical approach but borrow their concerns and techniques eclectically. The virtue of the three critics we discuss here, then, is simply that they are stimulating, and different from each other.

Emily Brontë's work has suffered from groundless speculations which have interfered with the business of criticism, since she and her family became a lucrative biographical and tourism industry. We noticed that biography and criticism have a habit of becoming confused when she is the subject, in Chapter 7. It is also true to say that *Wuthering Heights* had to wait a long time before its stature was properly recognised. It had enthusiasts and defenders, but the critical establishment took a patronising attitude until well into the twentieth century. For more than fifty years, *Wuthering Heights* was thought to be quite a powerful thing, but full of roughness and faults – a piece of writing not properly put together at all. Emily Brontë was treated as an odd, slightly mad genius who did not really know how to write a novel.

David Cecil

Our first critic was very influential in changing this view. David Cecil's comments on *Wuthering Heights* make one of the early examples of an academic recognising the novel's worth. His theory, which is summarised next, was also very influential: whether they agree with him, or disagree, many critics take Cecil's theory as a starting-point for their own investigations of the novel. Cecil's ideas appear in a general work called *Early Victorian Novelists.*[1]

According to Cecil, *Wuthering Heights* had not been appreciated as it deserved, because it had been judged as a Victorian novel – like a Dickens or a Thackeray. This was a mistake: it is not, and Brontë never meant it to be, anything like them. Emily Brontë is not typical of her time, because:

> She writes about different subjects in a different manner and from a different point of view. She stands outside the main current of nineteenth-century fiction as markedly as Blake stands outside the main current of eighteenth-century poetry.

---

[1] D. Cecil, *Early Victorian Novelists* (London, 1934). The commentary summarised in this chapter comes from between pages 161 and 169.

Cecil points out that Emily Brontë lived an isolated life at Haworth: he describes her environment as primitive and unchanging, saying that society had remained rugged and undeveloped in the less accessible areas of Yorkshire. So, Brontë did not write about, or for, the middle classes, but drew her picture of humanity from the 'grim race who inhabited the land of her childhood'. She is essentially unlike other authors of her time for another reason as well. Emily Brontë was not interested in social position, changing relationships, money, fame or any other incidental details of human life. Instead, she looked at humanity from 'a different point of view':

> Like Blake, Emily Brontë is concerned solely with those primary aspects of life which are unaffected by time and place. Looking at the world, she asks herself not, how does it work? what are its variations? – but what does it mean?

So, Brontë sees her characters 'in relation to time and eternity . . . and the nature of things', and nature figures as an important theme in her writing. Cecil describes the grand and archetypal effect of Brontë's figures:

> . . . they loom before us in the simple epic outline which is all that we see of man when revealed against the huge landscape of the cosmic scheme.

This concern with man's place in a 'universe' makes Cecil suggest a comparison with Hardy. He agrees that there is some similarity, but he thinks that the differences are more significant: Brontë was like Blake, and unlike any of her contemporaries including Hardy, because she was a mystic and experienced moments of vision:

> And it is in the light of these moments of vision that she envisages the world of mortal things; they endow it with a new significance; they are the foundation of the philosophy on which her picture of life rests.

Cecil acknowledges that this 'philosophy' is never made explicit or clear, and however hard we think about it, it still has 'dark places and baffling inconsistencies', but he does go on to explain its 'main features':

> The first is that the whole created cosmos, animate and inanimate, mental and physical alike, is the expression of certain living spiritual principles – on the one hand what may be called the principle of storm – of the harsh, the ruthless, the wild, the dynamic; and on the other the principle of calm – of the gentle, the merciful, the passive and the tame.
>
> Secondly, in spite of their apparent opposition these principles are not conflicting. Either – Emily Brontë does not make clear which she thinks – each is the expression of a different aspect of a single pervading spirit; or they are the component parts of a harmony.

David Cecil then follows his argument through, by showing that this vision of two spiritual principles leads Emily Brontë to avoid all the traditional 'antitheses' on which conventional novels are based. So, she does not show mankind in antithesis against nature, like Hardy. Cecil quotes young Cathy's description of her own and Linton Heathcliff's visions of heaven (see *Wuthering Heights*, p. 245), and comments that their choices represent 'the fundamental bias of their different natures' because they each feel an instinctive 'kinship' with one aspect of nature, the spiritual principle of which that character is the 'human counterpart'.

There is also no antithesis between good and evil in *Wuthering Heights*: 'The storm is as much a part of her universe as the calm.' Both principles, Cecil argues, are in conflict or appear destructive, only because they are diverted from their natural flow by the limitations of physical life; and even their fierceness is right and appropriate in the 'cosmic scheme'. For this reason, Cecil suggests that Emily Brontë's outlook is 'not immoral, but it is pre-moral'. This insight also extends to ideas of right and wrong. Brontë's characters do not act in a way which can be blamed or praised (although some are more or less sympathetic than others). Instead, they act 'according to the dictates of the principle of which they are the manifestation', or in other words, they are ruled by either 'storm' or 'calm' without reference to concepts of right and wrong.

Cecil then turns to the supposed antithesis between love and hate.

He points out that Catherine 'does not "like" Heathcliff, but she loves him with all the strength of her being'; and he quotes her celebrated descriptions of their bond, culminating in '"Nelly, I *am* Heathcliff!"' (see *Wuthering Heights*, pp. 80–2). Cecil's comment is: '. . . Catherine's love is sexless; as devoid of sensuality as the attraction that draws the tide to the moon, the steel to the magnet', and he again traces the necessary finality of their relationship to his spiritual principles by identifying the characters with one of them: 'For he, like her, is a child of the storm; and this makes a bond between them, which interweaves itself with the very nature of their existence.' Cecil uses the word 'affinity' to describe how Catherine and Heathcliff are linked, and says that this transcends conventional concepts of types of emotion, or antitheses of feeling such as love and hate.

Finally, he suggests that in *Wuthering Heights* the author has disposed of 'the most universally accepted of all antitheses – the antithesis between life and death'. He goes on to say that Brontë believes in the immortality of the soul, so that the 'spiritual principles' to which characters belong are immortal. Brontë, however, is unorthodox because she believes in 'immortality *in this world*'. The supernatural therefore plays a different role in *Wuthering Heights* from that allotted to it by other novelists. Other writers tend to see the supernatural as outside or against the laws of nature, whereas Brontë shows a supernatural dimension which is an expression of natural laws, so much so that it should not even be called supernatural, but 'is a natural feature of the world as she [Brontë] sees it'. The critic quotes Catherine's speech about her body as a 'shattered prison' (see *Wuthering Heights*, pp. 159–60), and Nelly's musings over her mistress's dead body, to show that the characters hold the same beliefs as their author.

David Cecil's interpretation, which is based on his concept of 'spiritual principles' of calm and storm, has been subjected to thorough critical analysis since it first appeared. For example, a number of more culturally or socially-minded critics have pointed out that 'calm', in particular, is a misnomer: the forces embodied in the Lintons are power and dominance, and are capable of vicious cruelty: their gentleness can be seen as hypocrisy, and they represent the oppressive power of capitalism, as the exploiting, ruling class. In our fourth chapter, in Part 1, we also criticised Cecil's ideas when we observed that the characters do not conform to any overarching duality such as 'storm' and 'calm'. Instead, we noticed that they act as themselves in all situations, partaking of opposing characteristics at different times, in a bewildering manner. We suggested that two different structural dualities exist in the novel – that between Wuthering Heights and Thrushcross Grange, and that between absolutes and limitations – but that the characters are extraordinarily free from, or immune to, these structures, and behave at all times as themselves.

On the other hand, we can appreciate what David Cecil sought to do. He attempted to define the 'archetypal' quality of the novel, the sense that it plays mankind within a 'cosmos' or 'universe' of elemental forces. This is something like the qualities we discussed in Chapter 8, when comparing *Wuthering Heights* with Shakespearian tragedy. Cecil's abiding achievement may, perhaps, be negative. His successive discussions of man/nature, good/evil, right/wrong, love/hate and life/death 'antitheses' dismissed conventional attacks on the novel, pointing out that the premises on which they were based are irrelevant to Brontë's aims. So, he influenced other critics to begin looking for another, more appropriate way to read *Wuthering Heights*.

Terry Eagleton

The second critic we look at is Terry Eagleton. His analysis of *Wuthering Heights* is an attempt to read the novel from a 'Marxist' point of view – that is, with a focus upon people in relation to social structures such as class, economic exploitation, and historical change. The argument we summarise can be found in his *Myths of Power: A Marxist Study of the Brontës*, which appeared in 1976.

Eagleton begins by saying that *Wuthering Heights* differs from Charlotte Brontë's novels, which seek to reconcile conflicts: '*Wuthering Heights*, on the other hand, confronts the tragic truth that the passion and society it presents are not fundamentally reconcilable – that there remains at the deepest level an ineradicable contradiction between them which refuses to be unlocked, which obtrudes itself as the very stuff and secret of experience.' He then states that the choice between Heathcliff and Edgar is the crucial, 'pivotal' event of the novel, which is decisive in bringing about the tragedy. Because this choice is the crucial event, he goes on:

> . . . the crux of *Wuthering Heights* must be conceded by even the most remorselessly mythological and mystical of critics to be a social one. In a crucial act of self-betrayal and bad faith, Catherine rejects Heathcliff as a suitor because he is socially inferior to Linton; and it is from this that the chain of destruction follows.

Heathcliff's lack of any defined place within the social and economic structure of Wuthering Heights makes him Catherine's natural companion, since she, as the daughter, 'who does not expect to inherit', is the least economically integral person in the family. Friendship with Heathcliff offers Catherine the relative freedom of being 'outside' the social structure of her family and class, because he enjoys the greater freedom from social constraints of those at the bottom of the class system, who are close to natural life: 'In loving Heathcliff, Catherine is taken outside the family and society into an opposing realm which can be adequately imaged only as "Nature"'. So, the relationship between the lovers represents a possibility of freedom beyond the restricting bounds of the Earnshaw family. However, Hindley's oppression of Heathcliff deprives him of this freedom by enslaving him as a farm-labourer, and also by giving him the freedom to run wild and so paradoxically restricting him by depriving him of culture:

> It is a contradiction which encapsulates a crucial truth about bourgeois society. If there is no genuine liberty on its 'inside' – Heathcliff is oppressed by work and the familial structure – neither is there more than a caricature of liberty on the 'outside,' since the release of running wild is merely a function of cultural impoverishment.

Heathcliff's response to the withdrawal of culture by Hindley, which is a mode of domination, is to acquire culture in order to acquire the power to fight back. Heathcliff, in effect, gathers enough 'gentility' during his absence so that when he returns he can turn the capitalists' weapons against themselves and dominate them by their own means. However, the power he thus gains is ultimately self-defeating, as his systematic revenge steadily 'drains him of blood, impels and possesses him as an external force'. Eagleton here implies that the dominating weapons of society destroy Heathcliff whether he is their victim or wielding them, and this accounts for his self-destructive decline and starvation at the end of the novel.

Eagleton discusses the social unit of Wuthering Heights in comparison with that of Thrushcross Grange. At Wuthering Heights social relations are inextricably tied to the work of the farm, which is the work of the family. They are regulated strictly, because of the arduous struggle to extract a living from a harsh environment, that the family must always engage in. However, Heathcliff is 'superfluous': he is put to work as a servant, and has no ordained place in the social and labour relationships of the unit. At Thrushcross Grange, on the other hand, the social unit survives 'on the basis of material conditions it simultaneously conceals'. When the bulldogs attack Catherine, 'The underlying truth of violence, continuously visible at the Heights, is momentarily exposed; old Linton thinks the intruders are after his rents. Culture draws a veil over such brute force but also sharpens it: the more property you have, the more ruthlessly you need to defend it'. Eagleton concludes this discussion with the point that nature and culture are in a complex relation to one another: they are enemies, yet the relationship outside society, away from the work-involvements of the Heights family, that Catherine and Heathcliff have found, is in some ways similar to the false 'heaven' of the Lintons' drawing-room with its gold-bordered ceiling and shimmering chandelier, which is also removed from the basic material condition of labour that sustains it.

We might think that the conflict between nature and culture (i.e., between Catherine-and-Heathcliff on the one hand, and the Lintons on the other) is one between the values of personal relationships and those of conventional society, and this would suggest a traditionally romantic conflict. However, this is not the case, because the relationship between Catherine and Heathcliff is different from the idealised 'personal' relationship of the romantic tradition: it is more and larger than that, because it 'seems to transcend the personal into some region beyond it'. 'Personal' may also suggest liberal humanism, but this – with its accent on 'pity, charity and humanity' – clearly denotes Edgar's understanding of relationships and does not cope with what we find between Catherine and Heathcliff. Their relationship suggests 'a depth inexpressible in routine social practice, transcendent of available social languages':

> What Heathcliff offers Cathy is a non- or pre-social relationship, as the only authentic form of living in a world of exploitation and inequality, a world where one must refuse to measure oneself by the criteria of the class-structure and so must appear inevitably subversive.

When they pursue their relationship, seeking union with each other, Catherine and Heathcliff are therefore trying to preserve 'the primordial moment of pre-social harmony, before the fall into history and oppression'. However, society itself forces their love into the periphery where there is no social mode or social language for it, so it is conventional society that projects their love into myth. Also, because their love is not possible to realise in the social world, it is paradoxically only possible in death: 'Death indeed, as the ultimate outer limit of consciousness and society, is the locus of Catherine's and Heathcliff's love, the horizon on which it moves.'

It may seem understandable to us, as a metaphor, that the Catherine–Heathcliff love is unacceptable within society, so it is pushed out into 'death' or 'myth'. However, Eagleton means something more precise than this. He explains the concept of 'possible consciousness', which he takes from Lukács and Goldmann, as:

> . . . those restrictions set on the consciousness of a historical period which only a transformation of real social relations could abolish – the point at which the most enterprising imagination presses against boundaries which signify not mere failures of personal perception but the limits of what can be historically said.

This suggests that there are experiences which – even if they are rebellious or subversive – are within reach of a society's 'normal' experiences, and so society does provide a language in which they can be expressed. These are experiences which seek to alter the point of view, or which change an element of convention by adopting a different opinion or life-style. By implication, Eagleton believes that the traditional romantic rebellion is like this: a rebellious attitude, but one society can comprehend, which therefore can be expressed. On the other hand, there are also experiences which are so totally alien that society has developed no language for them. They do not merely propose 'contrasting personal life-styles': they actually consist of 'an alternative world of meaning'. As a result they are outside 'possible consciousness' and cannot be expressed. Eagleton says that the bond between Heathcliff and Catherine is an experience of this second kind: 'the offered totalities of Nature, myth and cosmic energy are forced to figure as social worlds unable to engage in more than idealist ways with the society they subject to judgement'.

Eagleton next confronts the enigma of Heathcliff – and in particular discusses his relation to society in the second half of the novel. This leads to discussion of the declining 'yeoman' class of independent farmers, to which the Earnshaw family belongs; the 'agrarian capitalists' or 'squirearchy', a long-established ruling class in rural areas, to which group the Linton family belongs; and the new, aggressive class of 'bourgeois' and 'entrepreneurial industrialist'. Eagleton explains that this new class was struggling to supplant the 'squirearchy' by buying up their estates and adopting their cultured life-style, during Emily Brontë's lifetime. His suggestion is that Heathcliff belongs to this last type, and this makes the struggle between him and the Lintons in the second half of the novel an account of social changes which were happening at the time *Wuthering Heights* was written. Heathcliff, then, plays the role of entrepreneurial industrial capitalists, the new bourgeoisie which was aggressively taking over the agrarian economy and usurping the place of the older landed gentry during the nineteenth century. Eagleton is slightly hesitant in offering this interpretation, as Heathcliff is not an industrial entrepreneur and so does not conform to type. However, 'He belongs fully neither to Heights nor Grange, opposing them both; he embodies a force which at once destroys the traditional Earnshaw settlement and effectively confronts the power of the squirearchy'. Heathcliff's function in society is complicated in relation to the contrast between the Heights and the Grange. He uses the violence natural to the Heights, yet he also uses a knowledge of property, the power of the law, and ruthless economic exploitation which are properly the methods of the Grange, and so gains power over both. In this way he represents a 'turbulent form of capitalist aggression which must historically be civilised – blended with spiritual values, as it will be in the case of his surrogate Hareton'. In addition, the new bourgeoisie who were buying out the old landed gentry were both deeply hostile to the squirearchy, and at the same time keen to imitate their manners and life-style.

So Heathcliff is an 'indirect' embodiment of the aggressive industrial bourgeoisie which was growing in power and position in Emily Brontë's time. Eagleton then returns to his earlier analysis of the subversive pre-social relationship Heathcliff and Catherine assert in opposition to society. Society forced this relationship into an 'outside' area beyond the possible – into myth and death:

> The contradiction of the *novel*, however, is that Heathcliff cannot represent at once an absolute metaphysical refusal of an inhuman society and a class which is intrinsically a part of it. Heathcliff is both metaphysical hero, spiritually marooned from all material concern in his obsessional love for Catherine, and a skilful exploiter who cannily expropriates the wealth of others.

Eagleton explains that this contradiction in Heathcliff's role paradoxically contributes to the unity of the whole work. Heathcliff, for example, is 'a conflictive unity of spiritual rejection and social integration; and this, indeed, is his personal tragedy'. A discussion of the final scenes of the novel ensues, which traces the beginnings of convergence between the worlds of Heights and Grange, and between the aggressive capitalism of Heathcliff and the civilising of his surrogate, Hareton. However, even in the final pages, Eagleton finds that 'the quarrel between their [Cathy's and Hareton's] sedate future at Thrushcross Grange and the spectre of Heathcliff and Catherine on the hills lives on'.

Terry Eagleton, then, has shown that *Wuthering Heights* is both a subversive novel with a social/historical theme; and at the same time a tragedy in which a primordial, natural bond is ejected from this world into the area of myth and metaphysics, because it passes beyond 'possible consciousness'. According to Eagleton, it is the unflinching pursuit of both of these themes, without dilution, evasion or any reconciliation between them, that makes *Wuthering Heights* such an extraordinary and great work of literature. He finds that these two themes – the social and the metaphysical or 'mythical' – are particularly embodied in the unresolvable character of Heathcliff.

Sandra Gilbert

The third and final criticism we will look at is from 1979, and comes from Sandra Gilbert and Susan Gubar's influential book *The Madwoman in the Attic: The Woman Writer and the Nineteenth-Century Literary Imagination*.[2] Chapter 8 of this work is a study of Wuthering Heights by Sandra Gilbert, in which she both explores a feminist approach to the novel, in keeping with the overall aim of the book, and suggests a radical re-interpretation of Brontë's aims, which she compares with those of William Blake. We only have space here to summarise a part of her argument, that tracing the psychosocial development of the first Catherine.

Sandra Gilbert begins with two points which have been noticed by many critics: that *Wuthering Heights* is in some way about a fall; and that it is a novel with a 'visionary' quality. She points out Catherine's feelings, revealed in her delirium, of being 'an exile, an outcast', notices some of the evidence that suggests an ideal or Edenic childhood, and links these references to Milton's accounts of the Fall and Satan in *Paradise Lost*. In her discussion of the novel's 'visionary' element, she complains that most critics looking at Catherine's complaint of the 'shattered prison' and her 'wearying to

---

[2] New Haven, 1979.

escape into that glorious world' draw the conclusion that the novel
proposes a 'Romantic *Liebestod*'. Gilbert points out that these ideas
are similar to those of Nelly Dean. Brontë, like Blake, had another
more violent vision, which Gilbert calls her 'tigerish opposite'.
Sandra Gilbert then puts forward the thesis she will examine in the
remainder of her argument:

> . . . the sum of this novel's visionary parts is an almost shocking revi-
> sionary whole. Heaven (or its rejection), hell, Satan, a fall, mystical
> politics, metaphysical romance, orphanhood, and the question of
> origins – disparate as some of these matters may seem, they all cohere
> in a rebelliously topsy-turvy retelling of Milton's and Western
> culture's central tale of the fall of woman and her shadow self, Satan.
> This fall, says Brontë, is not a fall *into* hell. It is a fall *from* 'hell' into
> 'heaven', not a fall from grace (in the religious sense) but a fall into
> grace (in the cultural sense). Moreover, for the heroine who falls it is
> the loss of Satan rather than the loss of God that signals the painful
> passage from innocence to experience.

Gilbert then re-phrases this radical re-reading of the novel, in
Blakean terms, suggesting that Brontë goes as far as Blake in
asserting that the 'state of being patriarchal Christianity calls "hell" is
eternally, energetically delightful, whereas the state called "heaven" is
rigidly hierarchical, Urizenic'.[3] However, Brontë is different from
Blake because she reverses the terms of Milton's Christianity for
specifically feminist reasons.

The opening of the story has folk-tale or mythic qualities. Old Mr
Earnshaw's decision to walk sixty miles to Liverpool and back is
unexplained, like Lear's decision to divide his kingdom. It may be
that he is half-consciously preparing for death. His question to each
of the three children asks them to reveal their heart's desire, and they
do. Hindley reveals a longing for culture and some effeminacy by
asking for a fiddle, and Catherine reveals the yearning for power of a
powerless younger daughter, by asking for a whip. Gilbert suggests

---

[3] In William Blake's invented mythology, Urizen is the name given to an oppressive, aged,
impotent and white-haired tyrant-God whose rule is enforced with rigid laws and cruel
punishments.

that, metaphorically, Catherine gets her whip in the form of Heathcliff, because he 'functions just as she must have unconsciously hoped it [the whip] would' by enabling her to wield power in the family. Gilbert comments that following Heathcliff's arrival Catherine achieves 'an extraordinary fullness of being', and discusses Heathcliff as a completing 'alternative self or double' for Catherine:

> [Heathcliff is] a complementary addition to her being who fleshes out all her lacks the way a bandage might staunch a wound. . . . As devoid of sexual awareness as Adam and Eve were in the prelapsarian garden, she sleeps with her whip, her other half, every night in the primordial fashion of the countryside.

Catherine herself, during this happy period of her life, is 'unfeminine' and enjoys irritating all the other members of the family by ridiculing Joseph and 'doing just what her father hated most' (*Wuthering Heights*, p. 43). Gilbert points out that Milton's Eve was never allowed Catherine's talkative and sharp tongue.

Sandra Gilbert then turns her attention to the destruction of Catherine's 'paradise', her 'fall'. She shows that this coincides with Hindley's marriage, and likens Hindley and Frances to the stepparents of fairytales, like 'transformed or alien parents'. Her explanation is that Catherine enters puberty and begins adolescence at this point in her life, so her own new sexual awareness is at the root of her problems:

> . . . when the child gets old enough to become conscious of her parents as sexual beings they really do begin to seem like fiercer, perhaps even (as in the case of Hindley and Frances) younger versions of their 'original' selves. Certainly they begin to be more threatening (that is, more 'peevish' and 'tyrannical') if only because the child's own sexual awakening disturbs them almost as much as their sexuality, now truly comprehended, bothers the child.

Gilbert refers to Catherine's diary account of their punishment by Hindley, and his behaviour with his wife, to support this reading of the girl's development. Her point is that Catherine's separation from Heathcliff is not simply ordered by the authority of Hindley – it is also caused by her sexual development in puberty. In addition, we remember that Heathcliff is an 'alternative' being for Catherine herself. Sandra Gilbert puts her interpretation thus:

> For Catherine-and-Heathcliff – that is, Catherine and Catherine, or Catherine and her whip – have already been separated from each other, not just by tyrannical Hindley, the *deus* produced by time's *machina*, but by the emergence of Catherine's own sexuality, with all the terrors which attend that phenomenon in a puritanical and patriarchal society.

The myth of this part of *Wuthering Heights* is completed by the decline and death of Frances, and the birth of Hareton. Frances's example stands before Catherine as a lesson and a warning exemplifying the unavoidable fate of a woman in that society, and demonstrating that sex is a murderer. Frances indulges her 'billing and cooing' with Hindley, and the consequence is that she dies in childbirth, having fulfilled the female function allotted to her by a patriarchal society. At the same time, the baby she produces is Hareton, a 'resurrected version of the original patriarch whose name is written over the main door of the house, amid a "wilderness of shameless little boys"'. Gilbert suggests that Brontë has timed two events to coincide with each other: Catherine's separation from Heathcliff marks the beginning of the decline of her 'Satanic' female principle as she loses her 'whip', her enabling, powerful other half. At the same time, the old patriarchal line begins to reassert itself with the birth of Hareton.

Sandra Gilbert develops her thesis by following Catherine's psychosexual development through her introduction to Thrushcross Grange and her gradual 'fall' into feminine stereotype under the tuition of the Lintons. The analysis follows the classic lines of a feminist view of development in a patriarchal society. Having been forcibly divided from half of her own identity and restricted within a narrow 'feminine' stereotype by her acquiescence in this process, and her marriage to Edgar Linton, Catherine finds the return of Heathcliff is like a 'feverish infection' of the 'wound of femaleness that was inflicted at puberty'. The additional interest in this part of

Gilbert's interpretation lies in her analysis of the agents of Thrushcross Grange. We will look at her account of the first injury, which leads to Catherine's stay there, and at the view she takes of Edgar.

When Catherine is caught outside Thrushcross Grange, she is bitten by Skulker, 'a sort of hellhound posing as a hound of heaven', and the wound he inflicts 'is as symbolically suggestive as his role in the girl's forced passage from Wuthering Heights to Thrushcross Grange'. Gilbert enlarges on the significance of this wound, and Catherine's bleeding, in the heroine's pubescent development:

> Obviously such bleeding has sexual connotations, especially when it occurs in a pubescent girl. Crippling injuries to the feet are equally resonant, moreover, almost always signifying symbolic castration, as in the stories of Oedipus, Achilles, and the Fisher King. Additionally, it hardly needs to be noted that Skulker's equipment for aggression – his huge purple tongue and pendant lips, for instance – sounds extraordinarily phallic. In a Freudian sense, then, the imagery of this brief but violent episode hints that Catherine has been simultaneously catapulted into adult female sexuality *and* castrated.

Catherine's treatment in Thrushcross Grange – where we see her coddled and brushed and fed like a pampered pet – further suggests that she has been deprived of power; and Heathcliff's subsequent subjugation completes the division of her identity from her 'truer' self, and the destruction of that other self: 'her fall into ladyhood has been accompanied by Heathcliff's reduction to an equivalent position of female powerlessness, and Catherine has learned, correctly, that if it is degrading to be a woman it is even more degrading to be *like* a woman'.

When Sandra Gilbert discusses Edgar Linton, she dismisses the superficial view that he is gentle and weak:

> In fact, as Milton also did, Emily Brontë demonstrates that the power of the patriarch, Edgar's power, begins with words, for heaven is populated by '*spirits* Masculine', and as above, so below. Edgar does not need a strong, conventionally masculine body, because his mastery is contained in books, wills, testaments, leases, titles, rent-

rolls, documents, languages, all the paraphernalia by which patriarchal culture is transmitted from one generation to the next. . . . As a
figure in the psychodrama of Catherine's decline, then, he incarnates
the education in young ladyhood that has commanded her to learn
her 'place'. . . . Brontë shows that his patriarchal rule, like
Thrushcross Grange itself, is based on physical as well as spiritual violence. For her, as for Blake, heaven *kills*. Thus, at a word from
Thrushcross Grange, Skulker is let loose, and Edgar's magistrate
father cries 'What prey, Robert?' to his manservant, explaining that
he fears thieves because 'yesterday was my rent day'. Similarly, Edgar,
having decided that he has 'humoured' Catherine long enough, calls
for two strong men servants to support his authority and descends
into the kitchen to evict Heathcliff.

Gilbert points out various interesting paradoxes in this scene, such as
Catherine imprisoning herself when meaning to imprison Edgar, by
throwing away the key; and the fact that the 'gentle' Edgar frees
himself by striking a blow against Heathcliff 'that would have lev-
elled a slighter man'. She then supports this reading of Edgar as the
actual predator, despite his superficially gentle manners and
apparent submission to Catherine's will, by referring to Nelly's odd
simile on p. 71 of *Wuthering Heights*. When Edgar cannot bring
himself to leave Wuthering Heights during his courtship, the context
suggests that Catherine is trapping him. However, the image Nelly
uses is suggestively the other way around, with Edgar as the 'cat' and
Catherine as the 'mouse half killed' or 'bird half eaten'. In this way,
Nelly reveals that it is Edgar's predatory instinct as a patriarchal male
that enslaves him; and the true victim is actually the female prey –
Catherine.

This is as much of Sandra Gilbert's interpretation as we have
room for in the present chapter. Our own conclusions have been
similar to hers at various times in Part 1. For example, we noted
(although with a slightly different emphasis) the trauma of separation from Heathcliff, and the subsequent repression of Catherine's
'other side' under the pampering but superficial influence of
Thrushcross Grange (see Chapter 2), and thought of Catherine sym-
bolising a pampered pet of the household in Isabella's mind, when
we considered the hanging of the dog (see Chapter 3). There is a

great deal of fortuitous evidence for Gilbert's theory in the text, also – such as the details of Skulker's mouth and tongue and the Freudian interpretation she draws from these, and Nelly's odd simile on p. 71.

The difficulties of Gilbert's approach seem to be twofold. There are doubts about whether we are justified in reading so much from these details, because this seems to call into question how far we can justifiably go as critics. Do we analyse in order to understand Brontë's intentions in the novel? Or do we allow ourselves to suggest that the author unconsciously used symbols which she herself is unlikely to have consciously understood? Sandra Gilbert's approach allows a great deal of latitude in this respect, so we could say that it falls between literary criticism and cultural/psychosocial history: it divides its interest between *Wuthering Heights* itself, and Emily Brontë's psyche. Certainly, we have no evidence about Emily Brontë's awareness or ignorance about sexuality, and sexual symbolism.

Secondly, Sandra Gilbert seems in danger of distorting the novel, when she emphasises so strongly that Heathcliff acts as a completing 'alternative self' in Catherine's life. She seems to have a reduced awareness of him as a character in his own right. The strength of Sandra Gilbert's interpretation, however, lies in her undoubted success in making continuous sense of Catherine's psychosocial development; and her success in showing that Brontë's values are similar to Blake's, and are, as she says, 'an almost shocking revisionary whole' in which the conventional Hell and Heaven are seen 'oppositely'.

It is interesting that both Sandra Gilbert and Terry Eagleton present substantially the same analysis of Thrushcross Grange as a hypocritical and fundamentally oppressive embodiment of capitalist power. They also seem to agree with each other in saying that the novel as a whole contains a radically unconventional, or 'subversive' vision of the world. Gilbert calls this a 'shocking revisionary whole' and likens it to Blake's inversion of the concepts of heaven and hell; Eagleton suggests that this alternative vision of life passes beyond what he calls 'possible consciousness' and into myth, because it is so total and so alien to social convention. The different approaches of these two critics, however, are very distinct, and they bring different pre-existing theories to the study of literature: Eagleton applies Marxist ideas of society and history to the text, while Sandra Gilbert emphasises ideas about female psychosocial development, and symbolisms drawn from psychoanalytical theory. We may even be amused to notice that Eagleton (the male critic) devotes the main part of his analysis to unravelling the enigma of Heathcliff; while Gilbert (the feminist critic) hardly considers Heathcliff as a separate figure, and concentrates on Catherine.

The three critics we have discussed in this chapter are very different from each other, then. On the other hand, each of them has put forward valid and valuable insights into *Wuthering Heights*, and their ideas have all struck echoes from among the conclusions we reached in our own analysis in Part 1 of this book. For those interested in reading more literary criticism of *Wuthering Heights*, there are a number of suggestions to follow up, in 'Further Reading'. Most critical works also contain their own bibliography, and refer to other critics in their argument, so students can follow the trail of their own views or interests by following up these further leads.

Further Reading

Your first job is to study the text. There is no substitute for the work of detailed analysis: that is how you gain the close familiarity with the text, and the fully-developed understanding of its content, which make the essays you write both personal and convincing. For this reason I recommend that you take it as a rule not to read any other books around or about the text you are studying, until you have finished studying it for yourself.

Once you are familiar with the text, you may wish to read around and about it. This brief chapter is only intended to set you off: there are hundreds of relevant books and we can only mention a few. However, most good editions, and critical works, have suggestions for further reading, or a bibliography of their own. Once you have begun to read beyond your text, you can use these and a good library to follow up your particular interests. This chapter is divided into 'Reading Around the Text', which lists other works by Emily Brontë and her sisters, and some by other writers; 'Biography'; and 'Criticism', which will introduce you to the varieties of opinion among professional critics.

Reading around the Text

Emily Brontë wrote *Wuthering Heights*, a lost second novel (probably unfinished), and her poems: nothing else. However, her sisters Charlotte and Anne also wrote novels, and these are worth reading both for their own sakes, and for fuller understanding of the creative atmosphere of Haworth Parsonage, in which *Wuthering Heights* was produced. Charlotte's most famous novel – and the one most often directly compared with *Wuthering Heights* for its volatile passionate theme – is *Jane Eyre* (1847); and in *Shirley* (1849) the heroine was said to have been drawn from Emily Brontë herself. Charlotte's other major work is *Villette* (1853) which uses Brussels, where she lived with Emily during 1842, among its settings. Anne Brontë wrote *Agnes Grey* (1847) and *The Tenant of Wildfell Hall* (1848). Emily Brontë's poems have been collected in *The Complete Poems of Emily Jane Brontë*, edited from the manuscripts by C. W. Hatfield (New York, 1941), and this edition contains a number of useful features, such as a reconstruction of the Gondal story, and a list of the Gondal poems arranged – as far as can be ascertained – in their Gondal order.

Choosing novels analogous to *Wuthering Heights*, to read as a literary context for Emily Brontë's work, is difficult. As we remarked in earlier chapters, she stands outside the traditions of her time, and her novel is unique. This said, it may be interesting to look at some 'gothic' fiction. Mrs Radcliffe's *The Mysteries of Udolpho* (1794) is a good example of the genre; and *The Monk* (1796), by Matthew Lewis, is one of the most gripping and powerful productions of its kind. Mary Shelley's *Frankenstein, or The Modern Prometheus* (1818) is a classic tale worth reading on its own account. Emily Brontë was strongly influenced by Sir Walter Scott, who wrote a large number of novels and tales of the border country he loved. You could begin reading Scott by trying *Old Mortality* (1816) and *Rob Roy* (1817), particularly as some critics believe that *Rob Roy* suggested names and characteristics for *Wuthering Heights*.

Chapter 8 mentions a number of twentieth-century novels which experiment with, or make revisionary use of, the traditional novel form; and draws a comparison between these and *Wuthering Heights*. However, Thomas Hardy's great novelistic tragedies are more immediate analogues, and closer to Emily Brontë in time. These are *Tess of the D'Urbervilles* (1891) and *Jude the Obscure* (1896). As for twentieth-century novels, it is too far-fetched to suggest that any could be called 'background reading' specifically relevant to *Wuthering*

Heights. However, there is a minor interest in looking at E. M. Forster's *A Passage to India*, just because it uses the same device of a narrative blank covering the crucial event, as we find in *Wuthering Heights.*

Biography

Brontë biography is big business, and attracts a wide variety of odd theories and wild speculations about Emily's life and the lives of her siblings. There are a large number of biographies to choose from, therefore. The first major biography which told the story of the Brontë family was Elizabeth Gaskell's *The Life of Charlotte Brontë* (1857; now available as an Everyman paperback, 1997). Mrs Gaskell was a friend of Charlotte, and her narrative tends to adopt an uncritical view of Charlotte's character. None the less, this is where any biographical reading about the Brontës should begin. A recent biography of Emily is Katherine Frank's *Emily Brontë* (London, 1990; published in Penguin, 1992), which highlights the evidence that Emily was anorexic or a 'hunger artist'. *The Brontës*, by Juliet Barker (1994), is a meticulously researched account of the whole family; and Winifred Gerin's *Emily Brontë* (Oxford, 1971) is a highly-respected work which brought forward new evidence about Emily, and contributed to the reassessment of Mrs Gaskell's Charlotte-oriented view.

Criticism

The critical works sampled in Chapter 9 are: David Cecil, *Early Victorian Novelists* (London, 1934), pp. 161–9; Terry Eagleton, from pages 97–143 of his *Myths of Power: A Marxist Study of the Brontës* (London, 1976); and Sandra Gilbert, from Chapter 8 of Sandra Gilbert and Susan Gubar, *The Madwoman in the Attic: The Woman Writer and the Nineteenth-Century Literary Imagination* (New Haven, 1979).

Anthologies of critical essays and articles are a good way to sample the critics. You can then go on to read the full-length books written by those critics whose ideas and approaches you find stimulating. The New Casebooks series (general editors: John Peck and Martin Coyle), published by Macmillan, collects a variety of critical articles together, and provides an introduction which discusses the critical history of the text. The volume on *Wuthering Heights* is edited by Patsy Stoneman (1993). *Critical Essays on Emily Brontë*, edited by Thomas John Winnifrith (New York and London, 1997), contains a selection of earlier and more recent criticism of *Wuthering Heights*, as well as a selection from various biographies, and five articles about Emily's poems.

The following full-length critical works may also be of interest and should be stimulating whether you agree or disagree with the writer's analysis. Try Stevie Davies's *Emily Brontë: The Artist as a Free Woman* (Manchester, 1983), and Lyn Pykett's *Emily Brontë*, in the Women Writers Series (Basingstoke and London, 1989), both of which explore a feminist approach to the novel.

Some of the most influential criticisms of *Wuthering Heights*, however, have appeared within critical works with a wider scope than the one novel (like David Cecil's influential theory discussed in our last chapter, which appeared in his *Early Victorian Novelists*), or as articles in anthologies or periodicals. In this connection, it would be worthwhile to read some of the following: Queenie Leavis, 'A Fresh Approach to *Wuthering Heights*', from *Lectures in America* (London, 1969), pp. 86–104; Arnold Kettle, 'Emily Brontë: *Wuthering Heights*', from *An Introduction to the English Novel* (London, 1951), pp. 139–54; and C. P. Sanger, 'The Structure of *Wuthering Heights*', from *Hogarth Essay, 19* (London, 1926). The very useful bibliography at the end of the New Casebook on *Wuthering Heights* will add many further suggestions to this list, and is helpfully divided into sections covering different critical approaches such as Feminism, Psychoanalysis, Structuralism, and so on.

When you are in a library, use the catalogue system resourcefully to locate further interesting critical work on Emily Brontë. There are numerous books which appear to be on different subjects – the History of the Novel, Women Writers, and so on. A large number of these contain chapters or essays about Emily Brontë which may bring an illuminating angle to bear upon her writing.

Index